John Churton Collins

CW00815984

Jonathan Swift

A Biographical and Critical Study

Elibron Classics
www.elibron.com

Elibron Classics series.

© 2006 Adamant Media Corporation.

ISBN 0-543-90924-7 (paperback)
ISBN 0-543-90923-9 (hardcover)

This Elibron Classics Replica Edition is an unabridged facsimile
of the edition published in 1893 by Chatto & Windus, London.

JONATHAN SWIFT

JONATHAN SWIFT

A BIOGRAPHICAL AND CRITICAL STUDY

BY

JOHN CHURTON COLLINS

AUTHOR OF 'BOLINGBROKE, AN HISTORICAL STUDY' ETC

Ὁ τῶν ἄλλων ἐπεπωλεῖτο στίχας ἀνδρῶν,
Ἐγχεΐ τ᾽, ἄορί τε, μεγάλοισι τε χερμαδίοισιν.

London
CHATTO & WINDUS, PICCADILLY
1893

PRINTED BY
SPOTTISWOODE AND CO., NEW-STREET SQUARE
LONDON

TO MY MOTHER

I INSCRIBE

THIS VOLUME

PREFACE

DURING the last hundred years, and particularly during the last twenty years, so much has been written about Swift that some apology may seem necessary for the appearance of another volume on the subject. But to apologise for a very deliberate act would be affectation. Those who may do me the honour to read this book will, I think, find that, however open to question my views of the actions and character of this extraordinary man may be, they are at least the result of very careful study, and that if I have added little, I have added at all events something, to our knowledge of the details of his biography.

I hold no brief for Swift, but I have endeavoured to do him justice where justice has been either withheld or too grudgingly allowed. I have endeavoured to vindicate the consistency of his political principles, his character in all that related to practice and duty as a churchman, the purity of his motives as well as his wisdom as an Irish Agitator, and his conduct with regard to Stella and Vanessa.

In analysing his temper and his peculiarities I

have laid great stress upon one point. Ten years
ago, when I first began to study Swift, I felt convinced that not only was he never insane in the
proper acceptation of the term, but that the maladies
which he himself regarded as the germs and symptoms of gradually developing disease, and which had
been so regarded by all his biographers, had in truth
no connection with the state into which he latterly
sank. I accordingly wrote to Dr. Bucknill and placed
Swift's case fully before him, and he replied in a
letter corroborating my conjecture, and that letter he
has kindly allowed me to print.

It remains for me to thank Mr. Murray for allowing
me to draw very largely on two articles contributed
by me some years ago to the *Quarterly Review*, and
Mr. Percy Wallace for his valuable assistance in helping me to see this volume through the press. And
I should like also to take this opportunity of thanking the officials of the British Museum and the super-
intendent of the Dyce and Forster Library for the
more than courtesy with which they have always responded on this and on other occasions to my many
requests for assistance.

LONDON: *April* 30, 1893.

CONTENTS

CHAPTER I

BIOGRAPHICAL SOURCES AND BIOGRAPHERS

CHAPTER II

INJUSTICE OF THE POPULAR ESTIMATE OF SWIFT

CHAPTER III

THE EARLY LIFE OF SWIFT

CHAPTER IV

LIFE BETWEEN 1700 AND 1710

CHAPTER V

DURING THE ADMINISTRATION OF HARLEY, 1710–1714

I

II

CHAPTER VII

IRISH POLITICS

I

CHAPTER IX

LIFE IN IRELAND—LAST DAYS AND DEATH

I

II

CHAPTER X

CHARACTERISTICS

I

APPENDICES

I

II

JONATHAN SWIFT

CHAPTER I

BIOGRAPHICAL SOURCES AND BIOGRAPHERS

WE know Swift as we know no other of those eminent
men who have made the first four decades of the
eighteenth century memorable in literary history. A
mere glance at the materials to which his biographers
have had access will suffice to show that our information regarding him is of such a kind as to leave
scarcely anything to be desired. In the first place,
we have his own voluminous correspondence—a
correspondence which is, from a biographical point
of view, of peculiar value. For, as the majority of
his letters are addressed to intimate friends, and were
intended only for the eyes of those friends, they
exhibit him at times when the mask falls off, even
from the most guarded. They were, moreover,
written in all moods, without premeditation, without
reserve, with the simple object of unburdening his
mind, in no case with a view either to publication or
to display. 'When I sit down to write a letter,' he
used to say, 'I never lean upon my elbow till I have
finished it.' Again, in the *Journal to Stella* he has

not only left a minute record of his daily life during
a space of nearly three years, but he has with
unrestrained garrulity given expression to whatever happened at the moment to be passing through
his thoughts. Nor is this all.   He appears, like
Johnson and Coleridge, to have found an eccentric
pleasure in communing with himself on paper.   Many
of these soliloquies accident has preserved.   They
throw the fullest light on his innermost thoughts and
feelings.   They enable us to determine how far as a
Churchman he was honest, how far as a politician
he was consistent.   His Memoir of himself remains
unfortunately a fragment, but enough was completed
to illustrate that portion of his career during which
his correspondence is most scanty.   If to this mass
of autobiographical matter be added the innumerable
passages in his public writings which elucidate his
personal history, the evidence which is of all evidence
the least open to suspicion may be regarded as ample
even to superabundance.

But, if we owe much to the communicativeness of
Swift himself, we owe much also to the communicativeness of his friends.   Seven years after his death
appeared the famous *Letters* by John, Lord Orrery.
The indignation which this work excited among
Swift's admirers is well known.   The picture which
Orrery drew of the Dean was certainly not a pleasing
one, and he was accused of having malignantly
endeavoured to indemnify himself for the long and
not very successful court he paid to Swift when alive
by a series of calumnious attacks upon him when
dead.   Orrery is not entitled to much respect either
as a writer or as a man, but he may probably be

acquitted of any such intention. Careful study of the
letters must satisfy anyone that they are on the whole
what they profess to be. Orrery was, as we learn
from other sources, no favourite with Swift. He saw
him, therefore, not as he presented himself to the
fascinated eye of friendship, but as he presented himself to the impartial eye of critical curiosity. It should
be remembered, too, that he knew him only in his
decadence. Had Orrery's object been detraction, he
would have withheld praise where praise was due, and
when direct censure was hazardous he would have
resorted to misrepresentation. There is nothing of
this spirit discernible. He fully admits the greatness,
he fully admits the many virtues, of the man whose
portrait he has delineated in such harsh and disagreeable colours. What he painted was what he
saw, and what he saw were those features in Swift's
character which Delany and Deane Swift have piously
done their best to soften or conceal. The truth is
that the Swift of Orrery is the Swift of the *Voyage
to the Houyhnhnms*, and of the *Verses to the Legion
Club*. The *Letters* of Orrery elicited two years
afterwards the *Observations* of Delany. Few men
were better qualified to speak of Swift than Delany.
He had been on terms of intimacy with him for
upwards of a quarter of a century. He had been
his companion in business and recreation. He had
been acquainted with those who had known him from
early youth. But Delany's object was eulogy, and
for this due allowance must be made. He is, however,
one of those witnesses whose loquacity forms a per-
petual corrective to their prejudice, and his observations are so rich in reminiscence and anecdote that

a shrewd reader is in little danger of being misled. On the whole, we are inclined to think him the most trustworthy and valuable of all the original authorities. Delany's *Observations* were succeeded, at an interval of a year, by Deane Swift's *Essay*. This is a very disappointing book, though, as the writer was the son-in-law of Mrs. Whiteway, and had as a young man frequently conversed with Swift, what he says of the Dean's character and habits is of importance, and we are moreover indebted to him for many interesting particulars not preserved elsewhere. In Mrs. Pilkington, whose reckless indifference to truth was notorious among all who knew her, and in the compiler of the *Swiftiana*, no one could place any confidence. Hawkesworth's *Memoir*, which was published in 1755, and Johnson's *Life*, which was published in 1781, added little or nothing to what was already known. But in 1784 came out the *Memoir* by Thomas Sheridan—not, of course, the Thomas Sheridan who was the friend of Swift, but the son of Swift's friend. As Sheridan professed to have derived information from his father, and has on the authority of his father, and on the authority also of his own reminiscences as a boy, contributed new biographical matter, his name stands high, and, in spite of the wretched arrangement of his material, deservedly high, among Swift's biographers. With Monck-Berkeley's *Enquiry into the Life of Dean Swift*, prefixed to his *Literary Relics*, published in 1789, we have the last contribution to Swift's biography made by persons intimately acquainted with members of the Dean's circle. But, with the exception of an interesting account of Esther Johnson, obtained from her niece, Monck-Berkeley has added little to what was already known.

Then came the era of original research. This may be said to date from Dr. Barrett's *Essay on the Earlier Part of the Life of Swift*, which appeared in 1808. A few years afterwards Scott undertook to embody in a comprehensive narrative the information which lay scattered through the publications to which reference has been made. He did this, and he did much more. Indeed, he produced a work which still remains, with all its defects, the best complete biography of Swift in existence. Scott had many advantages. His editorial labours peculiarly fitted him for the office of biographer, and those labours had been greatly facilitated both by Hawkesworth and by Nichols, whose valuable editions of the Dean's collected writings had appeared at intervals between 1784 and 1808. Scott's own distinguished position in the world of letters gave, moreover, something of a national importance to his work. All who could in any way assist him eagerly proffered their services. Escritoires were ransacked, family archives explored. One gentleman placed at his disposal the correspondence between Swift and Miss Vanhomrigh; another lent him the memoranda of Dr. Lyons. Every year augmented his treasures, and on the completion of his task in 1814 he could boast that he had been able to add upwards of a hundred letters, essays, and poems to those which had already seen the light. In fine, had Scott made the best of his opportunities, had his information been as accurate as it was comprehensive, and had his patience and industry been equal to his genius and literary skill, any other Life of Swift would have been

a mere work of supererogation. But, unhappily, his
biography of Swift is marred by the same defects
which marred his biography of Dryden. It is essentially unthorough—the work of a man, of a very
great man, who was contented with doing respect-
ably what with a little more trouble he might have
done excellently. Hence, though he is always interesting and always instructive, he is seldom altogether
satisfactory. It may be doubted very much whether
any reader, after closing Scott's memoir, would have
any clear impression of Swift's character. Indeed, to
speak plainly, it may be doubted whether Scott had
himself taken the trouble to form any clear conception
of that character. But his most serious defect is his
careless credulity. To the relative value of testimony
he appears to attach little importance. He places,
for example, the same implicit confidence in statements which rest on no better authority than that of
Theophilus Swift and the younger Sheridan, as he
places in statements which rest on the authority of
Swift's own intimate associates. The result is that
what is authentic and what is apocryphal are so inter-
woven in his narrative, that it is never possible to
follow him without distrust and suspicion.

While Scott was busy with Swift, another writer
was similarly engaged. In 1819 Monck Mason published his *History and Antiquities of St. Patrick's
Cathedral*, a goodly quarto of some five hundred
pages. More than half of this formidable volume is
devoted to an elaborate biography of Swift. But
Monck Mason's quarto never succeeded in gaining the
ear of the world, and is now almost forgotten. Indeed,
it may be questioned whether even among professed

students of our literature two in twenty are aware of
its existence, still less of its rare merits. Nor is this
difficult to account for. A more unreadable book was
probably never written. It is arranged on that detestable method which originated, I believe, with Bayle—
a method the distinguishing feature of which is the
combination of the greatest possible confusion. The
style is equally repulsive ; it is at once harsh and
diffuse, as dull as the style of Birch, and as cumber-
some as that of Hawkins. But if Monck Mason
possesses none of the qualifications of an attractive
writer he possesses everything which constitutes an
invaluable authority. The extent, the variety, the
minuteness of his researches, his patience and acuteness in sifting evidence, his exact acquaintance with
the writings of Swift himself, and with the writings
of those who have in any way thrown light on Swift's
public and private life, his accuracy, his conscientiousness, his impartiality, are above praise. But our
obligations to this modest and laborious scholar extend still further. It was he who first proved, and
proved, it would seem, conclusively, that no marriage
was ever solemnised between Swift and Esther Johnson. To him we owe the first full and satisfactory
account of that long and important period in the
Dean's career which extends between the publication
of the pamphlet on the use of Irish manufactures and
the controversy with Boulter.

Such were the principal works bearing on Swift
which had, up to 1875, been given to the world. In
that year appeared the first volume of a biography
which would probably have superseded all that had
gone before, but which was unhappily destined to

remain a fragment. Of Mr. Forster's enthusiasm
and industry it would be superfluous to speak. His
devotion to Swift resembles the devotion of Lipsius
to Tacitus, and of Basil Montagu and Mr. Spedding
to Bacon. It amounted to a passion. To link his
name with the name of a man whom he had persuaded himself to believe one of the monarchs of
human kind was, till the last hours of his life, his
most cherished object. To zeal such as this we owe
perhaps nine-tenths of what is best in Biography and
History. But Mr. Forster's zeal was not always a
source of strength. It led him, in the language of
Shakespeare, to monster nothings, to attach undue
importance to the most trivial particulars. Nothing
that Swift did or said was in his estimation too unimportant to be chronicled. He pounced with ludicrous
avidity on matter which was not merely worthless in
itself, but of no value in its bearings on Swift. The
fact that a document had never before appeared in
print was, in his eyes, a sufficient justification for its
appearing in his pages. The fact that preceding biographers had in any portion of their narrative been
concise is the signal for Mr. Forster to become prepos-
terously diffuse. A biographer can, indeed, never be
too full when he is treating of anything which has
reference to what is in his hero distinctive and peculiar. But there are many things in which great men
and little men must necessarily act alike. There is
much in the constitution even of the most exalted
personages which is common to all mankind. On
these points a judicious biographer will be least com-
municative; but on these points Mr. Forster dilates
at insufferable length. That Swift played at cards and

made bad puns may possibly be worth recording, but
what man on earth cares to know the exact cards
he held, or the exact bad puns he made? No one
would wish to detract from the merits of Mr. Forster's
book, but it is assuredly doing him no injustice to
say that, had he paid more attention to the art of
suppression and selection, it would have been better
for his readers, and better for Swift's fame. But this
is not the only blemish in his work. It is animated
throughout by an unpleasantly polemical spirit. He
appears to have regarded the biographers who preceded
him as jealous lovers regard rivals. He is continually
going out of his way to exalt himself and to depreciate
them. Here we have a digression on the incompetence of Deane Swift, there a sneer at Orrery. Now
he pauses to carp at Delany; at another time he
wearies us with an account of the deficiencies of
Sheridan. He must himself have admitted that his
own original contributions to Swift's biography were
as a drop in the river, compared with those of Scott
and Monck Mason, and yet Scott rarely appears in
his pages, except in a disadvantageous light, and
to Monck Mason's work, though he draws largely
on it, he studiously refrains from acknowledging the
slightest obligation. But, to do him justice, Mr. Forster's fragment is a solid and valuable addition to
the literature of Swift. If he has added nothing of
importance to what was known before, he has scru-
tinised with microscopic minuteness all that was
known; he has thus accurately distinguished between
what was fiction and what was fact. He has confirmed
and illustrated what was established; he has for ever
set at rest what was doubtful; and he has rendered

it impossible for even the suspicion of error to attach itself to any portion of Swift's early history.

Lastly comes Mr. Henry Craik. His work is in many respects greatly superior to any preceding biography. It is more accurate, more critical, and much fuller, than the Memoir by Scott. It is written with more spirit, and it is executed with greater skill, than the Memoir by Monck Mason. It is, besides, enriched with material to which neither Scott nor Monck Mason had access, and which is altogether new. Such, for example, would be the diary kept at Holyhead by Swift, printed by Mr. Craik in his Appendix; such would be the correspondence between Swift and Archdeacon Walls, furnished by Mr. Murray; and such would be the Orrery Papers, furnished by the Earl of Cork.

But it is time to turn from the biographers to the Dean himself.

CHAPTER II

INJUSTICE OF THE POPULAR ESTIMATE OF SWIFT

THE injustice of the popular estimate of Swift is so glaring that it is surely high time for truth to be heard. That estimate, simply stated, resolves itself into this: that he was a gloomy and ferocious misanthrope, with a heart of stone and a tongue of poison; that, if not exactly a libertine, he revelled in impurity and filth; that he was an apostate in politics, a sceptic in religion, and a tyrant in private life; that he wrought the ruin of two women who passionately loved him, and that he paid the penalty for his inhumanity and selfishness by an old age of unutterable misery. Now the facts of Swift's life are, as has been already stated, matters of certain knowledge. In estimating his character a critic has at no point to resort to conjecture; his appeal lies to authentic evidence. That evidence, which is voluminous, few have leisure to survey; but a patient scrutiny of that evidence can scarcely fail to satisfy anyone that the popular picture of Swift has not even the merit of being a caricature, but that it is in truth a mere reckless daub, produced pretty much in the same way as Protogenes is said to have produced the foam on the mouth of his wearied hound.

In the first place, nothing is more certain than
that Swift's life, from the time he appears on the
stage of history to the time he ceased to be a responsible being, was a long course of active benevolence. While still a struggling priest, more than
one-tenth of what he expended he expended in
charity. As his fortune increased, his generosity increased with it. As soon as his political services gave
him influence, his first thought was for his friends.
'When I had credit for some years at Court,' he writes
to Lady Betty Germaine, 'I provided for above fifty
people in both kingdoms, of which not one was a
relative.' To his recommendation Congreve, Gay,
Rowe, Friend, Ambrose Philips, and Steele owed
remunerative offices. 'You never come to us,' said
Bolingbroke on one occasion, half angrily, ' without
bringing some Whig in your sleeve.' He obtained
for King, who had libelled and insulted him, a post
which relieved that facetious writer from the pressure
of want. His kindness to young Harrison and poor
Diaper would alone suffice to prove the goodness of
his heart. He made the fortune of Barber. He went
out of his way to serve Parnell and Berkeley. It was
through his influence that Trapp became Bolingbroke's chaplain. How greatly Pope profited from
his zealous friendship Pope has himself acknowledged. He was never known to turn a deaf ear to
sorrow or poverty; nay, it is notorious that he denied
himself the common comforts of life that he might
relieve the necessities of the paupers of Dublin. His
correspondence teems with proofs of his kindness and
charity. At one time we find him pleading for an
old soldier, at another time, when almost too ill to

hold the pen, for a poor parson ; now again for an unfortunate youth who had been treated harshly by his parents; [1] here he is soliciting subscriptions for a volume of poems, there he is stating the case of a persecuted patriot. ' He loved merit,' says Delany, ' wherever he found it.' His large-hearted philanthropy extended itself in all directions. He was the first who drew attention to the inadequacy of religious instruction in London, and suggested the remedy. He organised a club for the relief of distressed men of letters, and, visiting them personally in their cocklofts and cellars, dispensed with his own hand the money which his generous importunity had wrung from opulent friends. With the first five hundred pounds which he had been able to put by he established a fund which, advancing money without interest, saved many humble families from distress and ruin. He founded a charity school for boys, and at a time when he could ill afford it he built, at his own expense, an almshouse for aged women. Of that noble hospital which owes its existence to his munificent philanthropy we need scarcely speak. But, had he been in private life all that his enemies would represent him, his public services to Ireland would alone suffice to make him the peer of Burke and Howard. With regard to the charge of unbelief, which involves also the more serious charge of hypocrisy, there is not—and it may be said positively—a tittle of evidence to support it. His real attitude towards religion he has himself, with characteristic candour, accurately defined. In one of his private memoranda—the *Thoughts on Religion*—he writes—

[1] See the admirable letter addressed to William Fitzherbert, the father of the youth (Scott, xviii. 327).

I look upon myself, in the capacity of a clergyman, to be one appointed by Providence for defending a post assigned me, and for gaining over as many enemies as I can. I am not answerable to God for the doubts that arise in my own breast, since they are the consequence of that reason which He has planted in me, if I take care to conceal those doubts from others, if I use my best endeavours to subdue them, and if they have no influence on the conduct of my life.[1]

Again he writes—

To remove opinions fundamental in religion is impossible, and the attempt wicked, whether these opinions be true or false, unless your avowed design be to abolish that religion altogether. . . The proceedings of the Socinians are both vain and unwarrantable, because they will never be able to advance their own opinions or meet any other success than breeding doubts and disturbances in the world.[2]

And what sentence ever came from his pen, or what word is authentically recorded as ever having fallen from his lips, inconsistent with this statement? More than one-third of his voluminous writings, including the work on which the charge of infidelity is based, were in defence of the Protestant Church—the Church in which he believed Christianity to exist in

---

[1] Scott, viii. 175.

[2] *Id.* p. 174. See too particularly the sermon on the Trinity, Scott, viii. 28 *seq.* ; the sermon on the Wisdom of the World, in which he points out the superiority of Christianity to the systems of pagan philosophy, *id.* p. 147 ; and the admirable letter to a young clergyman (the paragraph beginning, ' I do not find that you are anywhere directed in the canons or articles to attempt explaining the mysteries of the Christian religion '), *id.* p. 355. Swift's attitude is precisely that of Dryden in the *Religio Laici*, and we may perhaps suspect a resemblance to that of Cotta in Cicero's *De Natura Deorum*. There is certainly a very marked absence of unction in all Swift's writings and recorded allusions to religion.

its purest form. It is certain that he devoted a portion of each day to religious exercises. It is certain that no scandalous or immoral action was, during his lifetime, ever seriously imputed to him. The ridiculous fable circulated by a poor lunatic at Kilroot was probably invented long after Swift's death.[1] It is very little to the credit of Nichols that he should have attempted to revive it, or to the credit of Monck-Berkeley that he should have thought it worth serious repetition. Into the question of his apostasy from the Whigs, and into the history of his relations with Esther Johnson and Hester Vanhomrigh, it will be more convenient to enter later on.

That the world, however, should misjudge Swift is not surprising, for he has had the misfortune to number among his assailants four writers who have done more than any other writers who could be named to mould public opinion on matters relating to the literary and political history of the last century. I allude, of course, to Jeffrey, Macaulay, Lord Stanhope, and Thackeray. Jeffrey's article on Swift, or, to speak more accurately, Jeffrey's libel on Swift, appeared in the *Edinburgh Review* for September 1816. It is a work which makes no pretension to impartiality. It is a mere party pamphlet. Its undisguised object was to render the great Tory satirist odious and contemptible. And the method employed is simple. The reviewer begins by attributing everything that Swift did to the lowest motives; he suppresses all mention of such actions in his life as were

---

[1] The curious volume published in 1730, entitled *Some Memoirs of the Amours and Intrigues of a Certain Irish Dean*, is, of course, an impudent fiction.

indisputably laudable ; he puts the worst possible construction on such actions as admitted of misrepresentation ; and he paints him as being during the whole course of his existence what he was only in his last sad years. Macaulay followed, and, to transcribe Macaulay's own words, ' the apostate politician, the ribald priest, the perjured lover, the heart burning with hatred against the whole human race,' [1] was again held up to the scorn and loathing of the world. Then came Lord Stanhope. We have no doubt whatever that that amiable and candid historian weighed well the bitter words in which he expressed his opinion of Swift's character,[2] but we believe him to have followed too implicitly what he found in Jeffrey and Macaulay, to have been insufficiently informed, and to have been too ready to think the worst of the adversary of Cowper and Somers. Of Thackeray's well-known lecture it need only be remarked that it abounds, as Mr. Hannay pointed out long ago, in erroneous statements and in utterly unwarrantable conclusions. It is shallow, it is flashy, it is unjust. The ignorance which Thackeray displays not merely of Swift's writings but of his temper and personal peculiarities is really extraordinary—and the more extraordinary when contrasted with the minute and extensive knowledge which he undoubtedly had of the social life and popular literature of the eighteenth century. Had he known Swift as well as he knew Addison and Fielding, he could scarcely have failed to do justice to virtues which no Englishman has possessed in larger measure than himself.

[1] Review of Mahon's *War of the Succession in Spain.*
[2] *History of England*, i. 48.

•

CHAPTER III

THE EARLY LIFE OF SWIFT

THE country in which Swift first saw the light, and
with whose history his name will be for ever associated, cannot number him among her sons. Of
unmingled English blood, he was descended on his
father's side from an old and gentle family. The elder
branch of that family had for many years been in possession of important estates in Yorkshire and Not-
tinghamshire, had intermarried with the Mulgraves
and the Creightons, and had, in the person of Barnam
Swift, been ennobled by Charles I. The younger
branch had settled in the Midland Counties, and from
this branch sprang Swift's immediate ancestors. His
great-grandfather, William Swift, was a divine of some
distinction. He married a woman of large property,
but of an irritable and malignant temper. The issue
of this marriage were two daughters and a son, Thomas.
The misfortunes of Thomas—and his long life was
destined to consist of little else than misfortunes—originated in his mother's capricious cruelty. She began
by disinheriting him, while still a schoolboy, for rob-
bing an orchard, and a few years later insulted him
so grossly that he was unable to remain under the
same roof with her. At last, having taken orders, he

C

obtained from his friend the Bishop of Hereford the
vicarage of Goodrich, in Herefordshire.   During the
Civil troubles he distinguished himself by his chivalrous devotion to the Royal cause.   Indeed, his loyalty
cost him his fortune and his liberty ; for, after being
repeatedly plundered by the Roundheads, who on one
occasion sacked his parsonage and half murdered his
family and servants, he was in 1646 deprived of his
preferment, stripped of his patrimony, and flung into
prison.   Some years before these events had occurred
he had formed an alliance which unites by the tie of
kindred the two most distinguished names in political
satire.   The wife of Thomas Swift was Elizabeth Dryden, the sister, not of the poet's father, as the earlier
biographers supposed, but of the poet's grandfather.
She bore her husband ten sons and four daughters.
Of these sons two only were, it seems, regularly educated and provided for.   The eldest, Godwin, a clever
and pushing youth, settled in Dublin, practised at the
Irish bar, married a connection of the Marchioness of
Ormond, and prospered.   Thither at various times
four of his brothers, attracted doubtless by his success,
followed him, and Godwin, to do him justice, appears
to have exerted all his influence to aid them.   One of
these brothers must, however, have sorely tried the
patience of the kind-hearted but worldly-minded law-
yer. This was Jonathan. Without any regular profession, without prospects, and with nothing but a miserable pittance of about twenty pounds a year to depend
upon, this thoughtless stripling had taken to wife a
young woman as poor as himself.   Jonathan's bride
was Abigail Erick.   She came of an ancient but decayed family in Leicestershire, which claimed as its

founder that wild Saxon patriot whose ferocity and
courage were long the terror of our Norman rulers ;
for in the veins of Swift's mother ran the blood of
Eadric the Forester. The imprudent couple soon
experienced the folly of the step they had taken. Mrs.
Swift had already a baby in her arms. Poverty and
the sordid miseries which follow in its train were before them. At last their prospects seemed to brighten.
The stewardship of the King's Inns fell vacant, and
Jonathan, who had occasionally assisted in the office,
was fortunate enough to obtain the post. This was in
January 1666. In the spring of the following year he
was in his grave.

He left his wife in deplorable circumstances. As
steward he had out of his scanty income been compelled
to advance money for commons, but the members of
the Inns now refused to refund it. He had died in
debt to the Benchers, and his widow was unable to
meet the claim. She owed money to the doctors who
had attended him ; she owed money to the very undertaker who had buried him. He had been taken from
her before she was aware that she was again to
become a mother. Every week her distress and
embarrassment increased. Her health was wretched,
her heart was breaking. In the midst of these
miseries her hour of agony drew on. On November
30, 1667, at No. 7, Hoey's Court, Dublin, was born
the child who was to make the name of his dead
father immortal.

Swift was always slow to confess obligations, but
there seems no reason for doubting that both Godwin
and William behaved kindly to their sister-in-law.
Indeed, it is stated on very good authority that it was

at his Uncle Godwin's house that Jonathan's birth
took place, and that the first months of his infancy
were passed there. However that may be, an event
occurred while he was still a baby which for some
years cast doubt on the country of his nativity. It
chanced that the nurse, a woman from Whitehaven,
to whose care he had been confided, was summoned
home to attend a dying relative from whom she expected a legacy. But the good soul had become so
attached to her charge that she could not bear to
part with it. Without saying a word, therefore, to
Mrs. Swift, she stole off with the baby to England,
and there for nearly three years the little fellow remained with his tender-hearted foster-mother. He
was sickly and delicate, but she watched over him
with maternal fondness; and she took such pains
with his education that by the time he was three
years old he could read any chapter in the Bible.
Under what circumstances he rejoined his mother in
Ireland we have no means of knowing, but in his
seventh year he was placed in the Foundation School
of the Ormonds at Kilkenny. One of his playmates
in this obscure Irish seminary was in a few years
destined to enter on a career of unusual brilliance, and
to leave a name as imperishable as his own; for his
playmate at Kilkenny was the future author of the
Way of the World and *Love for Love*. A few unimportant particulars are all that have survived of
this period of Swift's life. It seems, however, pretty
certain that there was nothing to distinguish him
either at school or at college from the general body of
his class-fellows. Parts like his are, indeed, rarely
remarkable for their precocious development. In his

fifteenth year he commenced residence at Trinity College, Dublin, being supported, no doubt, by his uncles Godwin and William. He was entered as a pensioner on April 24, 1682, and here he remained during those years which are perhaps of all years the most critical in man's life.

His career at Trinity was not creditable to him. Between the period of his matriculation and that of his degree, though he lived, he tells us, with great regularity and due observance of the statutes, he turned a deaf ear to his teachers, neglected the studies prescribed by the College, and, reading just as whim or accident directed, found himself, on the eve of his examination, very ill-qualified to face it. The subjects then required for a degree in Arts were, it must be admitted, sufficiently repulsive. Those noble works which form in our day the basis of a liberal education had had no place in the curriculum. The poetry, the oratory, the history of the ancient world, were alike ignored. Plato was a dead letter; Aristotle held the post of honour, but it was not the Aristotle who is familiar to us—the Aristotle of the *Ethics*, of the *Politics*, of the *Poetics*, of the *Rhetoric* —but the Aristotle of the *Organon*, the *Physics*, and the *Metaphysics*. Next in estimation to these treatises stood the dreary *Isagoge* of Porphyry, and the writings of two pedantic logicians whose names have long since sunk into oblivion, Smiglecius and Burgersdicius. Swift presented himself for examination, and failed. The examining Board, pronouncing him to be dull and insufficient, refused at first to pass him. Finally, however, they granted a degree *speciali gratiâ*, a term implying in that University that a candidate has gained by favour what he is not entitled to claim by merit. With this slur upon his name he resumed his studies, his object being to proceed to the higher degree of Master. His former irregularities were now aggravated by graver misdemeanours. He absented himself from chapel and from roll-call, neglected lectures, was out late at night, and became associated with a clique of youths who were not merely idle but dissolute. Indeed, he seems to have been in ill odour everywhere. Mr. Forster manfully endeavours to prove that Swift's college life has been greatly misrepresented. He is willing to admit that it was not all a fond biographer could wish, but he is, he says, convinced that it was by no means so discreditable as it has been painted. He produces, for example, a College roll, dated Easter, 1685, in which Swift is entered as having at a recent examination acquitted himself satisfactorily in Latin and Greek. From this Mr. Forster infers that neither incompetence nor idleness could be justly imputed to him. He is wel aware that in later years Swift never questioned, or, to speak more accurately, that he tacitly corroborated, the unfavourable verdict passed on him by the examiners at Trinity. But this Mr. Forster interprets as a touch of sarcastic irony. 'Famous as Swift then was,' he says, 'any discredit from the special grace would, as he well knew, go to the givers. In attempting to fix a stigma upon him, they only succeeded in fixing a stigma upon themselves.' Mr. Forster next points out that the most serious of Swift's alleged delinquencies during these years are purely supposititious—that he has been confounded with his cousin Thomas—and that it is to Thomas,

not to Jonathan, that the entries in the College re-
gistry may in many cases refer. This is undoubtedly true. Thus we have no means of determining
whether the Swift who, in November, 1688, was suspended for insubordination and contumacy was
Thomas or Jonathan, though the biographers have
in all cases assumed that the culprit was Jonathan.
That Jonathan was, however, publicly censured in
March, 1687, is certain, as in the entry which records
the censure—censure for 'notorious neglect of duties'
and for 'tavern-haunting'—the names of the two
Swifts occur together.[1] Whether he had any share
in the composition of a scurrilous harangue,[2] in which
some of the principal members of the Trinity Common
Room are treated with gross disrespect, and for the
delivery of which, in the character of Terræ Filius,
one of his college acquaintances narrowly escaped
expulsion, is still open to debate. Dr. Barrett is
convinced that it was Swift's production. Mr. Forster
sees no traces of his hand in any portion of it. Scott
is of opinion that it received touches from him, and
in that opinion I entirely concur. The heroic poem,
for example, in the third act of the piece is very
much in the vein of his maturer years; the doggerel
Latin recalls exactly the jargon in which throughout
his life he delighted to indulge; and, though we
search in vain for his peculiar humour, we find, we
regret to say, only too much of his peculiar indecency.
But the subject is scarcely worth discussing.

Whatever may have been the measure of his
delinquencies at College, it is not difficult to account

---

[1] See the subject fully discussed in Barrett's *Essay*, pp 10–19.

[2] Printed by Barrett *id.* pp. 46–77.

for their origin. His life had been poisoned at its
very source. Everything within and everything without combined to irritate and depress him. He was
miserably poor, he was inordinately proud ; he was
daily exposed to contumely and contempt, he was
sensitive even to disease. The wretched pittance
which was his sole support, and for which he was
indebted to the charity of relatives, was bestowed in a
manner which stung him to the quick. Of these
cruel benefactors his uncle Godwin was probably the
chief, and the patronage of Godwin he repaid with an
energy of hatred which no lapse of years could impair.
Ill-health and hypochondria added to his sufferings.
The solace of human sympathy was during the whole
of this dismal period unknown to him. His mother,
who was in England, he never saw. There is no evidence of his having been on affectionate terms with
any of his associates. He sought at first some allevia-
tion for his miseries in the perusal of light literature,
and he gave to poetry and history the time which
should have been devoted to severer studies. The
result of this was that, at an age when youths are
peculiarly sensitive about anything which casts
aspersion on their parts, he found himself branded
as a blockhead. What followed was natural. Angry
with himself, with his relatives, with his teachers, he
became reckless and dissolute. His misfortunes were
brought to a climax by the failure of his uncle Godwin,
who had for some time been in embarrassed circumstances, and was now on the verge of ruin.

Meanwhile events were occurring which terminated
in his abrupt departure for the mother-country
Ireland was in the throes of a dreadful crisis

Tyrconnel, at the head of the Celtic Catholics, was hurrying on a revolution which threatened to end in the extermination of the Saxon Protestants. The English, who held their lives in their hands, were preparing to abandon their possessions and fly. At the close of 1688 a report was circulated that there was to be a general massacre of the Saxons. A panic ensued. The ports were crowded. Many who were unable to obtain a place in commodious vessels embarked in open boats. Among these terrified emigrants was young Swift. On arriving in England he at once made his way to his mother, who was residing near her relatives at Leicester. She was not, as he well knew, in a position to offer him a home, but he found what he sought, affection and guidance. The glimpses which tradition gives us of this excellent woman suffice to show that the respect and love with which her illustrious son never ceased to regard her were not undeserved.[1] An unassuming piety pervaded her whole life. Though her fortune was scanty, even to meanness, she was, she used to say, rich and happy. Her spirit was independent, her mind cultivated, her manners gentle and refined. Her polite and sprightly conversation was the delight of all who knew her, and she was endowed with what is perhaps the rarest of all the qualities possessed by her sex—a keen sense of humour. From her Jonathan inherited no doubt many of the gifts which were to make him famous ; it was unfortunately not given her to transmit to him the gifts which would have made him happy. He remained at Leicester for some months, dividing his

---

[1] For the character of Mrs. Swift see Deane Swift's *Essay*, pp. 22–3.

time between forming plans for the future and toying with rustic beauties. His attentions to one of these young women, an intelligent but portionless girl, became so marked that Mrs. Swift, remembering the miseries of her own ill-advised union, was greatly alarmed. She found, however, some consolation in the fact that her scapegrace was amenable to reason.

The necessity for his quitting Leicester, where, if not dependent on herself, he was dependent on her relatives, and where he had no chance of obtaining employment, was obvious. But where that employment was likely to present itself was a problem on which the good lady was not able to throw much light. In truth, the future of a young man whose sole distinctions were a character for idleness and insubordination, a gloomy temper, an uncouth exterior, and the possession of a degree obtained under circumstances notoriously discreditable to him, might well have puzzled a far more experienced adviser. In this perplexity it occurred to her that the best course for Jonathan to take would be to consult Sir William Temple. That eminent man, though moving in a sphere very different from her own, had married one of her connections. His father, Sir Richard, had, moreover, been on terms of intimacy with Godwin Swift, and she thought it not unlikely, therefore, that Temple would, out of consideration for his father's friend, do what he could to assist that friend's nephew. Nor was she mistaken. Temple not merely received him with kindness but offered him a home, and at the beginning of the summer of 1689 we find him domesticated at Moor Park. The nature of Swift's connection with Temple and the circumstances of his residence at Moor

Park have been very variously related. Macaulay describes it as a period of unmingled humiliation and wretchedness, and represents his position as little better than that of an upper servant. Mr. Forster draws a different conclusion. There is, he contends, no evidence to show that Temple treated his young dependent in any manner calculated to wound his pride; and he is, he says, convinced that, whatever may have been the exact position held by Swift in Temple's household, it involved nothing which compromised either self-respect or independence. Swift's own account of the matter certainly corroborates Mr. Forster's view. 'I hope,' he wrote many years afterwards, in a letter to Lord Palmerston, 'you will not charge my living in Sir William's family as an obligation; for I was educated to little purpose if I retired to his house on any other motive than the benefit of his conversation and advice, and the opportunity of pursuing my studies.' Nothing, too, is more certain than that Temple introduced him to his most distinguished guests, an honour to which he would scarcely have been admitted, had he sat, as Macaulay represents, at the second table. Twice, indeed, during this period of alleged ignominious vassalage, we find him in conversation with no less a person than his Sovereign, who on one occasion condescended to teach him how to cut asparagus in the Dutch way, and on another listened to his arguments in favour of the Triennial Bill.

The conclusions of Macaulay and the conclusions of Mr. Forster may, however, without much difficulty be reconciled. Macaulay was no doubt right in asserting that the years passed by Swift under Temple's roof

were years during which his haughty and restless spirit
suffered cruel mortification.　Mr. Forster is no doubt
right in denying that Temple regarded him as a mere
parasite.　The truth probably is that he entered Moor
Park as Temple's amanuensis and secretary; that in
return for these services he was boarded and paid;
that his patron at first treated him not indeed with
indignity, but with the reserve and indifference which
a man of the world would naturally maintain towards
a raw and inexperienced youth of twenty-three.　But
as his genius developed, and as his extraordinary
powers began to display themselves—neither of which
would be likely to escape so acute an observer as Temple
—his relations with his employer assumed a new character.　Temple grew every day more condescending
and gracious.　He discoursed freely with him on public
affairs; he gave him the benefit of his own great experience as a diplomatist and as a courtier; and he entrusted him with business with which he would assuredly have entrusted nobody in whose tact and parts he
had not full confidence.　It was not in Temple's nature
to feel or assume that frank cordiality which puts dependents at their ease and lightens the burden of obligation, for his constitution was cold, his humour
reserved.　Partly also owing to ill-health, and partly
to congenital infirmity, his temper was often moody
and capricious.　Of his substantial kindness to Swift
there can, however, be no question.　Indeed, it seems
clear that Temple behaved from first to last with a
generosity which has never been sufficiently appreciated.　When, for example, in the spring of 1690, the
state of the young secretary's health rendered a change
to Ireland necessary, Temple at once exercised his in-

fluence to procure employment for him in Dublin. Two years afterwards he helped him to obtain an *ad eundem* degree in Arts at Oxford, and in 1694 he offered him a post—the only post it was in his power to bestow—in Ireland. He had already recommended him to the notice of the King, who had, as early as 1692, promised to assist him.

But, unhappily, the mind and body of the youth on whom these favours had been bestowed were so diseased that what was intended to benefit served only to irritate and distress him ; the more indulgence he received the more exacting and querulous he became ; the brighter appeared the prospect without, the deeper and blacker grew the gloom within. All that had haunted his solitude at Dublin with unrest and wretchedness now returned to torment him in scenes of less sordid misery. His pride amounted almost to monomania. Fancied slights and imaginary wrongs ulcerated his soul with rage and grief. No kindness availed either to soothe or to cheer him. What would in gentler spirits have awaked the sense of gratitude, awoke nothing in him but a galling sense of obligation. In an honourable employment his jaundiced vision discerned only derogatory servitude. The acute sensibility which had been his bane from childhood kept him constantly on the rack. A hasty word or even a cold look sufficed to trouble him during many days, and the inequalities of his patron's temper caused him pain so exquisite that it vibrated in his memory for years.[1] Nor were these his only miseries. The first symptoms, or what he

---

[1] For a vivid description of his miseries at Moor Park see his *Verses on Temple's Late Illness and Recovery*, Scott, xiv. 45.

believed to be the first symptoms, of that mysterious malady which pursued him through life, and which was, after making existence a misery to him, to end in bringing him, under circumstances of unspeakable degradation, to the tomb, had already revealed themselves. His chief solace during the earlier portion of this dismal time lay in scribbling verses and in teaching a little delicate, pale-faced, dark-eyed girl to read and write. The child was a daughter of a poor widow in the service of Temple's sister, Lady Giffard, and when Swift first saw her she was in her seventh year. Such were the circumstances under which he first met Esther Johnson, and such was the commencement of what was to afford him the only true happiness, perhaps, he was ever to know.

To poetic composition he appears at this time to have devoted himself with great diligence; but his success was by no means proportioned to his efforts. In truth, anything worse than the Pindarics of Swift would be inconceivable. They are not merely immeasurably below the vilest of Cowley's or Oldham's, but they are immeasurably below the vilest that could be selected from Yalden, Flatman, or Sprat. Indeed, they are so bad that, if we wish to judge of them relatively, we must judge them in relation to each other. If, for example, there is anything more insufferable than the *Ode to Archbishop Sancroft*, it is the *Ode to Sir William Temple*; and should the reader be inclined to wonder whether anything worse than the *Ode to Sir William Temple* could possibly exist, he has only to turn to the *Ode on the Athenian Society*. This last poem he submitted to his kinsman Dryden, requesting an opinion as to its merits. ' Cousin Swift,' was the

old man's blunt reply, 'you will never be a poet.' As
Dryden's literary judgments were held to be without
appeal, and carried among the wits of these times the
weight and authority of oracles, this was a severe
blow. And Swift felt it keenly. Its effect on him
was characteristic. He recognised, with the good
sense that always distinguished him, the justice of
the criticism, and he wrote no more ambitious verses.
But he indemnified himself for the blow his vanity
had received by seizing every opportunity to ridicule
and vilify his critic. To the end of his life he pursued
the memory of Dryden with unrelenting hostility.

He now determined to strike for independence.
His thoughts pointed towards the Church, for in the
Church he saw prospects such as no other walk in life
opened out, and the King had promised him preferment in the event of his taking orders. But Temple
was very unwilling to part with him. He counselled
delay; it would be wiser, he thought, to wait until
the King had offered what he promised. Swift was,
however, not to be evaded, and his importunity
appears to have ruffled his patron's temper. At last,
after some haggling, he boldly demanded what
Temple was prepared to do for him. 'I shall not,'
said the old statesman, 'pledge myself to anything;
but you may, if you please, take a clerkship in the
Irish Rolls.' 'Then,' replied Swift, 'as I have now
an opportunity of living without being driven into
the Church for a maintenance, I shall go to Ireland
and take orders.' And he quitted Moor Park in a rage.

He had, however, in all probability, fully considered
what he was about to do; and, though after events
must have caused misgivings as to the prudence of

this course, it is remarkable that he never, so far as
can be discovered, expressed, either in writing or in
conversation, regret for having taken a step which,
from a worldly point of view, he had assuredly ample
reason to repent. He was ordained by the Bishop of
Derry; his deacon's orders are dated Oct. 28, 1694,
his priest's orders Jan. 13, 1695. In his autobiography he is careful to tell us that it was not for the
mere sake of gaining a livelihood that he sought
ordination, but his correspondence makes it quite
clear that the expectation of preferment was, if not
his only, at least his primary motive. However that
may be, he accepted his position with all its responsi-
bilities. If the yoke galled him, none saw the sore.
If he had scruples, he concealed them. It would be
absurd to say that Swift was at any time a model
clergyman, but it is due to him to acknowledge that,
from the moment he entered the Church to the
moment disease incapacitated him for action, he was
the indefatigable champion of his order. Few ecclesi-
astics have, indeed, in any age, done more for the
body to which they belonged. To his efforts the
Irish Church owed the remission of First Fruits and
Twentieths. It was he who suggested, and it was
he who pleaded for, the erection of those churches
which still keep the memory of Queen Anne fresh
among Londoners. For upwards of thirty years he
fought the battles of the Church against the Catholics
on the one hand, against the Nonconformists and
Freethinkers on the other, with a vehemence and
intrepidity which savoured not merely of zeal but of
fanaticism. The meanest of his brethren, when persecuted and oppressed, was sure of his protection. Any

attempt on the part of the laity to tamper with the
rights of the clergy never failed to bring him into the
field. It was this which envenomed him against the
Whigs. It was this which involved him in a lifelong
feud with the Dissenters. It was this which inspired
the last and most terrible of his satires. Nor did his
anxiety for the interests of his order end here. There
can indeed be no question that the respectability of
the inferior clergy dates from him. What the position
of an unbeneficed priest was in those days we know
from innumerable sources. His existence was, as a
rule, one long struggle with sordid embarrassments.
Though he belonged to a learned profession, he was
not permitted even by courtesy to place himself on
an equality with gentlemen. He subsisted partly on
charity, and partly on such fees as his professional
services might accidentally enable him to pick up.
He officiated at clandestine marriages, he baptized
unfortunate children. He negotiated here for a
burial, and there for a sermon. In one family he
undertook to say grace for his keep; in another he
contracted to read prayers twice a day for ten shil-
lings a month. The result of this was that the minor
clergy, as Macaulay justly remarks, ranked as a body
lower than any other educated class in the community.[1]
To Swift belongs the double honour of having been the
first to kindle in his degraded brethren a new spirit,
and of having done more than any other single man
ever did to vindicate for them that rank in society
which happily they now hold. He strove to impress

[1] That Macaulay's well-known picture of the state of the clergy
at this time is substantially correct is shown by Mr. Lecky, *England
in the Eighteenth Century*, pp. 75-78.

on them a sense of the dignity of their calling. He
pointed out to them that to obtain the respect of the
world they must respect themselves. He taught them
to feel that a Christian and a scholar was in the truest
signification of the word a gentleman ; that there
need be nothing servile in dependence, nothing derogatory in poverty. How minutely he had studied the re-
quirements of his profession is evident in his *Essay on
the Fates of Clergymen*,[1] in the treatise he began *Concerning that Universal Hatred which prevails against the
Clergy*,[2] and in his *Letter to a Young Clergyman on taking
Orders* [3]—an admirable treatise which well deserves a
place in the library of every candidate for ordination.
Few things, probably, gave him more pleasure than
the reflection that his own social distinction had in a
manner contributed to raise the clergy in popular estimation. What is certain is that, the more famous he
became, the more studiously he identified himself with
his order. At Court, at the levee of the Lord Treasurer,
in the drawing-rooms of noble houses, he carried this
peculiarity to the verge of ostentation. It was observed
that whenever he went abroad, or gave audience to a
stranger, he was careful to appear in cassock and
gown. He would never permit even his most intimate
friends to forget the respect due to his cloth. If at
social gatherings festivity exceeded the limits of the
becoming, it was his habit to leave the table. Im-
modesty and impiety he regarded with abhorrence,
and he was once so annoyed at the levity of the conversation at Bolingbroke's table that he quitted his

[1] Scott, viii. 361.
[2] *Id*. p. 373. See too his tracts on the Irish Clergy
[3] *Id*. p. 335.

host's house in a rage. In his anonymous writings
he allowed himself, it is true, a licence which seems
scarcely compatible with this austerity; but his
anonymous writings must not be confounded with his
personal character. No profane or licentious expression was ever known to proceed from his lips. 'His
ideas and his style,' says Delany, 'throughout the
whole course of his conversation were remarkably
delicate and pure beyond those of most men I was
ever acquainted with.'[1] His morals were pure even to
asceticism. His deportment was remarkably grave
and dignified, and his conduct, though often singularly
eccentric, was never such as to degrade him in the
eyes of inferiors. The least charitable of his biographers admit that he performed his duties, both
as a parish priest and as head of the Chapter of
St. Patrick's, with exemplary diligence. He regularly
visited the sick, he regularly administered the Sacra-
ment, he regularly preached. For twenty years he
was never known to absent himself from early
morning prayer. Though he had personally no taste
for music, he took immense pains with the education
of the choir at St. Patrick's. At Laracor he instituted,
in addition to the ordinary Sunday services, extraordinary services on week-days; and these services,
whenever he was in residence, he conducted himself.
If between 1701 and 1714 he was frequently absent
from his parish, it must be remembered that his
congregation scarcely ever numbered more than
twenty, and that for this congregation, scanty though

---

[1] Delany's *Observations*, p. 75 ; and again, p. 83, 'He was remarkably guarded against anything that had the least appearance of
indecency.'

it was, he not only provided an incumbent, but took
care, even during his busiest time in London, to be
regularly informed of all that took place in his absence. He rebuilt at his own expense the parsonage ;
he laid out at his own expense the grounds ; he
increased the glebe from one acre to twenty. That
there was much in the temper and conduct of this
singular man which ill became an apostle of that
religion the soul and essence of which are humility
and charity, we must in justice acknowledge. But
no such admission should induce us to withhold the
praise to which he is righteously entitled. And that
praise is high praise.

Preferment, such as it was, was not long in
coming. A few days after he had been ordained
priest he was presented with the small prebend of
Kilroot. It was in the diocese of Connor, and was
worth about a hundred a year. Of his residence at
Kilroot few particulars have survived. One passage
of his life in this dismal solitude is, however, not
without interest. At Kilroot Swift sought, and
sought with importunity, to become a husband. For
the last time in his life he addressed a woman in the
language of passion. For the last time in his life
he was at the feet of a fellow-creature. The lady
who had the honour of inspiring this affection was
the sister of a college acquaintance. Her name was
Waryng, a name which her suitor, after the fashion
of gallants of those times, transformed into the
fanciful title of Varina. The correspondence between
the two lovers extended over a period of four years.
Of this nothing remains but two letters of Swift's,
and from these two letters must be gathered all that

can now be known of the woman whom Thackeray
absurdly describes as Swift's first victim. Now these
letters seem conclusive in Swift's favour. He had,
it is easy to see, acted in every way honourably
and straightforwardly. He offered to make great
sacrifices ; he expresses himself in terms of chivalrous
devotion. Miss Waryng, on the other hand, appears
to have been an inflammable but politic coquette,
who held out just so much hope as sufficed to keep
her lover in expectancy, and just so much encouragement as sufficed to make him impatient. For a
while he submitted to all the indignities which female
caprice can devise for the torture of men in his
unhappy condition. At last the spell was broken ;
he grew first languid and then indifferent. What
followed was what usually does follow in such cases.
As the lover cooled, the mistress melted. As he
wished to dissolve the tie, she wished to draw it
closer. Their correspondence terminated with a letter
on which it is needless to comment, but which it
would be well for all who may, like Varina, be
tempted to abuse the prerogatives of wit and beauty,
to peruse.[1] It would not be true to say that Swift
ever became a misogynist, but nothing is more certain
than that from this time the poetry of the affections
ceased to appeal to him. Henceforth love lost all its
glamour ; henceforth the passion which religion and
romance have ennobled into the purest and holiest
of human bonds awoke only nausea and contempt.
He never afterwards sought to marry ; he never afterwards permitted woman to be more to him than a
sister or a friend.

[1] Printed in Scott, vol. xv. 244.

Meanwhile his patron was anxious to have him back again at Moor Park. Temple was, it seems, busy preparing his *Memoirs* and *Miscellanies* for the press, and wanted assistance. Accordingly, at the beginning of 1696, he wrote to Swift inviting him to return. Swift, weary of Kilroot, and influenced, no doubt, by the hope of preferment in England, complied at once with the request. He completed his arrangements, indeed, with such expedition that gossip was busy with conjectures as to the reason of his sudden departure. Two legends, one to his credit and one to his discredit, but both equally unfounded and equally absurd, have been preserved by biographers. They are, however, scarcely worth a passing allusion.

Swift's second residence at Moor Park may be regarded as the turning-point of his life. During this period his character became fixed; the habits which ever afterwards distinguished him were formed; his real education commenced; his extraordinary powers first revealed themselves. Delany and others tell us that ever since his failure at the University he had vowed to devote at least eight hours in every day to study. Of this industry we find no very decisive proofs, either during his first residence with Temple or during his stay in Ireland. But between 1696 and 1700 it is certain that his application was intense. In one year, for example, in addition to several English and French works, he had perused the whole of Virgil twice, Lucretius and Florus three times, the whole of the *Iliad* and the *Odyssey*, the whole of Horace and Petronius, the *Characters* of Theophrastus, the *Epistles* of Cicero, much of Ælian; and

had not only read but analysed Diodorus Siculus,
Cyprian, and Irenæus. His classical attainments
were never, we suspect, either exact or profound. Of
his acquirements in Greek scholarship he has, it is
true, given us no opportunity of judging; but of his
acquirements in Latin we can only say that, if they
are to be estimated by his compositions, they were not
such as to give him a place among scholars. His
Latin prose is, as a rule, ostentatiously unclassical,
and his verses harsh and lumbering. The *Carberiae
Rupes* is indeed written with great vigour, and is not
inferior in point of Latinity to Johnson's verses on
completing his Lexicon, but it is not a poem which
Addison or Gray would have cared to own. But,
whatever may have been his deficiency in the niceties
of scholarship, his general acquaintance with the
writers of antiquity was undoubtedly considerable.
Of his familiarity with Homer there can be no question. He was his favourite poet, and he once said
of him that he had more genius than all the rest of
the world put together.[1] It would seem, too, that he
must have studied Demosthenes with great diligence.
It may sound paradoxical, but assuredly there is nothing in our literature more Demosthenean, in diction,
colour, and method at least, than the *Drapier Letters*
and such pamphlets as the *Conduct of the Allies* and
the *Public Spirit of the Whigs*.[2] Lucretius was always

[1] Deane Swift's *Essay*, p. 237.
[2] Dr. Jowett, in the Introduction to his translation of Plato's *Republic*, says that there are no traces of a knowledge of Plato in Swift.
This is not correct. In the *Sentiments of a Church of England Man*
there is an allusion to a passage in the *Apology*; in his 31st *Examiner*
the substance of Aristophanes' speech in the *Symposium* is given
(the unknown correspondent being a common fiction); there is a

a favourite with him, and the Roman satirists he
knew intimately. Indeed, he was so sensible of the
value of such studies, that, when political duties
had for a while suspended them, his first care, on
becoming master of his time, was to betake himself
to the History of the Persian Wars and to the *De
Rerum Naturâ*.

While he was thus storing his mind with the
treasures of Temple's library, an incident occurred
which gave birth to the first characteristic production
of his genius. For some years a most idle controversy
as to the relative merits of ancient and modern writers
had been agitating literary circles both in England
and on the Continent; and in 1692 Temple had, in
an elegantly written but silly and flimsy dissertation,
taken up the gauntlet in favour of the ancients. In
this dissertation he had selected for special eulogy a
series of impudent forgeries which some late sophist
had attempted to palm off on the world as the *Epistles
of Phalaris of Agrigentum*. Competent scholars had
long treated them with the contempt they deserved.
But Temple, with a dogmatism which was the more
ludicrous as he was probably unable to construe a
line of the language in which they were written, not
only pronounced them to be genuine, but cited them
as proofs of the superiority of the ancients in epis-
tolary literature. Nothing which bore Temple's name
on the title-page could fail to command attention, and

reference to the *Republic* in the *Advice to a Young Poet*; Plato is
quoted in the sermon on the Wisdom of this World; in *Gulliver's
Travels*, Part IV., he is quoted on the subject of conjectural knowledge; and the account of the principle on which selections for
marriage are made in the Commonwealth of the Houyhnhnms is
plainly taken from the fifth book of the *Republic*.

the treatise speedily became popular. The general
public, who knew little more about Phalaris than that
he roasted people in a brazen bull and was afterwards
roasted himself, grew curious about these wonderful
letters. As there was no accessible edition, Aldrich,
the Dean of Christ Church, induced his favourite
pupil, Charles Boyle, a younger son of the Earl of
Orrery, to undertake one, and in 1695 the volume
appeared. The book was as bad as bad could be, and
would have been forgotten in a fortnight, but it
chanced that in the preface the young editor had
taken occasion to sneer at Richard Bentley, then fast
rising to pre-eminence among scholars. Bentley, in
revenge, proved the letters to be what in truth they
were, the worthless fabrication of a late age. To the
public expression of this opinion he had been urged
by his friend Wotton, who had already broken a lance
with Temple in defence of the moderns, and was only
too glad to find so weak a point in his opponent's
armour. Temple, naturally angry at the aspersion
thus cast on his taste and sagacity, and the digni-
taries of Christ Church, feeling that the reputation
of their College was at stake, made common cause.
Temple prepared a reply, which he had the good
sense to suppress. Boyle, or rather Boyle's coadjutors,
Atterbury and Smalridge, united to produce a work
now only memorable for having elicited Bentley's
immortal treatise. Some months, however, before
the Christ Church wits were in the field, Swift had
come to his patron's assistance. The *Battle of the
Books* is surely the most original and pleasing of
Swift's minor satires. The humour is in his finest
vein, austere and bitter, but without any of that

malignity which in later years so often flavoured it.
Every clause is pregnant with sense and meaning.
The occasional parodies of the Homeric style are felicitous in the extreme.   The allegory throughout is
admirably conducted, full of significance even in its
minutest details.   Nothing could be happier than the
Apologue of the Spider and the Bee, nothing more
amusing than the portrait of Bentley, and assuredly
nothing more exquisitely ludicrous than the episode
of Bentley and Wotton.   Historically the work is of
great interest.   It initiated a new style of satire.   It
opened out a new field for satire.   It sounded the first
note of the famous war waged by Wit and Humour
and Good Sense against Pedantry and the Abuse of
Learning—a war in which so many of the foremost
men of the eighteenth century were to engage.   Out
of the *Battle of the Books* grew the dissertations in
the *Tale of a Tub,* and out of those dissertations grew
the great Scriblerus Satire and the Fourth Book of
the *Dunciad.*[1]   For the idea, but for the idea only, of
this work, Swift was perhaps indebted to De Callières,
a French writer, whose *Histoire poétique de la Guerre
nouvellement déclarée entre les Anciens et les Modernes*
appeared in 1688, and is now one of the rarest
volumes known to bibliographers.[2]

[1] It is perhaps worth noticing that the *Battle of the Books* supplied Matthew Arnold with the phrase which has since become so
popular, ' Sweetness and Light ' ; and Gray with the hint of his sub-
limest couplet—

'Amazement in his van, with Flight combin'd,
And Sorrow's faded form, and Solitude behind.'

Cf. where Swift says of Bentley, ' On he went, and in his van Confusion and Amaze, while Horror and Affright brought up the rear.'

[2] The authorship of this work was formerly attributed to an apo-

Swift soon discovered where his strength lay. His genius developed itself with astonishing rapidity. In 1696 he had not, so far as is known, produced a line which indicated the possession of powers in any way superior to those of ordinary men. In the following year he suddenly appeared as the author of a satire of which the least that can be said is that it would have added to the reputation of Lucian or Erasmus; and before the year was out he had written the greater part of a work which is allowed to be one of the first prose satires in the world. The *Tale of a Tub* was composed immediately after the *Battle of the Books*, and it forms, as Mr. Forster rightly observes, part of the same satirical design. In the *Battle of the Books* he had satirised, in the person of the Moderns, the abuses of learning; in the *Tale of a Tub* he satirises in the body of the narrative the abuses of religion, and in the digressions he returns to his former theme. It is scarcely necessary to say that the immediate object of the Apologue of the Three Brothers was to trace the gradual corruption of primitive Christianity, to ridicule the tenets and the economy of the Church of Rome, to pour contempt on the Presbyterians and Nonconformists, and to vindicate the superiority of that section of the Reformed Church to which he himself belonged. But, though the Apologue of the Three Brothers is the most celebrated portion of the satire, and forms, so to speak, the nucleus of the work, it is not here that the key is to be found. If we would seek the key we may find it in the ninth section :—

cryphal Coutray. It was reserved for Mr. Craik to assign it to its proper author. See his interesting note, *Life of Swift*, p. 71.

How fading and insipid do all objects accost us that are not
conveyed in the vehicle of delusion! How shrunk is everything
as it appears in the glass of nature! So that, if it were not for
the assistance of artificial mediums, false lights, refracted angles,
varnish and tinsel, there would be a mighty level in the felicity
and enjoyments of mortal men. . . . In the proportion that credulity is a more peaceful possession of the mind than curiosity, so
far preferable is that wisdom which converses about the surface
to that pretended philosophy which enters into the depth of things.

He tells us in the Apology that he had endeavoured to strip himself of as many real prejudices
as he could—in other words, not to be the dupe of
illusions ; and in this temper the work is composed.
The satire rests on the same foundation as *Gulliver's
Travels*—a deep-seated and intense conviction of the
hollowness and nothingness of life, a profound contempt for all the objects to which the energies of
mankind are usually directed, and a profound contempt for all that is supposed to constitute human
eminence. That the satire falls chiefly on ' those
strange beasts which in all tongues are called fools ' is
true, but the mockery, as in *Gulliver*, knows no distinction. The very dedication is ironical, and could scarcely
have been agreeable to Somers. Martin is every whit
as ridiculous as his brethren, and, whatever Swift may
himself have thought or designed—and that he was
the last man in the world to be guilty of intentional
profanity is certain—the effect of the work is undoubtedly to place all ceremonial religion in a ludicrous
light. Against the charge of profanity he anxiously
defended himself in an elaborate Apology prefixed
to an edition of the work which appeared in 1710.
After frankly admitting that he ' had given a liberty
to his pen which might not suit with maturer years or

graver characters '—for he was ' a young gentleman '
when he wrote the work—he yet maintains that
nothing can be fairly deduced from it which is contrary
to religion and morality. He is, he says, at a loss
to understand why any clergyman of the English
Church should be angry to see the follies of fanaticism
and superstition exposed, though in the most ridiculous
manner. So far from the satire containing anything
to provoke them, 'it celebrates the Church of England
as the most perfect of all others in discipline and
doctrine ; it advances no opinion they reject, nor
condemns any they receive.' Religion, it is true,
ought not to be ridiculed, but surely, he continues, its
corruptions are proper subjects for satire. ' Il y a
bien de la différence,' he might, indeed, have said with
Pascal, ' entre rire de la religion et rire de ceux qui
la profanent par leurs opinions extravagantes. Ce
serait une impiété de manquer de respect pour les
vérités que l'esprit de Dieu a révélées ; mais ce serait
une autre impiété de manquer de mépris pour le
faussetés que l'esprit de l'homme leur oppose.' [1]
But, though he argued thus, and contended that what
was reprehensible in the work could have been easily
corrected with a very few blots, those very few blots
were never made. He was, no doubt, perfectly aware
that the removal of what pious people might with
justice take exception to as profane would be as disastrous to the fabric of his work as his own Jack's
removal of the gold lace and embroidery from the
primitive coat. He adopted, therefore, in the interests of his work, the policy of Martin, but in his own
professional interests he compromised the matter by

[1] *Lettres Provinciales*, xi.

never acknowledging the authorship of the satire. To this day the authorship of the *Tale of a Tub* rests only on presumptive evidence.

No other of his satires is so essentially Rabelaisian, but it is Rabelaisian in the best sense of the word. In the phrase of Voltaire, it is Rabelais in his senses; in the still happier phrase of Coleridge, it is the soul of Rabelais in a dry place. Without the good canon's buffoonery and mysticism, it has all his inexhaustible fertility of imagination and fancy, all his humour, all his wit. But it has them with a difference. The humour of Rabelais is that of a man drunk with animal spirits; the humour of Swift is that of a reflective cynic. The essence of Rabelais's wit is grotesque extravagance; the wit of Swift is the perfection of refined ingenuity. The one revels without restraint in licentious drollery; the other, sobered and measured, delights most in dry and bitter irony. In the *History of Gargantua and Pantagruel* there is no attempt at condensation; the ideas are, as a rule, pursued with wearisome prolixity to their utmost ramifications. But the power manifested in the *Tale of a Tub* is not merely power expressed, but power latent. Its force is the force of reserve. Every paragraph is pregnant with innuendo; every page teems with suggestion. There is much in Rabelais which conveyed, we suspect, as little meaning to Du Bellay and Marot as it conveys to us. There is nothing in Swift's allegory which would puzzle a schoolboy who has Scott's notes, brief though they are, in his hand. The *Tale of a Tub* is, in the opinion of many of Swift's critics, his master-piece. 'It exhibits,' says Johnson, 'a vehemence and rapidity of mind, a copiousness and vivacity of diction, such as he never afterwards possessed, or never exerted.'

It is curious that it should have escaped all Swift's biographers and critics that he was probably indebted for the hint of this famous work to a sermon written by Archbishop Sharp, the very prelate who succeeded a few years later in persuading Anne that, as the author of such a satire as the *Tale*, Swift was not a proper person for a bishopric. Sharp's sermon is entitled, *A Discussion of the Question which the Roman Catholics much insist upon with the Protestants, viz. in which of the different Communions in Christendom the only true Church of Christ is to be found. With a refutation of a certain Popish argument handed about in manuscript in 1686.* Now, as this sermon had attracted great attention, because it had given occasion to James II.'s mandatory letter to the Bishop of London to suspend Sharp, then Rector of St. Giles' in the Fields, it is very likely indeed to have come under Swift's notice.[1]

[1] Sharp's allegory is this (he is disputing the claims of the Church of Rome to consider itself the primitive and Catholic Church) :—' A father bequeaths a large estate among his children and their children after them. They do for some generations quietly and peaceably enjoy their several shares without disturbance from each other. At last one branch of this family (and not of the eldest house neither) starts up, and, being of greater power than the rest, and having got some of the same family to join with him, very impudently challengeth the whole estate to himself . . . and would dispossess all the rest of the descendants, accounting them no better than bastards, though they be far more in number than his own party. . . . Upon this they contest their own right against him, alleging their father's will and testament and their long possession, and that they are lawfully descended from their first common ancestor. But this gentleman who would lord it over his brethren offers this irrefragable argument for the justice of his claim.' The argument is that they cannot show

Swift's indifference to literary distinction, at an age when men are as a rule most eager for such distinction, is curiously illustrated by the fate of these works. For eight years they remained in manuscript, and, when they appeared, they appeared not only anonymously, but without receiving his final corrections.

At the beginning of 1699 Temple died. 'He expired,' writes Swift with mingled tenderness and cynicism, ' at one o'clock this morning, January 27, 1699, and with him all that was good and amiable in human nature.' When the will was opened, he found that his patron's provision for him, though not liberal, was judicious. In addition to a small pecuniary legacy, he had appointed him his literary executor, with the right to appropriate such sums as the publication of his posthumous papers—and they were voluminous—might realise. These papers Swift published in three instalments, the first appearing in 1700 and the last in 1709.

that any opposition was made to his claim by others of the family setting up a claim of their own; *therefore* he is lord of the inheritance. The reply is that they were at first all living in peace together, and that they did not oppose his claim for the simple reason that he never advanced it, but that they are perfectly prepared, now that he has advanced it, to resist him. ' Tell us by what right or justice you can pretend to be sole lord of this inheritance. Let the will of our common parent be produced, and this will plainly show that we have as much a share in this estate as you have.' Sharp's *Works*, vii. 94. Nor is it at all unlikely that Swift may have been indebted still further to Sharp. The sermon referred to is one of fourteen which are devoted to an elaborate exposure of the errors and corruptions of the Church of Rome, furnishing indeed, even to minute details, the whole text for Swift's satire, which follows Sharp's commentary step by step. My attention was directed to this interesting parallel by a letter in the *Gentleman's Magazine* for July, 1814, signed ' Indagator.'

It was probably with no regret that Swift turned his back on Moor Park. He was in the prime of youth, the world was before him, and he had assuredly every reason to think that the removal of such obstacles as lay in the road to success would not, to one equipped as he was equipped, prove a very arduous task.

E

CHAPTER IV

LIFE BETWEEN 1700 AND 1710

During the next fourteen years Swift's life was one long and fierce struggle for pre-eminence and dominion. To obtain that homage which the world accords, and accords only, to rank and opulence, and to wrest from fortune what fortune had at his birth malignantly withheld, became the end and aim of all his efforts. 'I will tell you,' he wrote many years afterwards to Pope, 'that all my endeavours from a boy to distinguish myself were only for want of a great title and fortune, that I might be used like a lord by those who have an opinion of my parts, whether right or wrong it is no great matter.' In those days literary distinction was not valued as it is valued in our time. If a man of letters found his way to the tables of the great, he was treated in a manner which offensively reminded him of the social disparity between himself and his host. The multitude regarded him, if he was poor, as was only too likely, with contempt; if he was well to do, with indifference. Hence men ambitious of worldly honour and worldly success shrank from identifying themselves with authorship, and employed their pens only as a means of obtaining Church preferment or political influence. It was so with some of the most distinguished writers of those times—with Burnet, with Addison, with Sprat, with Rowe, with Price, with Parnell. 'I desire,' said Congreve to Voltaire, 'to be considered not as an author, but as a gentleman.' This perhaps accounts for Swift's carelessness about the fate of his writings, and for the fact that, with two or three unimportant exceptions, nothing that came from his hand appeared with his name. Indeed, on no body of men have the shafts of his terrible scorn fallen so frequently as on those whom we should describe as authors by profession. But, if distinction in literature was not his end, he knew well its value as a means. Many adventurers with resources far inferior to his had already fought their way into the chambers of royalty and to the Episcopal Bench. With what patience under disappointment, with what long-protracted assiduity, with what tact and skill, with what tremendous energy, with what unscrupulous versatility, with what vast expenditure of genius and ability he pursued this object, is now matter of history.

The death of his patron found him without preferment and without a competency. As the King had, however, on the occasion of one of his visits to Moor Park, promised to confer on him a prebend either of Canterbury or of Westminster, he was by no means inclined to despond; and he hastened up to London to remind the King of his promise. His request took the form of a petition, which the Earl of Romney, one of the Lords of the Council, promised to present. This, however, he neglected to do, and Swift, weary of hanging about Kensington, and angry, no doubt, at the King's neglect, accepted an invitation

E 2

from the Earl of Berkeley, then one of the Lords
Justices of Ireland, to accompany him as chaplain
and secretary to Dublin. Berkeley, little knowing the
character of the man with whom he had to deal,
attempted at first to treat him as superiors were in
those days wont to treat dependents. Finding it
convenient on his arrival in Ireland to bestow the
private-secretaryship on a layman, he suddenly informed Swift that his services as a chaplain were all
that would henceforth be expected from him. The
deprivation of this office was, however, accompanied
with a promise of ecclesiastical preferment. In a
few months the rich deanery of Derry chanced to fall
vacant. It was in the disposal of Berkeley, and Swift
at once applied for it ; but the person, one Bushe,
who had superseded him in the secretaryship, now
prevailed on Berkeley to confer the deanery on another
candidate. Swift's rage knew no bounds. Bursting
into Berkeley's room, and thundering out to the
astonished secretary and his no less astonished principal ' God confound you both for a couple of scoun-
drels,' he abruptly quitted the Castle. Nor did his
wrath end here. He gibbeted his patron in a lampoon
distinguished even among his other lampoons by its
scurrility and filth. Whether this came to Berkeley's
ears is not known. It probably did, and in that case
Berkeley's subsequent conduct is in all likelihood to
be attributed, not to a sense of justice, nor, as Mr.
Forster supposes, to the influence of Lady Berkeley
and her daughters, but to a sense of fear. He had
probably the sagacity to see that no public man could
afford to make an enemy of a writer so powerful and
so unscrupulous as Swift. What is certain is that

his Excellency lost little time in appeasing his in-
furiated chaplain. In a short time Swift was again
the inmate of the Castle, and in a few weeks he was in
possession of preferment, not indeed equivalent in
value to the deanery, but sufficient to maintain him
in decency and independence. In March, 1699, he
was presented with the rectory of Agher and the
vicarages of Laracor and Rathbeggan, in the diocese
of Meath. In the following year the prebend of Dun-
lavin, in St. Patrick's Cathedral, was added to his other
preferments. A few months later he took his Doctor's
degree in the University of Dublin. For the present,
however, he continued to reside as domestic chaplain
at the Castle.

In the spring of 1701 Berkeley was recalled, and
Swift accompanied him to England. He found the
country convulsed with civil discord ; the unpopularity
of the King was at its height ; disgraceful feuds
divided the two Houses; a war with France was
apparently imminent. This latter disaster the Tories
attributed to the Partition Treaties, and, as the Tories
had just won a great victory, they were determined to
indemnify themselves for their recent depression by
giving full scope to resentment and vengeance. With
this object they were hurrying on impeachments
against the four Whig Ministers, who were, it was
supposed, responsible for the second of these obnoxious
treaties. Swift was not the man to remain a mere
spectator where he was so well qualified to enter the
arena, and in the summer of 1701 appeared his first
contribution to contemporary politics. It was a
treatise in five chapters, entitled *A Discourse of the
Contests and Dissensions between the Nobles and the*

Commons in Athens and Rome; and it was written
to vindicate the Whig Ministers, to defend the King's
foreign policy, and to allay the intemperate fury of
party.   It points out that what ruined States in
ancient times is quite as likely to ruin States in
modern times, that political liberty can only be preserved by the just equilibrium of power at home and
power abroad, and that dissension between the ruling
bodies in commonwealths must ultimately result either
in anarchy or in despotism; and it selects from the
political history of Rome and Athens incidents ana-
logous to the incidents then occurring in England.
Orford has his analogue in Miltiades and Themistocles,
Halifax in Pericles and Alcibiades, Somers in Aristides,
and Portland in Phocion.   The tone is calm and
grave, the style simple, nervous, and clear, but somewhat heavy.   What distinguishes it from Swift's other
political tracts is its ostentatious parade of classical
learning, and the fact that it is purely didactic, that it
is without humour and without satire.   The work at
once attracted attention.   Some ascribed it to Burnet,
others to Somers; but Swift, for a time at least, kept
his own secret and returned to Ireland.   Next year,
however, he acknowledged the authorship, and was
received with open arms by the Whig leaders, who,
confessing their obligations to him, promised to do all
in their power to serve him.   In 1704 appeared a
volume which at once raised him to the highest place
among contemporary prose writers.   It contained the
Tale of a Tub, the *Battle of the Books*, and the *Discourse on the Mechanical Operation of the Spirit*, a singularly powerful satire, in which he returns again to
the sectaries, or modern saints as he calls them, whom

he had lashed so unmercifully in the *Tale of a Tub.*
The contempt and loathing with which Swift regarded
these fanatics are not difficult to explain. They were
the enemies of the Church. They were republicans
and levellers in politics. They were distinguished as
a body by characteristics which are and always will
be particularly odious to men of honesty and good
sense. With 'enthusiasm,' even when it was not
simulated, he had little sympathy, for he knew its
perilous proximity to mere hysterics; but enthusiasm
deliberately affected for disguising ignorance and
masking lewdness or avarice, as by these people it
habitually was, provoked him to fury. The Saints
had long been the butts of wits and satirists. South
had covered them with ridicule from the pulpit;
Butler and Dryden had lashed them in the press.
But the vehement vituperation of the sermons on the
Christian Pentecost and the Education of Youth, the
caustic sarcasm of *Hudibras* and of the *Hypocritical
Nonconformist,* and the trenchant raillery of the
Religio Laici and the *Hind and Panther,* are tame and
merciful compared with the cataclysm of filth and
vitriol with which the scorn and contempt of Swift
overwhelmed them.

The volume containing these pieces was published
anonymously. But it was probably soon known, or at
least suspected, in literary circles that Swift was the
author. From this moment he became a distinguished
figure in what were then the favourite haunts of wits
and politicians. He renewed his acquaintance with
his old schoolfellow Congreve. He grew very friendly
with Addison. He did all in his power to ingratiate
himself with the Whig leaders; and not without

success. Somers, indeed, contented himself with
being civil, but with the more genial Halifax acquaint-
anceship soon ripened into intimacy. The very remarkable words in which Addison inscribed to him
a copy of his *Travels in Italy* sufficiently prove in
what estimation the Vicar of Laracor was, even as
early as 1705, held by those whose praise was best
worth having. ' To Dr. Jonathan Swift '—so runs
the inscription—' the most agreeable companion, the
truest friend, and the greatest genius of his age.'

The next five years form perhaps the most unsatisfactory period in Swift's life. They were spent
partly in Ireland, where he divided his time between
Laracor and Dublin, and partly in London, where he
passed his mornings in scribbling pamphlets which
he never published, his afternoons in dancing attendance on the Whig Ministers, and his evenings in
gossiping with Addison and Addison's friends in
coffee-houses. The preferment which his new patrons
had promised never came, though it appeared to be
always on the way. At one moment it seemed probable that he would be promoted to the see of Waterford, at another moment he had some hope of Cork.
Then he expressed his willingness to accompany Lord
Berkeley as Secretary of the Embassy to Vienna, and
at last talked half seriously of going out as a colonial
bishop to Virginia. But nothing succeeded, and the
fact that nothing succeeded he attributed neither to
the cross accidents of fortune nor to the obstinate
opposition of the Court, but to the treachery and
ingratitude of his friends. Though he still continued
to jest and pun with Pembroke and the Berkeleys, to
discuss the prospects of the Whigs with Somers, and

to lend an additional charm to the splendid hospitality
of Halifax at Hampton Court, his temper grew every
day more soured ; every day he became more suspicious and sore.

In truth, a breach with the Whigs was inevitable.
Even apart from motives of self-interest—and it
would be doing Swift great injustice to suppose that
motives of self-interest were the only, or indeed the
chief, motives which at this time guided him—he had
ample cause for dissatisfaction. If there was one
thing dear to him, it was the Established Church.
To preserve that Church intact, intact in its ritual,
intact in its dogmas, intact in its rights, was in his
eyes of infinitely greater importance than the most
momentous of those questions which divided party
from party.   As a politician, he found no difficulty in
reconciling the creed of Halifax and Somers with the
creed of St. John and Harcourt.   He was at one with
those who dethroned James and set up William ; he
was tender with those who spoke respectfully of the
doctrines of passive obedience and non-resistance.
He figures in history, indeed, as a furious partisan,
but nothing is more remarkable than the moderation
and tolerance which he always displays in discussing
the principles of political opinion.   In his own creed
he shunned all extremes ; it was of the essence of
compromise. ' No man,' he says in one of the most
admirable of his minor tracts, ' who has examined the
conduct of both parties for some years past, can go to
the extremes of either without offering some violence
to his integrity or understanding.' [1]   Again he writes :

[1] *Sentiments of a Church of Englan Man.*

'In order to preserve the Constitution entire in Church
and State, whoever has a true value for either would
be sure to avoid the extremes of Whig for the sake of
the former, and the extremes of Tory for the sake of
the latter.'[1]   But all traces of this moderate spirit
disappear the moment the Church is in question.   As
an ecclesiastic, he was intolerant even to ferocity.
The Reformed Protestant Church was in his eyes the
only religious institution which civil authority should
recognise ; its doctrines the only doctrines which
should be held to constitute the faith of Christians.
' The Church of England,' he says, and has said
over and over again in almost the same words,
should ' be preserved entire in all her rights, power
and privileges ; all doctrines relating to her government discouraged which she condemns ; all schisms,
sects and heresies discountenanced.'[2]   The depth and
sincerity of his convictions on this point are strikingly
illustrated by the fact that when, as leader of Irish
opposition to England, it was plainly his interest to
unite men of all religions against the Government,
his hostility to such as lay outside the pale of the
Protestant Church was as obstinate and uncompromising as ever.   In his writings he makes no distinction between Papists and Atheists, between Presbyterians and Free Thinkers.   He was in favour of the
Penal Laws.   He upheld the cruellest of those statutes
which excluded Nonconformists from the rights of
citizens.   On these points his opinion was at variance
with that of the party to which he was politically
attached, and entirely in harmony with that held by the

[1] *Sentiments of a Church of England Man.*
[2] *Free Thoughts upon Present Affairs.*

party to which he was politically opposed. It was not, however, till 1708 that Swift began to see clearly that the interests of his order and the interests of his party were irreconcilable. In that year it became evident that the Church was in danger. The Whigs were, in truth, more and more identifying themselves with her enemies. They had already agitated a repeal of the Test Act in favour of the Protestant Dissenters in Ireland, and its repeal would probably soon be moved in England. The contempt in which many of them held the religion of the State was notorious. Indeed, Cowper, the Chancellor, Somers, the President of the Council, and Wharton, the Viceroy of Ireland, were popularly regarded as little better than infidels. Nor was this all. In the Whig ranks were to be found that odious clique—at the head of which were Toland, Tyndal, and Collins—a clique whose avowed object was the demolition of orthodoxy. Under these circumstances Swift published, in 1708, his *Sentiments of a Church of England Man*, a pamphlet in his best manner, temperate in tone, forcible and luminous in style. He here defines his position, and here for the first time his dissatisfaction with his party is discernible. This was succeeded by that inimitable satire on Free Thinkers, the *Argument against Abolishing Christianity*. Never, perhaps, has the truth of Horace's remark that pleasantry is, as a rule, far more efficacious than vehemence and severity been more strikingly illustrated than in this short piece.

But it was not as a satirist only that he designed to combat the enemies of Christianity. He had gathered materials for an elaborate refutation of one

of the most obnoxious of Tyndal's publications, an
interesting fragment of which may be found in the
eighth volume of his collected writings.[1]

Meanwhile, the Whigs in Ireland were pushing on
the repeal of the Test Act, and in December appeared
Swift's famous letter concerning the Sacramental
Test.   The defeat of the Bill followed.   It was believed
that Swift's pamphlet had turned the scale against
Repeal; and from this moment all cordiality between
himself and his party was at an end.   In his next
treatise, *A Project for the Advancement of Religion*,
there was, no doubt, as much policy as piety.   It
appears to have been written partly to ingratiate himself with the Queen, partly to insinuate that Whig
dominion was inimical alike to morality and religion,
and partly to confirm the reaction which was now
beginning to take the turn in favour of the Church
party.   No man who knew the world as the author of
this work knew it could have seriously entertained
many of the schemes which he here gravely propounds.
To find Swift in Utopia is to find him where we never
found him before and where we shall never find him
again.   It is not unlikely that he suspected, or had
perhaps been informed, that the *Tale of a Tub* might
injure his prospects of preferment, and that this tract
was written to remove any unfavourable impression
which this work may have made on the Queen and
other orthodox people.   What is certain is that the
work is designed to show that the writer is an enthusiast in the cause of religion and orthodoxy, and that

---

[1] *Remarks upon a Book entitled The Right of the Christian
Church, &c.*

religion and orthodoxy should be necessary qualifications for favour and preferment.[1]

While he was busy with these works, his humour and drollery were convulsing all London with laughter. Though astrological quackery had long been on the decline, it still found credit with the multitude. Its most distinguished professor at this time was John Partridge, a charlatan who was in the habit of publishing each year an almanack, in which he predicted, with judicious ambiguity, what events were in the course of the year destined to take place. In February, 1708, appeared a pamphlet of a few pages, informing the public that Partridge was an impostor, that a rival prophet was in the field, and that it was the intention of that rival prophet to issue an opposition almanack. The writer then proceeded with great gravity to unfold the future. He scorned, he said, to fence himself, like Partridge, with vagueness and generalities ; he should be particular in everything he foretold ; he should in all cases name the day ; he should often be enabled to name the very hour. 'My first prediction,' he goes on to say, 'is but a trifle ; ' it relates to Partridge, the almanack maker. 'I have consulted the star of his nativity by my own rules,

[1] This conjecture as to Swift's object in the tract is, it may be added, rendered the more probable by the remarkable notice of the work inserted by Steele, then on friendly terms with him, in the fifth number of the *Tatler*. Compare these sentences : 'It is written with the spirit of one who has seen the world enough to undervalue it with good breeding. The author must certainly be a man of wisdom as well as piety and have spent much time in the exercise of both. . . . The whole air of the book, as to the language, the sentiments, and the reasonings, shows it was written by one whose virtue sits easy about him, and to whom vice is thoroughly contemptible.'

and find he will infallibly die upon the twenty-ninth
of March next, about eleven o'clock at night, of a
raging fever ; therefore I advise him to consider of it
and settle his affairs in time.' The pamphlet was
signed 'Isaac Bickerstaff,' but it was soon known in
literary circles that Isaac Bickerstaff was none other
than Jonathan Swift.   The thirtieth of March arrived,
and out came *The Accomplishment of the First Part
of Bickerstaff's Predictions, being an Account of the
Death of Mr. Partridge upon the 29th instant.*   Here
we read how, towards the end of March, Mr. Partridge
was observed to droop and languish ; how he then
grew ill and took to his bed ; how, as the end drew
near, his conscience smiting him, he sorrowfully confessed that his prophecies were mere impositions, and
that he himself was a rogue and a cheat ; how the
unhappy man ' declared himself a Nonconformist and
had a fanatical preacher to be his spiritual guide,'
and how, finally, he breathed his last just as Bickerstaff
had predicted.   To this, in his almanack for 1709,
Partridge was fool enough to reply, ' thanking God
that he was not only alive, but well and hearty,' and
unluckily adding that he was alive also on the day of
his alleged demise.   Upon that Bickerstaff, in an exquisitely humorous pamphlet, proceeded to assure
Partridge that if he imagined himself alive he was
labouring under hallucination ; alive he may have
been on March 29, for his death did not occur
till the evening, but dead he most assuredly had been
ever since, for he had himself candidly admitted
it.   ' If,' added Bickerstaff, ' an uninformed car-
case still walks about, and is pleased to call itself
Partridge, I do not think myself in any way answer-

able for that.' The jest had now become general.
The life of the unhappy almanack maker was a
burden to him. At home facetious neighbours pes-
tered him with questions as to whether he had left
any orders for a funeral sermon, whether his grave
'was to be plain or bricked.' If he appeared in the
street he was asked why he was sneaking about without his coffin, and why he had not paid his burial
fees. So popular became the name assumed by Swift
in this humorous controversy that when, in April,
1709, Steele published the first number of the *Tatler*,
it was as Isaac Bickerstaff that he sought to catch the
public ear.[1]

But controversies of another kind were now fast
approaching. The latter half of 1709, and the greater
part of 1710, Swift spent in sullen discontent in
Ireland. And sorrow also was to visit him. In the
spring of 1710 he received the news of his mother's
death. 'It was,' he writes with touching particularity,
' between seven and eight on the evening of May 10,
1710, that I received a letter in my chamber at
Laracor . . . giving an account that my dear mother
died that morning, Monday, April 24, 1710. . . . I
have now lost my barrier between me and death. God
grant that I may be as well prepared for it as I confidently believe her to have been. If the way to Heaven
be through piety, truth, justice, and charity, she is
there.' He had the consolation of knowing that he

---

[1] See, for the whole controversy, *Predictions for the Year 1708 :
an answer to Bickerstaff. By a Person of Quality. The Accomplishment of the First Part of Bickerstaff's Predictions. Squire Bickerstaff Detected. A Vindication of Isaac Bickerstaff, Esq. A Famous
Prediction of Merlin.* All printed in Scott's *Swift*, vol. ix.

had been an affectionate and dutiful son, the best and perhaps the only solace in one of the bitterest of human afflictions. Meanwhile, every post was bringing important tidings from London. At the beginning of March had come the news of the impeachment of Sacheverell. In the summer arrived a report that the Ministry were to be turned out. By June 15 Sunderland had been dismissed. By August 23 Godolphin had resigned, the Treasury was in commission, and the ruin of the Whigs imminent. In less than a month—on September 7—Swift was in London. The business which carried him thither was business which had for two years been occupying him. At the suggestion of Bishop Burnet, Anne had, shortly after her accession, consented to waive her claim to the First Fruits and Tenths. The remission extended only to the English clergy, but the Irish Convocation, thinking themselves entitled to the same favour, had petitioned the Lord Treasurer to lay their case before the Queen. With this object they had, in 1708, appointed Swift their delegate. Session after session he had pleaded and importuned, but he had been able to obtain nothing but evasive answers. It was now hoped that an application would be more successful, and this application Swift, in commission with the Bishops of Ossory and Killaloe, was directed to make.

On his arrival in London he found everything in confusion. The Whigs were in panic, the Tories in perplexity. Harley was at the head of affairs, but on which of the two parties Harley intended to throw himself was as yet known to no man. Many believed that few further changes would be made. Others

were of opinion that a Coalition Ministry would be
formed. What seemed certain was that no Tory
Government would have the smallest chance of standing for a month. By the majority of the Whigs the
appearance of Swift was hailed with joy. ' They
were,' he writes to Esther Johnson, ' ravished to see
me, and would lay hold on me as a twig while they
are drowning.' [1]   But by Godolphin he was received
in a manner which bordered on rudeness, and when
he called on Somers it was plain that all he had to
expect from the most eminent of the Whigs was cold
civility. And now he took a step of which he probably
little foresaw the consequences. With Harley he was
already slightly acquainted, and at the beginning of
October he called on him, explaining the business
which had brought him to town, and requesting the
favour of an interview. The interview was granted,
and in less than a fortnight Swift was the friend and
confidant of the leader of the Tories, was assailing
his old allies, was fighting the battles of his former
opponents.

No action of his life has been so severely commented on as his defection from his party at a crisis
when defection is justly regarded as least defensible.
But what are the facts of the case ? In deserting
the Whigs he deserted men from whom in truth he
had long been alienated, who were in league with the
enemies of his order, who were for factious purposes
pursuing a policy eminently disastrous and immoral,
and who had treated him personally not merely with
gross ingratitude but with unwarrantable disrespect.
He was bound to them neither by ties of duty nor by

[1] *Journal to Stella*, Sept. 9, 1710.

F

ties of sentiment. He owed them nothing, he had promised them nothing. Nor did his apostasy involve any sacrifice of political principle. On all essential points he was, as we have seen, a moderate Whig, and in all essential points a moderate Whig he continued to remain. Whoever will take the trouble to compare what he wrote under the Administration of Godolphin with what he wrote under the Administration of Harley will perceive that he was never, even in the heat of controversy, inconsistent with himself. What he declared to be his creed in his *Sentiments of a Church of England Man*, and in his *Letter concerning the Sacramental Test*, he declared to be his creed in his contributions to the *Examiner*, in his *Free Thoughts on Public Affairs*, in a remarkable letter which, six years after Anne's death, he addressed to Pope,[1] and in his *Memoirs relating to the Change in the Queen's Ministry*. Who ever accused Godolphin and Marlborough of treachery when they deserted the Tories and identified themselves with the Whigs? And yet

---

[1] This important letter, which is dated Dublin, Jan. 10, 1720-1, is an elaborate exposition of Swift's political creed. In his letter on the Sacramental Test he defines what he calls a Whig: 'Whoever bears a true veneration to the glorious memory of King William as our great deliverer from Popery and Slavery: whoever is firmly loyal to our present Queen, with an utter abhorrence and detestation of the Pretender: whoever approves the succession to the crown in the House of Hanover and is for preserving the doctrine and discipline of the Church of England, with an indulgence for scrupulous consciences; such a man, we think, acts upon right principles and may be justly allowed a Whig.' So in a letter written in 1733 he writes to Lady Betty Germaine: 'As for me, I am of the old Whig principles, without the modern articles and refinements.' So, too, in a letter to Mr. Grant, dated March, 1734, he speaks of 'the old Whig principles which always have been mine.' See, too, his *Letter to a Whig Lord* (*Works*, Scott's edition, iv. 255).

there is nothing which tells against Swift which does
not tell with infinitely greater force against them.
They deserted the Tories in the interests of the War;
he deserted the Whigs in the interests of the Church.
They sacrificed principles for party: he sacrificed
party for principles.   If conclusive proof of his
honesty and sincerity were needed, it would be furnished indeed by his conduct and writings during
the dominion of the Whigs.   Had he allowed motives
of self-interest to guide him, he would never have
opposed, and opposed to their great annoyance, measures to which the policy of the Whig leaders was
pledged.   But to Occasional Conformity, and to all
other attempts to relax, much more to rescind, the
provisions of the Test Act, his attitude had, since
1706, been that of determined and uncompromising
hostility. And he had made no secret of his opinions.[1]
He had embarrassed his party by opposing toleration in Ireland and by opposing it in Scotland. 'No
prospect of making my fortune ' — such was his
language to Archbishop King in 1708—'shall ever
prevail on me to go against what becomes a man of
conscience and truth, and an entire friend of the
Established Church.'[2] Nor was this all. As the friend
of the Church, he was the friend of the throne ; as
a minister of religion and as a patriotic citizen, he
was opposed to the superfluous sacrifice of life and
money.   The disrespect with which the Whigs habitually treated the Queen was as notorious as the fact
that for party purposes they were protracting, and

[1] See particularly *Memoirs relating to the Change in the Queen's
Ministry.*
[2] Letter to King, Nov. 9, 1708.

unnecessarily, a sanguinary and ruinous war. To describe, therefore, as Macaulay and others have done, Swift's defection from the Whigs as the conduct of an interested and unscrupulous renegade, is as absurd as it is unjust. He went over to Harley, it is true, at a time when the Whigs were in trouble, but it ought in justice to be remembered that he went over to him at a time when there were probably not ten men in London who believed that the new Ministry would stand. But here apology must end. The rancour and malignity which mark his attacks on his old associates, many of them men to whose probity and disinterestedness he had himself given eloquent testimony, admit of no justification. He had, we may be sure, honestly persuaded himself that it was his duty, both in the interests of the State and in the interests of the Church, to break with the Whigs, but it would be absurd to deny that his hostility on public grounds was sharpened by private animosity.

CHAPTER V

I

No other man of letters has ever occupied a position similar to that which Swift held during the Administration of Harley. Ostensibly a mere dependent, the power which he virtually possessed was autocratical. Without rank, without wealth, without office, rank, wealth, and authority were at his feet. The influence which he exercised on all with whom he came in contact resembled fascination. Men little accustomed to anything but the most deferential respect submitted meekly to all the caprices of his insolent temper. Noble ladies solicited in vain the honour of his acquaintance. The heads of princely houses bore from him what they would have resented in an equal. Indeed, the liberties which he sometimes took with social superiors are such as to be scarcely credible. On one occasion, for example, he sent the Lord Treasurer to fetch the principal Secretary of State from the House of Commons, 'For I desire,' he said, 'to inform him with my own lips, that if he dines late I shall not dine with him.' On another occasion, when the Lord Treasurer at one of his levees asked him to present Parnell, Swift coolly replied : ' A man

of genius, my lord, is superior to a lord in high
station, and it is becoming therefore that you should
seek out Dr. Parnell and introduce yourself.'   And
so Lord Oxford, ' in the height of his glory,' as Delany
puts it, ' had to walk with his Treasurer's staff from
room to room through his own Levy enquiring which
was Dr. Parnell.' [1]   On another occasion, when informed that the Duke of Buckinghamshire—a nobleman whose pride had passed into a proverb—was
anxious to be introduced to him, he coolly replied : ' It
cannot be, for he has not made sufficient advances.'
' I use them like dogs,' he writes to Stella, ' because
I expect they will use me so.'   By Harley and
St. John, the one the Lord Treasurer, the other the
principal Secretary of State, he was treated not merely
as an equal but as a brother.   He was their companion at home and in business.   They indulged him
in all his whims.   They bore with patience the sallies
of his sarcastic humour.   They allowed him a licence,
both of speech and of action, which they would never
have tolerated in a kinsman.   When we remember
that at the time Swift attained this extraordinary
dominion over his contemporaries he was known only
as a country priest with a turn for letters, who had
come to London partly as an ambassador from the
Irish clergy and partly to look for preferment, it may
well move our wonder.   But it is not difficult to explain.   No one who is acquainted with the character
of Swift, with his character as it appears in his own
writings, as it has been illustrated in innumerable
anecdotes, and as it has been delineated by those who
were familiar with him, can fail to see that he belonged

---

[1] Delany's *Observations*, pp. 28-9.

to the kings of human kind.   Like Innocent III. and
like Chatham, he was one of those men to whom the
world pays instinctive homage.   Everything about
him indicated superiority.   His will was a will of
adamant ; his intellect was an intellect the power and
keenness of which impressed or awed everyone who
approached him.   And to that will and to that intellect was joined a temper singularly stern, dauntless,
and haughty.   In all he did, as in all he said, these
qualities were obtrusively, nay, often offensively,
apparent, but nowhere were they written more legibly
than in his deportment and countenance.   Though
his features had not at this time assumed the severity
which they assume in the portrait by Bindon, they
were, to judge from the picture painted about this
time by Jervis, eminently dignified and striking.
The portrait is a familiar one—the lofty forehead, the
broad and massive temples, the shapely semi-aquiline
nose, the full but compressed lips, the dimpled double
chin, and the heavy-lidded, clear blue eyes, 'with the
very uncommon archness in them,' [1] rendered peculiarly lustrous and expressive by the swarthy complexion and bushy black eyebrows which set them
off.   He was, we are told, never known to laugh ; his
humour, even when most facetious, was without
gaiety, and he would sit unmoved while his jest was
convulsing the company round him.   The expression
of his face could never, even in his mildest moods,
have been amiable, but when anger possessed him it
was absolutely terrific.   'It would,' says one who
knew him well, 'be impossible to imagine looks or
features which carried in them more terror and

---

[1] Pope's description in Spence's *Anecdotes*, p. 119 (edit. Singer).

austerity.'[1] 'He kept,' writes Delany, ' every one in
awe.'[2]   His manner was imperious and abrupt; to
inferiors or to those whom he disliked, contemptuous
or insolent. A harsh and unsympathetic voice corresponded with his manner and with his speech. His
words—few, dry, and bitter—cut like razors. In his
conduct and in his speech lurked a mocking irony,
which rendered it impossible even for those who were
familiar with him to be altogether easy in his society.
What he felt he seldom took pains to conceal, and
what he felt for the majority of his fellow-men was
mingled pity and contempt.

The biography of Swift between the winter of 1710
and the summer of 1714 is little less than the history
of four of the most eventful years in English annals.
For during the period which began with the triumph
of Harley and ended with the discomfiture of Bolingbroke nothing of importance was done with which he
is not associated. So fully, indeed, did he enter into
the political life of those stirring times, that a minute
history of the Administration of Oxford might without
difficulty be constructed from his correspondence and
pamphlets.

To one portion of that correspondence a peculiar
interest attaches itself. Twenty-one years had passed
since Swift first saw Esther Johnson at Moor Park.
She was then a child of seven, he a young man of
twenty-two. In spite of this disparity in years the
little maid and himself had soon grown intimate.
Her innocent prattle served to while away many a sad
and weary hour. He would babble to her in her own
baby language. He would romp and play with her,

[1] Orrery's *Remarks*, Letter ix.   [2] *Observations*, p. 18.

and, as her mind expanded, he became her teacher.
From his lips she first learned the principles which
ever afterwards guided her pure and blameless life.
By him her tastes were formed, by him her intellect
was moulded.   For a while their intercourse was interrupted.   Time rolled on.   Temple died in 1699.
Esther had settled down with a female companion at
Farnham.   She was then on the eve of womanhood,
and rarely has woman been more richly endowed
than the young creature who was about to dedicate
her life to Swift.   Of her personal charms many
accounts have survived.   Her pale but strikingly
beautiful face beamed with amiability and intelligence.
Neither sickness nor sorrow could dim the lustre of
her fine dark eyes.   Over her fair and open brow
clustered hair blacker than a raven.   Though her
figure inclined, perhaps, somewhat too much to
embonpoint, it was characterised by the most perfect
grace.   Her voice was soft and musical, her air and
manner those of a finished lady.   But these were not
the qualities which in the eyes of Swift elevated
Esther Johnson above the rest of her sex.   What he
dwells on with most fondness, in the description
which he has left of her, are her wit and vivacity, her
unerring judgment, her manifold accomplishments,
the sweetness and gentleness of her temper, her
heroic courage,[1] her large-hearted charity.   ' She

---

[1] It is curious that none of Swift's biographers should in the
accounts they have given of Esther Johnson have referred to the very
remarkable anecdote which he has recorded to illustrate her courage
and presence of mind.   ' She and her friend having removed their
lodgings to a new house, which stood solitary, a parcel of rogues,
armed, attempted the house, where there was only one boy.   She
was then about four-and-twenty; and having been warned to

excelled in every good quality that can possibly accomplish a human creature,' wrote Swift to Stopford.[1] Delany tells us that he 'had often heard a man of credit and a competent judge declare that he never passed a day in Stella's society wherein he did not hear her say something which he would wish to remember to the last day of his life.[2] Few men would have been proof against charms like these. But to Swift Esther Johnson was at eighteen what she had been at seven. To her personal beauty he was not, indeed, insensible, but it formed no link in the chain which bound him to her. Many of the qualities which attracted him were qualities not peculiar to woman, and of the qualities peculiar to woman those which attracted him most were those which form no element in sexual love. Coleridge has conjectured with some plausibility that the name Stella, which is a man's name with a feminine termination, was purposely selected by him to symbolise the nature of his relation with Miss Johnson.[3] That

apprehend some such attempt, she learned the management of a pistol; and the other women and servants being half dead with fear, she stole softly to her dining-room window, put on a dark robe to prevent being seen, primed the pistol afresh, gently lifted up the sash, and taking her aim with the utmost presence of mind, discharged the pistol, loaded with bullets, into the body of one villain who stood the fairest mark. The fellow, mortally wounded, was carried off by the rest, and died the next morning; but his companions could not be found. The Duke of Ormond had often drunk her health to me upon that account.' *Character of Mrs. Johnson.* So much for Thackeray's sentimental picture of 'the Saint of English Story,' of the tender drooping victim of unrequited love.

[1] See *Correspondence*, letter dated July 20, 1726. See, too, Swift's *Character of Mrs. Johnson* (*Works*, Scott, ix. 489).

[2] Delany's *Observations*, p. 66.

[3] *Table Talk*, p. 106. The name is, of course, merely the Latinised form of · Esther.'

he was more attached to that lady than he was to
any other human being seems clear, but the love was
purely platonic, and there is not the shadow of a
reason for believing that a marriage was ever even
formally solemnised between them.   Of marriage,
indeed, he scarcely ever speaks without expressions
indicative either of horror or of contempt.   He delighted in the society of women ; he even preferred
their society to that of men.   The truth is that, with
all his austerity and cynicism, no man was more
dependent on human sympathy.   That sympathy he
found in woman—he sought nothing more.   To
approach him nearer was to move his loathing.   Of
the poetry of passion he knew nothing.   The grace
and loveliness over which an artist or a lover would
hang entranced presented themselves to him as they
might present themselves to a thoughtful physician.
Where the rest of his sex saw only the blooming
cheek and the sparkling eye, he saw only the grinning
skull behind.   Where all else would be sensible of
nothing but what was pleasing, he would be sensible
of nothing but what was disagreeable.   His imagination grew not merely disenchanted but depraved.   He
appears, indeed, to have been drawn by some strange
attraction to the contemplation of everything which
is most offensive and most humiliating in our common
humanity.   But it was the fascination of repulsion.
It was of the nature of that morbidity which tortured
the existence of Rousseau.[1]   His fastidious delicacy

[1] The subject is not a pleasing one, but if the reader will turn to
the second volume of the *Confessions*, Part 2, Book 7, p. 210 *seqq.*, he
will find a passage which seems curiously illustrative of Swift's
peculiarities of temperament.   Cf., too, Ovid, *Remed. Amoris*, 429-40 ;
Burton's *Anatomy of Melancholy*, Part 3, Memb. 6, Sect. 3 ; Browne's
Religio Medici, Part 1, Sect. 9.

was such that the conditions of physical being seemed
to him inexpressibly revolting, and his mind, by continually dwelling on noisome images, became so pol-
luted and diseased, that he looked upon his kind pretty
much as the Houyhnhnms of his terrible fiction
looked upon the Yahoos.

It was probably with the understanding that she
could never be more to him than a sister that, at the
beginning of 1701, Miss Johnson consented to settle
near him in Ireland. And now commenced that
curious history the particulars of which have excited
more interest and elicited more comment than any
other portion of Swift's biography. What he desired
was to establish free and affectionate relations with
his young favourite, without compromising either her
or himself. It was agreed, therefore, that she was to
continue to reside with her companion Mrs. Dingley,
and with Mrs. Dingley she continued to reside till
her death. The rules which regulated their intercourse never varied. When Swift was in London,
the two ladies occupied his lodgings in Dublin; when
he returned, they withdrew to their own. At Laracor
the arrangements were similar : he never passed a
night under the same roof with them. At all his
interviews with Miss Johnson Mrs. Dingley was
present. It would, says Orrery, be difficult if not impossible to prove that he had ever conversed with her
except in the presence of witnesses. With the same
scrupulous propriety, what he wrote he wrote for the
perusal of both. If Miss Johnson nursed hopes that
she might some day become his wife, these hopes
must have been speedily dispelled. As early as 1704
the nature of his affection was submitted to a crucial

test.   One of his friends, a Mr. Tisdall, sought Esther
in marriage.   He consulted Swift with the double
object of ascertaining whether Swift had himself any
idea of marrying her, and, in the event of that not
being the case, of soliciting his assistance in further-
ing his own suit.   Swift replied that he had no
intention at all of entering into such a relation with
her, and, on being assured that Tisdall was in a
position to support a wife, expressed his willingness
to serve him.   It is not unlikely that the whole of
this transaction was a stratagem of Miss Johnson's.
A bright and lively girl, in the bloom of youth and
beauty, is scarcely likely to have adopted by choice
the mode of life prescribed by Swift.   She wished—
who can doubt it ?—to be bound to him by dearer
ties.   If anything could win him, it would be the
fear of losing her.   If anything could induce him to
make her his wife, it would be the prospect of her
becoming the wife of another man.   She now knew
her fate.   She accepted it ; and Swift was never again
troubled with a rival.   In Swift's conduct in this
matter we fail to see anything disingenuous ; he
appears to have acted throughout honourably and
straightforwardly.[1]   Each year drew the bonds of
this eccentric connection closer.   In Ireland the three
friends were daily together, and though, as we have
seen, Swift was frequently absent in England, it was
always with reluctance that he set out, as it was
always with impatience that he looked forward to
returning.   At last the friends were destined to be
separated.   From the time of Swift's arrival in

---

[1] See Swift's letter to Tisdall, *Corresp.* ; Scott's *Swift*, xv. 256 ; and
Foster's remarks, *Life of Swift*, pp. 136-39.

England at the beginning of September, 1710, till his
return to Ireland as Dean of St. Patrick's in June,
1713, he saw nothing either of Esther or of her companion. But absence was not permitted to interrupt
their communion. A correspondence was exchanged
as voluminous as that which passed between Miss
Byron and Miss Selby. Of this correspondence the
portion contributed by Swift is extant, ànd constitutes, as everyone knows, the *Journal to Stella*. Of
the value of those letters, both as throwing light on
the political and social history of the early eighteenth
century and as elucidating the character and conduct of their writer, it would be superfluous to speak.
There is, indeed, no other parallel to them but
the parallel which immediately suggests itself—the
Diary of Pepys. Like Pepys, Swift writes with
absolute unreserve. Like Pepys, he is not ashamed
to exhibit himself in his weakest moments. Like
Pepys, he records—and seems to delight in recording
with ludicrous particularity—incidents trivial even to
grotesqueness—how he dined and where he dined,
what he ate and what he drank, what clothes he
bought and what they cost him, what disorders he
was suffering from and what disorders his friends
were suffering from, what medicine he took and how
that medicine affected him, what time he went to bed
and on what side of the bed he lay. Side by side
with these trivialities we find those vivid pictures of
Court and City life in which, as in a living panorama,
the London of Anne still moves before us. Nothing
escaped his keen and curious glance, and nothing
that he saw has he left unrecorded. Indeed, these
delightful letters reflect as in a mirror all that was

passing before his eyes and all that was passing in his mind.

On his accession to power, Harley found himself beset with difficulties. The war with France was raging. Little more than a year had passed since the bloodiest and most obstinate of Marlborough's battles had appalled Europe by its carnage. Disaster after disaster had humbled France and shattered her power. Abjectly as she had sued for peace, her proposals had been rejected, and her ruthless foes had broken up the Conference at Gertruydenberg to pursue their destructive course. Mons had succumbed, and the capture of Mons had been succeeded by the fall of Douay and Bethune. In Spain fortune had equally favoured the Allies, and two disastrous defeats had for the moment appeared to render the cause of the Bourbons desperate. But the burden of a struggle in which the sole gainers were Austria and Holland fell on England, and the burden did not fall equally. To the moneyed classes, as they were then called, it was a source of profit, for it raised the value of money; but the landed class suffered, for it depreciated the value of land. And, as the first belong as a rule to the Whig party and the second to the Tory, it is not surprising that this question linked itself inseparably with other articles in the creed of faction. Indeed, war had now become the touchstone of party feeling. The Tories were bent on bringing it with all expedition to an end; the Whigs, in league with the Allies, were furious for its continuance. It was obvious that without a peace the Ministry must collapse. It was equally clear that to conclude a peace, except on terms highly advantageous to England, might cost Harley not his place

merely but his head. The task before him was therefore twofold. It was necessary to take measures to
prosecute the war with vigour, that France might
be induced to offer such terms as would satisfy the
pride and cupidity of the English, and it was necessary at the same time to render the war and the war
party unpopular. In this embarrassing position he
was surrounded by colleagues in whom he could place
little confidence, and who were divided among themselves. Every day as it passed by increased his
perplexity. A great schism had already torn his
party into two sections. With the moderate Tories he
knew how to deal, and could rely on their hearty
co-operation. Over the extreme Tories—and the
extreme Tories were in the majority—he had little or
no control. Nor was this all. The finances were in
deplorable confusion; there was a panic in the City;
and so bad was the credit of the new Government
that he found it impossible to negotiate a loan sufficient even for the pressing necessities of the moment.
Such was the position of affairs when, in the autumn
of 1710, Swift joined the Tories.

The secret of Harley's extraordinary civility to
Swift soon became apparent. He had had the sagacity
to discover what no English minister had discovered
before—the power of the press as an engine of political
influence; and he had had also the sagacity to foresee
that all that that engine could effect it would effect
in the hands of his new ally. There was no time for
delay. In November Swift undertook the editorship
of the *Examiner*. This famous periodical, which was
the organ of the Tories, was published weekly.
Thirteen numbers had already appeared. Though

written by men whose names stood high both in
literature and in politics, none of the papers had
made much impression on the public mind. Indirectly, indeed, they had done more mischief than
service to the Tory cause, for they had provoked the
Whigs to set up an opposition journal, the *Whig
Examiner*, and the superiority of the papers in the
Whig Examiner was so striking that it was admitted
even by the Tories themselves. But in Swift's hands
the *Examiner* rose to an importance without precedent
in journalism. It became a voice of power in every
town and in every hamlet throughout England. It
was an appeal made, not to the political cliques of the
metropolis, but to the whole kingdom, and to the
whole kingdom it spoke. In a few months Swift had
attained his purpose. He had turned the tide against
the Whigs, he had made Harley popular, he had
rendered the policy of the Ministry practicable. No
one who will take the trouble to glance at Swift's
contributions to the *Examiner* will be surprised at
their effect. They are masterpieces of polemical
skill. Every sentence—every word—comes home.
Their logic, adapted to the meanest capacity, smites
like a hammer. Their statements, often a tissue of
mere sophistry and assumption, appear so plausible,
that it is difficult even for the cool historian to avoid
being carried away by them. At a time when party
spirit was running high, and few men stopped to
weigh evidence, they must have been irresistible. To
one part of his task it is evident that Swift applied
himself with peculiar zest. He had now an opportunity for avenging the slights and disappointments of
years, and he made, it must be admitted, the best of

G

his opportunity. Nothing can exceed the malignity and bitterness of his attacks on his old allies. He assails them sometimes with irony, sometimes with damning innuendo, sometimes in the language of ribald scurrility, and sometimes in the language of fleering scorn. Descending to the grossest personalities, he charges Somers with immorality and atheism ; he holds up to contempt the low tastes of Godolphin ; he taunts Cowper with libertinism and bigamy. Then, spurning meaner adversaries under his feet, disposing of one with an epithet, of another in a parenthesis, he strikes full at the towering crest of Marlborough. One paper dilates on his avarice, another on his unprincipled ambition ; here he reproaches him with being the slave of a harridan consort, there he lashes him as a traitor to William and an ingrate to Anne. But his onslaughts on these distinguished men are mercy compared with those terrible philippics in which he gave vent to his rage against Wharton. Of all the Whigs, Wharton was the most odious to him. It was Wharton who had deprived him of his place at the Court of the Lord Lieutenant ; it was Wharton who had spoken lightly of his personal character ; it was Wharton who had agitated the repeal of the Test Act. In his second *Examiner* Swift was at the throat of his victim, and with each number his satire gathers animosity and venom. Every crime which can load a public man with obloquy, every vice and every folly which in private life sink men in contempt and shame, are described as uniting in this abandoned noble. He is the Verres of Ireland, with a front more brazen, with a nature fouler and more depraved, than that of the

arch-villain of Cicero ; he is a public robber, a pol-
troon, a liar, an infidel, a libertine, a sot.   The merci-
less satirist then goes on to accuse him of atrocities
too horrible to specify.   With these charges he dealt
at length in a separate pamphlet ; for, not content
with flaying his enemy in the *Examiner*, he published
at the end of November, 1710, *A Short Character of
Thomas, Earl of Wharton*, a satire absolutely appalling
in its malignity and force.

It was not likely that the Whigs would suffer
their leaders to be thus maltreated with impunity.
Though the *Whig Examiner* had died, the *Medley* and
the *Observator* were in vigorous activity.   The staff of
both papers was a powerful one, and Swift soon found
himself front to front with assailants as rancorous
and as unscrupulous as himself.   During seven
months the paper war raged with a fury never before
known in the history of political controversy, and
during seven months Swift engaged single-handed
with the whole force of the Whig press ; wielding,
like Homer's Agamemnon, spear, sword, and boulder-
stone—

ὁ τῶν ἄλλων ἐπεπωλεῖτο στίχας ἀνδρῶν,
Ἔγχεΐ τ᾽, ἄορί τε, μεγάλοισί τε χερμαδίοισιν.

But, in spite of all the efforts of their indefatigable
champion, the Ministry appeared to be engaged in a
losing battle, and were almost in despair.   ' They are,'
wrote Swift to Stella,[1] ' upon a very narrow bottom,
and stand like an isthmus between the Whigs on one
side and the violent Tories on the other.   They are
able seamen, but the tempest is too great, the ship too

---

[1] *Journal*, March 4, 1711.

rotten, and the crew all against them.' Suddenly, however, an event occurred which gave a new turn to affairs. A French adventurer who had become acquainted with St. John had, on his friend's accession to office, obtained from him the promise of 500*l.* a year. This pension Harley had reduced, and had declined also to guarantee its permanence or its regular payment. The fellow, angry with the minister, and desperate from poverty, had entered into treasonable correspondence with France. It was discovered. He was arrested and brought before a Committee of the Privy Council at the Cock-pit. In the course of his examination he had requested to be allowed to speak privately with St. John. The request was refused. Upon that he suddenly produced a penknife, and stooping forward stabbed Harley, who was sitting near him, just above the heart. The blade broke against the breast-bone, and the wound was fortunately not fatal. There is not the smallest reason for supposing that Guiscard—for that was the assassin's name—had any other motive for what he did than rage and chagrin at what he conceived to be private wrongs. But Harley and Swift at once saw how much political capital could be made out of an incident which naturally enough caused immense public excitement. Swift at once set to work. He furnished Mrs. Manley with facts for *A True Narrative of what passed at the Examination of the Marquis de Guiscard*, instructing her how to treat them and how to colour them. The affair became his leading theme in four papers of the *Examiner*. With admirable skill he manages, without actually falsifying facts, to create a totally false im-

pression of the whole transaction. The grievance of
a private man on private grounds was transformed
into the hostility of a public enemy. He had not
indeed the audacity to state that Guiscard had been
suborned by the Whigs, the Papists, and the French,
but he insinuates it. It was probably, he says,
Guiscard's design to assassinate the Queen as it was
certainly his design to assassinate St. John, but, as
these 'enemies of France and Popery' had not come
within his reach, he had been obliged to content
himself with a single victim. He then proceeds to
enlarge on all that could intensify the sympathy
naturally felt for Harley, on his heroism at the awful
moment when he received, as he then thought, his
death-blow, on his patriotism, on his loyalty, on his
magnificent public services. Though Harley had
escaped with his life, his sufferings were severe and
his recovery slow. When he reappeared in public it
was at once apparent that the knife of Guiscard and
the pen of Swift had done him yeoman's service. A
reaction had set in in his favour. He found the
Queen cordial, the people enthusiastic, his colleagues,
with one exception, more tractable. On May 24 he
was Earl of Oxford and Mortimer, on the 29th Lord
Treasurer.

In the middle of July, 1711, Swift's contributions
to the *Examiner* ceased. A series of pamphlets now
flowed from his pen in rapid succession. In his
Remarks on a Letter to the Seven Lords he retorts
with great asperity on certain Whig journalists, who
had in a recent publication accused him of circulating calumnious reports against the committee who
examined Greg in 1708. But these controversies

were only preliminary to the most important of his
services to the Ministry. The pivot on which the
political fortunes of his party turned was peace with
France. It was the measure to which on their accession to power they were pledged ; it was the measure
on which their continuance in power depended.
Without peace their fall was certain. So enormous
and complicated were the difficulties in which the
protraction of the war was even now involving them,
that the Ministry were already beginning to despair.
'We have nothing,' wrote St. John, 'in possession,
and hardly anything in expectation ; our government
is in a consumption, our vitals are consuming, and we
must inevitably sink at once.' But, tremendous as
these difficulties were, the attempts of Harley and
St. John to extricate themselves and their party by
pressing on the conclusion of the war had involved
them in difficulties of a still more formidable kind.
As early as the autumn of 1710 clandestine negotiations had been opened with France. During the
winter of that year, and all through the spring and
summer of 1711, a surreptitious correspondence had
been carried on between Harley and St. John and
the agents of the French King. In September eight
Preliminary Articles of Peace had, with the privity
and consent of the Queen, been secretly signed. By
an unfortunate accident these dishonourable negotiations had been very nearly publicly detected. Prior,
who had been sent on a clandestine mission to France,
was on his return detained at Deal. It was known
that he was in the confidence of the Ministry, and
that he was ordinarily employed in diplomatic business.
The officer who arrested him was not discreet. The

news soon spread. The suspicion of the Whigs was
aroused. Harley and St. John, thankful, no doubt,
that nothing more had been discovered than that
peace with France was contemplated, thought it best,
probably with the object of sounding public opinion,
to allow what was practically the ministerial organ,
the *Post Boy*, to hazard conjectures as to the terms
on which peace was likely to be settled. It is clear
from the *Journal to Stella* that up to this point at
least Harley and St. John had not taken Swift into
their confidence, and that he knew nothing of these
negotiations.[1] But it was probably at their instigation that he wrote that pleasant *jeu d'esprit, A New
Journey to Paris*, in which he endeavoured to throw
public curiosity on a false scent by pretending to give
a detailed account of Prior's adventures and business
in France. The two ministers now, as the *Journal*
shows, concealed nothing from him but the trans-
actions in which they were engaged with the Pretender
and his agents.[2] Towards the end of September it
was known throughout the country that negotiations
for peace were in progress. The Whigs and the
Allies were furious. It was in vain for the Tories to
retort, in answer to taunts of treachery and perfidy,
that the war had reduced the country to the point of
bankruptcy; that what had in 1702 cost England less
than four millions was now, in consequence of the
failure of the Allies to supply what they had under-
taken to supply, costing her eight millions; that we
had entered into it merely as auxiliaries, that we had
for some years been engaging in it as principals; that
the original objects of it had long been attained; and

[1] *Journal to Stella*, Aug. 24, 1711.   [2] *Id.*, Sept. 28.

that to protract it further was to ruin England for
the aggrandisement of Austria and Holland abroad,
and for the profit of stock-jobbers and usurers at
home. The Whigs were as impervious to the testimony of facts as they were deaf to reason and argument. Every artifice of sophistry and rhetoric was
employed to cast discredit on the advocates for peace
and to swell the clamour for war. Again the Ministry had recourse to the pen of Swift. At the end
of November appeared *The Conduct of the Allies.* It
appeared anonymously, but in forty-eight hours the
first edition had run out; in five hours a second
edition was exhausted, and within a few days no less
than five editions were in circulation. Nor is this
surprising. Levelled to the capacity of the meanest
understanding, it urged with irresistible power and
cogency all that could be advanced against the war
party on the side of testimony, and all that could be
deducted, for their refutation, on the side of argument. The style and tone of this masterly pamphlet
are adapted with great skill both to the popular taste
and to the reason of thoughtful men. Nothing, for
example, could bring home to the vulgar the folly of
glorying in war that posterity might be proud of us
more forcibly than the following: ' It will no doubt
be a mighty comfort to our grandchildren to see a few
rags hung up in Westminster Hall which cost a hundred millions, whereof they are paying the arrears, to
boast, as beggars do, that their grandfathers were rich
and great.' The influence of this pamphlet was co-
extensive with its popularity. It touched the nation
to the quick. From that moment the fate of Marlborough and the Allies was sealed. From that

moment victory, however it fluctuated, declared for
the Tories.

II

Up to this time the writings of Swift had, since
the publication of the *Tale of a Tub*, dealt almost
entirely with subjects of ephemeral interest. In pure
literature he had produced little or nothing. A few
copies of occasional verses—such verses, for example,
as *Baucis and Philemon*, an adaptation of the well-
known story in Ovid (suggested, perhaps, by Chaucer's
similar transformation of the story of Apollo and
Coronis from the same work), the *Description of a
City Shower*, a few unimportant contributions to the
Tatler,[1] and one or two short trifles scarcely intended,
perhaps, for the public eye—would probably exhaust
the list. But in the summer of 1711 an incident
occurred which recalled him for a moment from
politics to letters. That incident was the foundation
of the famous Brothers' Club,[2] one of those institutions

[1] In the *Tatler* his only entire paper was No. 230, on 'Popular
Corruptions of Language.' He contributed to No. 9 the verses on
'A Morning in Town'; to No. 32 the 'History of Madonella'; to
No. 63 the letter ridiculing the college for young damsels; to No. 35
the letter signed 'Eliz. Potatrix'; to No. 59 the letter signed 'Oba-
diah Greenhat'; to No. 66 the remarks on pulpit oratory in the first
part of the paper; portions of Nos. 67 and 68; to No. 70 the letter
on pulpit eloquence; to No. 71 the admonitory letter to the vicar and
schoolmaster; to No. 238 the verses on the 'City Shower'; to No. 258
the letter on the words 'Great Britain'—this he wrote in conjunction
with Prior and Rowe. In the *Spectator* he supplied hints for No. 50,
and was, perhaps, the author of a paragraph in No. 575. See Drake's
Essays on the Tatler and Spectator, vol. iii., and Scott's *Swift*, vol. ix.

[2] This club must be distinguished from the meetings held at
Harley's house, generally on Saturdays, and occasionally on the same
day (Thursday) on which the Brothers met. The company here

which shed peculiar lustre on the reign of Anne.
It was a club founded by the leaders of the Tory
party, and it numbered among its members the most
distinguished Tories then living.   Its object was, in
the words of Swift, to encourage literature by the
judicious dispensation of patronage, to improve conversation, and to temper party ardour with humanity
and wit.   In its meetings all those artificial distinctions which separate caste from caste and man
from man were ignored.   Its members met and
mingled on terms of fraternal equality.   As brothers,
indeed, they addressed each other.   Among the
brethren were — in addition to Swift, Arbuthnot,
Friend, and Prior—the heads of three ducal houses,
Ormond, Beaufort, and Shrewsbury, the Lord Treasurer Oxford, St. John, then leader of the Lower
House, the Solicitor-General Raymond, Lords Arran,
Dupplin, Lansdowne, Bathurst, and the Earl of
Orrery.   Nothing illustrates more pleasingly than

consisted of the Lord Keeper Harcourt, Earl Rivers, the Earl of Peterborough, and St. John, to whom were subsequently added the Dukes
of Ormond, Shrewsbury, and Argyle, Earl Poulett, and the Earls of
Anglesey, Dartmouth, and Berkeley. Swift was the only person without title and without office who was admitted as a regular guest at these
meetings. ' They had,' said Mr. Forster, ' the character of Ministerial
meetings, and the day when Swift was admitted to them was practically that of his appointment as a minister without office.' *Life of
Swift*, p. 359.   This is very doubtful ; it is certainly difficult to reconcile with Swift's statement in the *Journal to Stella*, Feb. 26,
1712–13, ' I know less of what passes than anybody because I go to
no coffee-houses nor see any but ministers and such people, *and
ministers never talk politics in conversation.*' Cf. too *Id.*, Dec. 26,
1712.   In his *Memoirs relating to the Change* he seems exactly to
describe his position : ' My early appearance at these meetings, which
many thought to be of greater consequence than they really were,' &c. ;
see Scott's *Swift*, iii. 246–7.

this society the most charming feature in the social
life of that age. Never, since the gatherings at which
Augustus and Mæcenas assembled on the Palatine the
wit and genius of Rome, had the alliance between the
class which governs and the class which adorns a
nation been so close and so honourable. From the
reigns of Elizabeth and James men of letters had
never, it is true, lacked patrons either in the Ministry
or among the aristocracy. At the Revolution, and
during the early years of Anne, they had grown in
favour and reputation. Some of the leading Whig
statesmen—Somers, for example, and Halifax—had
prided themselves on their connection with letters.
Indeed, at no period had literary merit been so muni-
ficently rewarded. But the relative position of the
two classes had never changed. The barriers which
fortune had placed between them had always been
jealously guarded. The language in which Addison
addresses Halifax and Somers differs in no respect
from the language in which Spenser addressed
Leicester; Shakespeare, Southampton; and Dryden,
Dorset or Rochester. It is the language of respectful
homage; it sometimes savours of servility; it is in
all cases that of an inferior addressing a superior. It
may be doubted whether any of the ordinary nobility
condescended to associate even with the most distinguished of their clients as friend with friend. The
reserve and hauteur displayed by Somerset, Buckinghamshire, and Nottingham in their intercourse with
men of letters were proverbial. When Prior was
appointed to act with the Earl of Strafford as Ambassador Extraordinary and Plenipotentiary for the
Peace of Utrecht, Strafford refused to be joined in

commission with a commoner, and caused much
inconvenience by doing so. To the members of the
Brothers' Club belongs the honour of having been
the first to recognise in men of parts and genius not
objects of patronage merely, but companions and
equals. Though Swift was not, as Scott erroneously
supposes, the founder of this society, he was undoubtedly one of its most influential members. He was
treasurer; he dispensed its charity; he proposed
candidates for election; he prevented the election of
candidates proposed by others. He was its presiding
genius. In the *Journal to Stella* the meetings of the
club are regularly chronicled, and nothing is more
characteristic of Swift than these records. To indemnify himself for the want of fortune and title
by seizing every pretext for slighting and mortifying
their more favoured possessors was to him a source
of the most exquisite pleasure. And in that pleasure
he could now indulge to the full. He opposed the
election of the Lord Keeper and the Lord Treasurer,
though their sons were members. He excluded the
Earl of Jersey, he attempted to exclude the Duke of
Beaufort. He 'opposed Lord Arran to his face.'
The election of the Duke of Beaufort was carried in
spite of him, but when the Duke 'had the confidence to
propose his brother-in-law, the Earl of Danby,' Swift
opposed the application so strongly that it was waived.
It is amusing to find him—and in all gravity—
'holding out hopes' to the Duke of Shrewsbury.

In his conversations with the brethren he had
often discussed a scheme which had long been in his
mind. This was the foundation of an Academy for
fixing and correcting the English language. The

scheme was no doubt suggested by the Italian and
French Academies, but the idea was not new, even in
England. Towards the end of Charles II.'s reign,
Dillon, Earl of Roscommon, had not only proposed
the same scheme, but had made some progress in
carrying it out. With the assistance of Dryden and
others he had begun to form a society on the model
of an institution to which he had been introduced at
Caen,[1] 'for the refining and fixing the standard of our
language.' But the design had been interrupted by
the civil troubles at the commencement of James II.'s
reign, and on the Earl's death, shortly afterwards, it
had collapsed. Then De Foe attempted to revive it,
and gave it, in his *Essay on Projects*, a prominent
place among the institutions which he hoped to see
established. But De Foe had little authority and no
influence. Roscommon had found an ally in the
Marquis of Halifax. Swift hoped to find an ally and
patron in Harley. His cause was a good one and he
pleaded it powerfully. He was, he said, convinced
that, if some stand was not made against the tide of
corruption which was from all sides pouring in upon
our language, that language would in less than two
centuries be an unintelligible jargon. From the time
of the civil struggles its pollution had been systematic.
First it had been invaded by the cant of the Puritans,
then by the still more offensive cant of the Cavaliers.
Later on it had been vitiated by licentious abbrevi-
ations. Its grammar was unsettled and abounded in
solecisms. It fluctuated, in fact, with every colloquial
fashion ; and with every colloquial fashion it would,

---

[1] See the *Memoirs of Roscommon*, compiled from Fenton's notes,
and cf. Johnson's *Life of Roscommon.*

unless proper measures were taken, continue to
fluctuate. He proposed, therefore, that a committee
should be formed, composed of such persons as should
be generally admitted to be most qualified for the
task, that they should meet at an appointed place,
that their expenses should be defrayed by the State,
and that they should be authorised to ascertain and
fix our language. This proposal he embodied in a
letter to the Lord Treasurer, which was published in
May, 1712, and was much discussed in literary circles.
The Lord Treasurer professed to be greatly interested
in the scheme. He would give it, he said, his most
serious consideration. But his encouragement extended only to words, and the project fared as such
projects always have fared at the hands of English
statesmen.

Out of the Society of Brothers sprang the still
more famous Scriblerus Club. This undoubtedly
owed its origin to Swift, though Arbuthnot seems to
have been the creator of the hero who gave the club
its name. The Scriblerians, like the Brothers, had no
settled place for assembling. When they met they
met at each other's houses. The topics discussed
were as a rule purely literary, and seldom have men
so well qualified to shine in such discussions gathered
together at the same table. First in reputation, and
first in colloquial ability, stood Congreve, who, though
comparatively young in years, had already taken his
place among classics as the Molière of England. He
had won his laurels when Dryden still presided at
Will's, and he had lived among the flower of an age
now fast becoming historical. With a weakness not
uncommon among men of his class, he affected in

general society to attach more importance to his reputation as a man of fashion and gallantry than to his
fame as a writer.   But Congreve as he revealed himself to the world, and Congreve as he revealed himself
in the Scriblerus meetings, were very different persons.
The wit which blazes in his comedies sparkled in his
discourse.   He overflowed with anecdote and pleasantry.   His mind had been assiduously cultivated.
He was not only an accomplished Latinist, but he
was one of the few Englishmen then living who were
familiar with the poetry of Greece.   Sixteen years
junior to Congreve was Pope, whose *Essay on Criticism* and *Rape of the Lock* had given fine promise
of the great future before him.   He was now busy
with the translation of the *Iliad*.   Under what circumstances and at what period he became acquainted
with Swift we have now no means of knowing.   They
were certainly on intimate terms in the winter of 1713.
Another distinguished Scriblerian was Atterbury.   In
Atterbury the Universities of that day recognised
their most finished product.   His graceful scholarship,
his refined taste, his varied acquirements, his polished
and luminous eloquence, had placed him in the first
rank of literary churchmen.   The part he had played
in the Phalaris Controversy, and the part he had
played still more recently in the controversy with
Wake, had proved that his superior in polemical skill
was not to be found.   His learning, indeed, if we may
judge from his dissertations and sermons, was neither
exact nor deep, but it was elegant, curious, and extensive.   French he both spoke and wrote with Parisian
purity.   In the vernacular and Latin poetry of
modern Italy he was probably better versed than any

other man in England.   But it was not as a scholar or
as a controversialist that Atterbury was most valued by
those who knew him.   On all questions pertaining to
the niceties of criticism he was an unerring guide,
for his judgment was clear and solid, his perception
fine, and his taste pure even to fastidiousness.   In no
contemporary critic had Pope so much confidence.
Atterbury's approving nod relieved his mind of any
doubt he might have about the excellence of a verse.
It was at Atterbury's advice that he committed to the
flames a work on which he had expended great labour
and on which he had himself passed a more favourable
verdict.   Of a very different order were the genius
and character of John Gay.   The early part of his
life had been passed behind a linendraper's counter
in the City.   He had received no regular education,
and had, on emerging from obscurity, been too indo-
lent to remedy the defect.   A smattering of Latin
and a smattering of French and Italian constituted all
his stock as a scholar ; but, if he owed little to the
schools, he owed much to nature—a rich vein of
genial humour, wit less abundant, indeed, and less
brilliant, than that of his friends Congreve and Pope,
but scarcely less pleasing, native grace, and, what
were rare with the poets of that age, spontaneity and
simplicity.   His first experiment had been made in
serious poetry, and in serious poetry Gay never rises,
even in his happiest moments, above mediocrity.
But this poem he had judiciously dedicated to Pope,
then fast rising into reputation ; and Pope, charmed
with his young admirer's unaffected modesty, sprightly
conversation, and amiable temper, took him under
his protection.   The favourable impression which he

made on Pope he made on Swift; and when the
Scriblerus Club was formed, Gay, though he had as
yet produced nothing which entitled him to so high
an honour, was invited to join it.   Next came Thomas
Parnell.   Few things in literary history are more
remarkable than the fate which has befallen this once
popular poet.   The praises of his personal friends,
though these friends were Pope and Swift, may be
suspected of partiality,[1] but so late as 1760 Hume
placed Parnell among the very few poets whom a
reader of mature taste would delight in re-perusing for
the fiftieth time.   His biography was written in a
laudatory strain by Goldsmith, and the eulogies of
Goldsmith were repeated by Johnson.   Since then,
however, his fame has been rapidly declining, and is
now almost extinct.   But his poetry has not deserved
this fate.   It has often a charm which makes Hume's
remark perfectly intelligible.   His touches of sentiment and his pictures of nature are sometimes exquisite.   His *Hermit* is, in point of execution, a perfect
gem.   His *Fairy Tale* is delightful, and no reader
of taste and sensibility could peruse such poems as
the *Night Piece* and the *Hymn to Contentment* without feeling that he was in communion with genius,
if not of a high, certainly of a fine order.   He seems
to anticipate Goldsmith on one side and Gray on
another.   To his brother-poets Parnell owed nothing.
He chose his own themes, he treated those themes in
his own way, and never conventionally.   His versification—and his versification is peculiarly his own—is
singularly soft and musical.

[1] Swift says of him, *Journal to Stella*, 'He passes all the poets of
the day by a bar's length.'

H

But the member who fills the largest space in the history of Swift's Club remains to be mentioned. This was Dr. John Arbuthnot. Arbuthnot is one of those figures on which the memory loves to dwell. If we are to credit the testimony of men little prone either to exaggeration or to delusion, his character approached as near to perfection as it is possible for humanity to attain. His charity, his benevolence, his philanthropy, were boundless. He possessed, says Swift, every quality and every virtue which can make a man either amiable or useful. Ill-health and adverse fortune were powerless to ruffle his gentle and equable temper.[1] But the beauty of his character was equalled by the vigour and amplitude of his mind. 'I think Arbuthnot,' said Johnson, speaking of the wits of Anne's reign, 'the first man among them ; he was the most universal genius.'[2] His literary and scientific attainments were immense. While a mere youth he distinguished himself in a controversy with the veteran geologist Woodward. His *Tables of Ancient Coins, Weights, and Measures* long remained a standard work, and, though his medical writings have, like all the medical writings of past time, been superseded, they entitle him to an honourable place among the fathers of his profession. To one of his treatises particular praise is due, for in his *Dissertation on the Regularity of Births in the Two Sexes* he may be said to have laid the foundation of the science of Vital Statistics. Nor is he without striking merit as a poet. His Γνῶθι Σεαυτὸν, published in *Dodsley's Collection*,[3] which would have done honour to Dryden

[1] For a beautiful picture of Arbuthnot see Chesterfield's *Characters*.

[2] Boswell's *Johnson*. Croker's one-vol. ed. p. 145.

[3] *Supplement*, i. 192 *seqq*.

and Pope, has a condensed energy of thought, an originality, and a vigour of expression, such as few other poems of that age possess. In addition to these accomplishments he was an amateur musician, and an anthem by him, *As pants the Hart*, is in the collection of the Chapel Royal.[1] But it is not as a man of science, nor as a writer, that the world is most familiar with Arbuthnot's name. The lustre of that name is still indeed untarnished by time, but it shines now rather with reflected light than with light emanating from itself. By modern readers he is remembered chiefly as the friend of Pope and Swift; to modern readers he lives, not so much as the author of the *History of John Bull*, as the dedicatee of the *Prologue to the Satires*. Very different was the position he held among those who knew him, and among those who had inherited the traditions of those who knew him. Of his wit and humour both Pope and Swift speak in terms of extravagant praise. 'He has,' said Swift, 'more wit than we all have.' 'In wit and humour,' observed Pope, 'I think Arbuthnot superior to all mankind.' Half a century later Johnson rated him almost as highly. And in our own time Macaulay has not hesitated to pronounce the *History of John Bull* the most ingenious and humorous satire extant in the English tongue. The truth is that Arbuthnot's literary fame has suffered from causes which must sooner or later preclude any writer from permanent popularity. With two exceptions, the first book of the *Memoirs of Scriblerus* and the inimitable *Epitaph on Chartres*, his satires must be unintelligible to a reader not minutely versed in the politics of that

---

[1] Macmichael's *Gold-headed Cane*, p. 83.

time. No satire in itself so intrinsically excellent is so little capable of universal application. His wit, his humour, his sarcasm, exhausting themselves on particular persons and on particular events, now require an elaborate commentary. There is, moreover, nothing either striking or felicitous in his style. The *History of John Bull* and the *Art of Political Lying* will probably not find half a dozen readers in as many years, but we venture to think that out of these readers there will be one or two who will have no difficulty in understanding the position which Arbuthnot once held.

Last of this illustrious group of wits comes William Fortescue, afterwards Master of the Rolls. A descendant of the celebrated Chief Justice, and a man of ample fortune, he had joined the Bar to divert his mind from the grief occasioned by the loss of his wife. Gay, who is said to have been his schoolfellow at Barnstaple, introduced him to Pope, and Pope to the Scriblerians. At what time he became a member of the Club does not appear, but he is described as their legal adviser.[1] He was an accomplished and good-natured man, and so great a lover of mirth that Jervas has in one of his letters to Pope described him as laughing Fortescue. When Pope imitated the first satire of the second book of Horace he very happily substituted Fortescue for Trebatius.

Such were the men in whose society Oxford and Bolingbroke forgot the cares of State, whose gatherings have been immortalised by Pope, and whose diversions have enriched literature with compositions which the world will not readily let die. For out of these diver-

---

[1] *Suffolk Papers*, i. 202.

sions grew many years afterwards *Gulliver's Travels* and the fourth book of the *Dunciad*.

The project with which the Scriblerians sought to amuse themselves was the production of a comprehensive satire on the abuses of human learning. These abuses were to be satirised in the person of one Martinus Scriblerus, a foolish and conceited pedant who, with a head replete with learning, was entirely devoid of taste, discrimination, and good sense. The germ of the work may perhaps be traced in the *Tale of a Tub*. Martin is not indeed the counterpart of Swift's fictitious author, who is represented not as vain and stupid only, but as ignorant and illiterate. He is, however, Swift's pretentious blockhead refined into a really learned fool. Both are satires on the abuse of learning, but with this difference: Martin is to Swift's author what Don Quixote is to Sancho and Hudibras to Ralph. He is an enthusiast without judgment but without assumption. He is all that he pretends to be; he possesses what he misapplies. Swift's author is three parts charlatan. Deprive Martin of his learning and he becomes the picture of Swift's author; give Swift's author learning and he becomes the picture of Martin. To this satire, which found perhaps its models in *Don Quixote* and the *History of Mr. Ouffle*, each Scriblerian was to contribute a portion. Pope, Gay, and Parnell undertook to depict Martin in his relation to polite letters, Arbuthnot in his relation to science, and Swift in his relation to the world. Whether Atterbury and Congreve had any share in the design we have now no means of knowing. The work was unfortunately never completed. What remains of it first appeared in the

Miscellanies published by Pope between 1727 and 1732, and in the quarto edition of Pope's Prose Works published in 1741. The exquisitely humorous memoir of Martin, which furnished Sterne with a model for Mr. Shandy, and Lord Lytton with a model for Mr. Caxton, was written mainly if not entirely by Arbuthnot. To Pope, assisted perhaps by Gay and Swift, we owe the amusing parody on the *De Sublimitate*, the *Treatise on the Bathos*. In the *Virgilius Restitutus* attributed also to them, it is not unlikely that Atterbury had a hand. It is among the very best things produced by the Scriblerians, and is indeed inimitable. The pleasant parody of Bishop Burnet's *History of his Own Time*, the *Memoirs of P. P., Clerk of this Parish*, was the joint production of Pope and Gay. The *Annus Mirabilis*, a rapid and feeble compound of dulness and indecency, may be assigned with some confidence to Arbuthnot. The specimen of *Scriblerus's Reports, Stradling versus Stiles*, was written by Pope with the assistance of Fortescue. To Pope, Arbuthnot and Parnell, so Spence tells us, we owe the *Essay on the Origin of the Sciences*. Such are the pieces which represent all that remains of a work which might have been monumental.

III

More than two years had yet to elapse before the war with France was finally terminated. During the whole of this time the storms of faction raged without intermission. The Whigs, conscious that they were fighting a losing battle, fought with the fury of despair. The Tories, thwarted and on their mettle, fought with like passion for victory. De Foe gives us a terrible picture of the state of England at this crisis. 'We fight,' he says, 'not like men but like devils, like furies ; we fight not as if we would kill one another only, but as if we would tear one another's soul out of our bodies ; we fight with all the addition of personal envy, revenge, hellish rage, irreconcilable, implacable malice. Nor do we fight with cudgels only, as at Marlow, Whitchurch, &c., with swords and staves, as at Coventry, but we fight with the poison of the tongue, the venom of slander, the foam of malice and the poison of reproach.'[1] Few elections passed without bloodshed, and it was only with imminent peril to limb and even to life that a man could push his way through the yelling savages who surrounded the hustings, to record his vote. An attempt was made to assassinate Prince Eugene. Two attempts were made to assassinate Harley, and anonymous threats of assassination were frequently conveyed to him through the post.[2] It is a remarkable proof of the panic in which men who were prominently connected with politics lived, that when Swift received a present of oranges directed to him in an unknown hand he refused to touch them, for fear that they might have been poisoned.

Nine days after the publication of the *Conduct of the Allies* Parliament met. Marlborough had arrived in London, and the Whigs prepared to make a tremendous effort to defeat the Government. They could hardly expect victory in the Commons, where the majority against them was very large. But they

[1] *Review*, vii. 335–337.
[2] *Journal to Stella*, Nov. 14, 1711. *Id.*

had reason to hope that a motion against the Peace
might be carried by the Lords.   Harley had recently
made an enemy of one of the most influential men of
his own party, the Earl of Nottingham.   Nottingham,
who had been passed over in all the recent nomina-
tions, had expected to succeed Rochester as Lord
President, but Harley fearing his extreme views had
not invited him to take office.   Nottingham, determining to avenge himself for this slight, prepared to
make terms with the Whigs.   His heart had long
been set on passing the Bill against Occasional Conformity, but the opposition of the Whigs had over
and over again prevented the Bill from becoming law.
He had now the opportunity of gratifying his pique,
and of attaining a cherished object.   If the Whigs
would consent to withdraw their opposition to the
Bill, he was willing, he said, to introduce a motion
against the Peace.   The bargain was struck.   Parliament assembled.   In the Speech from the Throne it
was announced that time and place had been appointed for opening the treaty of general peace,
'notwithstanding the arts of those who delight in
war.'   Then Nottingham rose, and, after denouncing
the proposed peace as derogatory and mischievous,
concluded by moving 'that no peace could be safe or
honourable to Great Britain or Europe if Spain and
the West Indies were allotted to any branch of the
House of Bourbon.'   A long and intemperate debate
followed; Nottingham was supported by the whole
strength of the Whig party, and the motion was
carried by 62 votes against 54.   This crushing blow
was succeeded by an omen of equally disastrous
import.   No one at this time stood so high in the

Queen's favour as the Duchess of Somerset, and the Duke of Somerset had been the loudest and most vehement of those who had supported Nottingham. The Queen had been present during the debate, and on leaving the House surprised everyone by giving her hand to the Duke of Somerset to escort her to her carriage. This was naturally interpreted as indicating that her sympathies were not with the advocates for peace but with the war party, especially when it was known that she had refused the proffered escort of the Lord Chamberlain. The Whigs were now confident of victory, the Tories in despair. Swift believed that all was lost. 'I look upon the Ministry,' he wrote to Stella, 'as certainly ruined.' Prior was of opinion that the Government would resign in a week.

But the crisis was not so formidable as the Tories in their panic thought. The pen of Swift had done its work. If in Parliamentary circles the spirit of party was proof against reason and ridicule, the world outside these circles was not. To that world he had appealed in the *Conduct of the Allies*, and to that world he now prepared again to appeal. During the next fourteen months his pen was scarcely ever idle, now gibbeting, in lampoons and Grub Street ballads, obnoxious individuals, now explaining and defending in elaborate pamphlets the policy and measures of the Ministry, now assailing in almost every form which satire and argument can assume the aims, the tactics, the characters of the Opposition.

His warfare was systematic. He began by attempting to turn into ridicule those who had been most prominent in supporting the motion against

peace. His first victim was Nottingham, who was so
stung by the ludicrous ballad in which his infirmities
were exposed that he had the printer arrested. Next
he assailed, in the lampoon which is said to have cost
him a bishopric, the Duchess of Somerset. Marlborough, who had just been deprived of all his offices,
came third, and when we read the *Fable of Midas* we
shall not suspect the Duke's sincerity when he said
'that there was nothing he desired so much as to
contrive some way to soften Dr. Swift.'[1] He now
proceeded to more serious work. The great obstacle
in the way of the Peace—the measure on which the
existence of the Ministry depended—was the Allies,
and in the exposure of their unwarrantable demands,
and of the calamities in which, for their own aggrandisement, they were involving England, lay, as the
impression made by his former tract had shown, the
argument most likely to be of service to his party.
He determined therefore to follow up the *Conduct of
the Allies*, which had been an attack on them generally,
by a particular attack on the Dutch. No point had
been urged with more emphasis by the opponents of
the Peace, both within Parliament and without, than
the obligations imposed on us by the Barrier Treaty.
By this absurd treaty, which even Marlborough had
had the sagacity to oppose,[2] England had, in addition
to other provisions, bound herself to place Holland
not only in possession of the most important cities
in the Spanish Netherlands then[3] conquered, but of

[1] Recorded with much complacency by Swift, *Journal to Stella*,
Jan. 8, 1712.

[2] Marlborough to the Duchess, Aug. 19, and to Godolphin, Aug. 26.
Coxe, *Life of Marl.* iv. 413–14.

[3] October 1709.

every town which should in the course of the war be
conquered from France, stipulating also to guarantee
the possession of these cities to the Dutch, and engaging to come with an adequate force to their defence,
should the enemy attack them. In return for these
immense concessions, Holland was to guarantee the
Protestant succession in England.

Nothing could exceed the skill with which the
Remarks on the Barrier Treaty is composed. It well
deserves to be studied by all who would understand
the power of simplicity as an artifice of rhetoric. We
rise from its perusal persuaded and convinced, glowing
with indignation, as in sympathy with some invective,
settled and resolute, as in accordance with irresistible
argument. And yet it appears to consist of little
more than the plain statement of plain facts, so
obvious as to appear self-evident. But analyse it and
the art is apparent—it is the art of which Demosthenes
was so consummate a master.

But it was not the Allies and Whigs alone who
were embarrassing the Ministry. Harley was regarded
with disfavour by certain malcontents among his
own supporters, and Swift never did his patron more
service than in the tract entitled *Some Advice to the
October Club*. The October Club was a clique of
country gentlemen and Members of Parliament who
belonged to the extreme section of the Tory party, and
who, having long expressed dissatisfaction with their
chief, were now assuming a very menacing attitude.
Constitutionally cautious and moderate, dilatory also,
and with the fortunes of his party so often on the
razor's edge, Harley had always preferred a trimming
to a decided policy. He never entirely trusted the

Tories; he cherished to the last a hope of coalition
with the Whigs.[1] To his procrastination, indecision,
and half-heartedness his party attributed, and no
doubt justly, the recent defeat in the debate on the
Peace. That disaster had for a moment roused him
to take, or at least to allow his colleague St. John to
take, decisive measures.

The simultaneous creation of twelve peers had
turned the Tory minority in the House of Lords into
a majority. The dismissal of the Duke of Somerset,
the disgrace of Marlborough, the incarceration of
Walpole, and the expedition with which the Treaty
with France was progressing, had indeed delighted the
Club. But they were not satisfied. What had been
begun, they said, should be completed. A clean sweep
ought to be made of the Whigs from all places of post
and power ; there should be no more compromise, no
more half measures. To pacify and if possible to
gain the confidence of these malcontents was at this
moment of more urgent importance than anything
else. But how to do so without at the same time
making concessions which it was of almost equal
importance not to make was a problem by no means
easy to solve. It was solved by Swift in a pamphlet
which Scott justly calls a masterpiece of political tact.
The *Letter to the October Club* is perhaps the best

---

[1] It was no doubt impossible for Harley, even had he been so
inclined, to adopt any other policy, for it was the policy which the
Queen, who equally distrusted the Tories, had made up her mind to
adopt. 'She had,' says Swift, 'entertained the notion of forming a
moderate comprehensive scheme, which she maintained with great
firmness, nor would ever depart from until half a year before her
death.' *Enquiry into the Behaviour of the Queen's Last Ministry.*
See, too, *Journal to Stella, passim.*

example to be found in Swift's writings of the rare skill with which he could perform the nicest offices of diplomacy. He regarded it himself with much satisfaction. It was one of the few works with which he confessed that he was pleased. The *Letter to the October Club* was succeeded by a very powerful tract, the *Letter to a Whig Lord*. This lord is said, though on doubtful evidence, to have been Lord Ashburnham. Originally a Whig, he had joined the Tories. He was now fluctuating, and it was feared that he would again go over to the Whigs. But, if the pamphlet is ostensibly addressed to an individual, it is really addressed to that large class of whom a man in the position of Ashburnham may be regarded as typical. It is an appeal to the waverers. Its design is to confirm the Tories in their allegiance to their chief, and to make converts of the doubtful Whigs. Artfully arguing that there is nothing incompatible between the principles and interests of the moderate Tories and those of the moderate Whigs, he proceeds to show that what separates the two parties is simply the dispute ' between those who would support and those who would violate the royal prerogative '; that what were in question were not measures but men, not principles but factious brangles. ' There is no opinion properly belonging to you as a Whig wherein you may not still continue and yet deserve the favour and continuance of the Court, provided you offer nothing in violation of the royal prerogative, nor take the advantage in critical junctures to bring difficulties upon the administration, with no other view but that of putting the Queen under the necessity of changing it.' But the object of the tract was not merely to confirm the waverers; it is in effect an elaborate defence and justification of Harley's policy of compromise. It was probably written at his suggestion, and there is a sentence in it which looks very like an interpolation. If Swift promised that ' the ministers will second your utmost zeal for securing the indulgence to Protestant dissenters,' it must have been with a wry face.

Side by side with these pamphlets he was keeping up an incessant fire of squibs and broadsides, sometimes in verse and sometimes in prose, pelting Marlborough when he left England, and Prince Eugene when he came to England. Raking into the scandals of private life and noting all that passed in public, he kept a vigilant eye for every incident that could be turned to account against the Whigs. No man was probably ever so much feared. For neither age, rank, nor sex afforded any protection from his bitter and often filthy raillery. Some of these lampoons find a place in his collected writings. But the greater portion of them have certainly escaped the diligence of his editors, and lurk unidentified among the broadsheets preserved in the British Museum. It would be easy to point to many in these collections which bear his sign manual. What is certain is that he was engaged, as we know from his correspondence, on pieces of which in his republished works not a vestige remains.

Incessant as these occupations were, they did not exhaust his extraordinary energy. Towards the end of 1712 he commenced his *History of the Peace of Utrecht*, which appeared many years afterwards, when completed, under the title of the *History of the Four Last Years of the Queen*. He had vindicated the policy and conduct of the Ministry in these ephemeral publications, which were for the purposes of the moment addressed to his political contemporaries, and he was now anxious to vindicate them as a historian to the world generally and to posterity. He had access to documents and correspondence of the most secret kind. The manuscript was submitted to Harley, who corrected portions of it with his own hand. Swift frequently speaks in the *Journal to Stella* of the pains he took with its composition, and we learn from the same source that it was completed on May 16, 1713.

Seven weeks before he had put the finishing touches to his work, that other work for the furtherance of which he had toiled so much and had toiled so long had at last been accomplished. His party had triumphed; the Peace of Utrecht had been signed.

IV

If the measure of a man's importance be the measure of the influence he exercises on contemporaries, it would be no exaggeration to say that, in the spring of 1713, no Commoner in England stood so high as Swift. He dictated the political opinions of half the nation. He had turned the tide of popularity against the Whigs. He had done more than any single man then living to confound the designs of Austria and Holland, to crush Marlborough, to paralyse Marlborough's coadjutors.[1] A war, splendid

---

[1] 'This day se'ennight, after I had been talking at Court with Sir William Wyndham, the Spanish Ambassador came up to him, and said he heard that was Dr. Swift, and desired him to tell me that

beyond parallel, he had rendered odious. At two
perilous junctures he had saved the Ministry. For
every step in the negotiations with France, for every
measure in the domestic policy of Oxford, he had
paved the way. He had indeed done more for his
party, and for the leaders of his party, than any man
of letters had ever done for any patron or for any
cause. And what he had done he had done gratui-
tously.[1] 'I never,' he says, 'received one shilling
from the Ministers, or any other present except that
of a few books, nor did I want this assistance to
support me.'[2] All this had been acknowledged in
terms flattering even to fulsomeness. Nothing therefore was more natural than that he should expect
some substantial mark of ministerial favour. That
he expected preferment though he never solicited it,[3]
and that Harley and St. John were perfectly aware of
the tacit contract into which by accepting his services
they had entered, is abundantly clear from the *Journal to Stella*. He was neither impatient nor unreasonable. It is not until May 1711 that he begins to

his master, and the King of France, and the Queen, were more obliged
to me than any man in Europe.'—*Journal to Stella*, Dec. 21, 1712.

[1] It is remarkable that Swift, though he was one of the most voluminous and popular writers of his age, never troubled himself to
negotiate with publishers. 'I never got a farthing for anything I
writ,' he says in a letter to Pulteney, dated May, 1735, 'except once,
about eight years ago, and that by Mr. Pope's prudent management
for me'—a fact which Jeffrey, when taxing him with sordid avarice,
found it convenient to suppress.

[2] *History of the Four Last Years, &c.* Preface.

[3] His reasons for not doing so he characteristically explains in a
letter to Archbishop King, Oct. 1, 1711. *Works* (Scott), xv. 445-6.
See, too, King's letter, earnestly urging him to conquer his mischievous
pride. *Id.* pp. 451-2.

express dissatisfaction. 'To return,' he writes, 'without some mark of distinction would look extremely little, and I would likewise gladly be somewhat richer than I am. Everything here is tasteless to me for want of being where I would be. And so a short sigh and no more of this.' And no more of this there is for another year. Then expressions of querulousness and discontent become frequent. 'Less of civility and more of interest,' he adds bitterly, after telling Stella that the Lord Treasurer had chidden him for not having visited him for three days. 'Ministers,' he observes on another occasion, 'never do anything for the companions of their pleasures.' His first great disappointment was the deanery of Wells, which was vacated in the spring of 1712, and which everyone expected would have been conferred on him. In November the death of Dr. Humphrey Humphreys left the See of Hereford vacant. For a moment it seemed not unlikely that Swift would be selected to fill it. There is reason to believe that he was strongly recommended to the Queen. But the Queen, whose natural dislike to him is said to have been sharpened by the Archbishop of York and by the Duchess of Somerset, whom, as we have seen, he had grossly libelled, turned a deaf ear to the recommendations of her Ministers.[1] She probably thought, as a pious and sensible woman might reasonably think, that the

---

[1] This story is contradicted by King, who was informed by Bolingbroke that the Queen had herself assured him that she ' had never received any unfavourable character of Swift, nor had the Archbishop or any other person endeavoured to lessen him in her esteem.' And Bolingbroke added that it was a story invented by Oxford to deceive Swift and make him contented with his deanery in Ireland.—King's *Anecdotes*, pp. 60–61.

I

author of such a treatise as the *Tale of a Tub*, and of such verses as the *Windsor Prophecy*, was scarcely the man for a place among the Fathers of the Church. This feeling appears to have been understood and respected by Swift himself, for, though he was well aware that Anne had been the only obstacle between himself and the prize he most coveted, it is remarkable that in speaking of her—and he often has occasion to speak of her—he never betrays the smallest ill-will or vindictiveness. Other disappointments followed. ' This morning ' (April 13, 1713), he wrote to Stella, ' my friend Mr. Lewis came to me and showed me an order for three deaneries, but none of them for me.' And now he lost all patience. ' Tell the Lord Treasurer,' he said, ' that I take nothing ill of him but his not giving me timely notice, as he promised to do, that the Queen would do nothing for me.' Oxford, no doubt as mortified as himself, hearing that he was in the Under Secretary's office, came in to see him. In the course of a long conversation Swift plainly told him that unless he had ' something honourable ' immediately conferred on him he should at once leave for Ireland. Oxford, without informing Swift at the time, stopped the warrants, and they both dined that night at the Duke of Ormond's. The object of this visit appears to have been to induce Ormond to exercise his influence in persuading the Queen to confer the vacant See of Dromore on Sterne, then Dean of St. Patrick's, Dublin. This would leave the deanery, which was in the gift of Ormond, open, and it was hoped that the Queen would allow Ormond to confer it on Swift. But preferment at the price of exile from all that made life,

as he said, tolerable to him, was by no means to his
mind or to the mind of his friends.   Oxford, not yet
in despair of the Queen's conversion, still kept back
the warrants.   Lady Masham, who on hearing of the
proposed arrangement burst into tears, had an interview with the Queen.   Then Oxford, who saw that
higher preferment in England was, in the Queen's
present mood, out of the question, suggested as a last
resource that a prebendaryship at Windsor, which
then happened to be vacant, should be conferred on
his friend.   But the Queen was inexorable.   It should
be the deanery of St. Patrick's or nothing.   Meanwhile even this had become uncertain and appeared
to be eluding him.   Ormond had changed his mind
and refused to consent to Sterne's promotion.   Sterne
had, he said, not treated him with respect, and he
disliked Sterne, and Sterne was under the influence
of the Archbishop of Dublin.   He desired Swift, therefore, to name some other deanery.   'I desire,' replied
Swift, with quiet dignity, 'that your Grace will put
me out of the case, and do as you please.'   Ormond
was a gentleman and, though irascible, a kind-hearted
man.   He probably read in a moment the full meaning of what Swift had said, and perhaps a glance at
the face of the speaker assisted the interpretation.
He replied with great kindness, 'I will consent,'
adding that he would not have done so for any other
man alive.   How inexpressibly galling all this must
have been to a man of Swift's temper may well be
imagined.   He had not only the humiliation of feeling
that what he ought to have owed to simple desert he
had owed to extorted favour, but that, in securing a
prize which it was almost an indignity to accept, he

had secured for another—and that an inferior—the prize which he himself most coveted.

Under these mortifying circumstances, he accepted what he was not in a position to refuse, and, swallowing his chagrin, set out early in June for Ireland. His reception in Dublin was not calculated to raise his spirits. He was grossly insulted as he passed along the streets, and on the morning of his installation a copy of verses, which is still extant,[1] taunting him with apostasy and infidelity, is said to have been posted on the door of the cathedral.

In a few weeks he was again in London. He had been summoned to mediate, as he had so often done before, between Oxford and Bolingbroke, whose internecine feuds were now causing grave alarm. He soon found, however, that the differences between them were not such as admitted either of reconciliation or of compromise; for who can reconcile rivals, or who negotiate compromise when the struggle is for supremacy? But what it was possible to do he did, and his correspondence amply shows that he acted at this unhappy crisis in a manner that reflects the highest credit both on his heart and on his judgment.

Meanwhile he had not permitted those terrible weapons which had already done so much execution among the Whigs to rust in idleness. Of all the Whig journalists, none were at that moment carrying scurrility and intemperance to greater length than Richard Steele. In an evil hour he had abandoned literature for politics, had dropped the *Spectator* to set up the *Guardian*, and had recently entered Parliament.

---

[1] Printed in Monck Mason's *Annals of St. Patrick's Cathedral*, p. 269.

Between Swift and himself there had existed for some
years cordial friendship, a friendship which political
differences had subsequently cooled, but which both
had been, even in the heat of controversy, careful to
respect. To Swift he was under great obligations.
At Swift's intercession he had been permitted to
retain a lucrative office under Government. He had
been assisted by him in his literary ventures; he had
on more than one occasion been protected by him
from slander and insult. But, shortly before Swift's
departure from Ireland, Steele, now drunk with party
spirit, had so far forgotten himself as to insert in the
Guardian a coarse and ungenerous reflection on his
old friend. Upon that, Swift sought through Addison
an explanation. Steele's reply was pert and rude.
Swift, in spite of this double provocation, displayed at
first singular forbearance. Nothing indeed could be
more dignified and becoming than his conduct at the
beginning of this rupture. A reference to the correspondence which passed between the two men will
show how greatly Mr. Forster has, in his Essay on
Steele, misrepresented the facts. The letters of Swift
are those of a man calm, just, and candid. The letters
of Steele are those of a blustering egotist, who, without
reason himself, will listen to reason in nobody else.
Swift was, however, seldom insulted with impunity.
The castigation which Steele now received was due no
doubt immediately to his prominence as a party writer,
but it is easy to see that private animosity glows in
every paragraph of that cruel pamphlet—*The Importance of the ' Guardian ' Considered* [1]—in which the

---

[1] *Works* (Scott), iv. p. 369

Member for Stockbridge was held up to the mockery of his constituents.

While busy with Steele, he was busy also with Burnet. That turbulent prelate, who was on the point of bringing out the third volume of his *History of the Reformation*, had, with the double object of whetting public curiosity and of gratifying his own absurd vanity, published by anticipation the *Preface*. In this he had taken occasion to taunt the Tories with Jacobitism and Popery. Swift's reply, which assumed the form partly of a parody, and partly of a running commentary of a parody on the Bishop's *Preface,* is one of the most amusing, as it is assuredly one of the most severe, of his polemical pieces. He had long suspected, he said, that Steele and the Bishop were working in co-operation, for, 'though that peculiar manner of expressing themselves which the poverty of our language forces us to call their style' presented points of difference, their notions were precisely similar. 'But I will confess,' he goes on to say, 'that my suspicions did not carry me so far as to conjecture that this venerable champion would be in such mighty haste to come into the field and serve in the quality of an *enfant perdu,* armed only with a pocket pistol before his great blunderbuss could be got ready, his old rusty breastplate scoured, and his cracked head-piece mended.' But the whole pamphlet is inimitable. Its irony, its humour, its drollery, are delicious.

And now the country was tossing under the storms which shook the last year of Anne. The Whigs taunted the Tories with designing to bring in the Pretender, and the Tories taunted the Whigs with treachery to the Throne and the Constitution. In the spring of 1714 appeared Steele's *Crisis*.   Swift, whose wrath against Steele had been sharpened by their recent controversy, at once replied to it in the *Public Spirit of the Whigs*.   Nothing which ever came from his pen appears to have exasperated his opponents so much as this tract.   The attention of the Legislature was directed to it.   The Scotch Peers, with the Duke of Argyle at their head, complained personally to the Queen.   The bookseller and the printer were arrested.   A proclamation offering a reward of three hundred pounds to any one who would reveal the author was issued.   Swift, with the fate of Tutchin and De Foe before his eyes, became alarmed and meditated flight.   But the tact of Oxford averted discovery, and the danger blew over.

The catastrophe which he had long feared was, however, fast approaching.   The feud between Oxford and Bolingbroke was about to terminate in the ruin of both.   In May he met his two friends for the last time under the same roof, and he made a final effort to recall them to reason and duty.   He pleaded, he argued ; but expostulation, warning, counsel, were vain.   He now saw clearly that all was over.   ' I can no longer,' he sighed, ' do service in the ship, and am able to get out of it.   I have gone through my share of malice and danger, and will be as quiet the rest of my days as I can.   So much for politics ; ' [1] and he had hurried away sick at heart to hide his sorrow and chagrin at Letcombe.   Two troubled months passed by.   Though he was out of the world, numerous correspondents kept him fully informed of all that occurred. Each step in the rapid decline of Oxford, each step in

[1] Letter to Walls, Mr. Murray's MSS., quoted by Mr. Craik.

the fallacious triumph of Bolingbroke, was at once communicated to him. Indeed, his correspondence at this period forms the best account extant of the momentous weeks which preceded the death of Anne.[1]

The history of that crisis reflects indelible infamy on the leaders of Swift's party; it is pleasing to add that the conduct of Swift himself may be regarded with unalloyed satisfaction. When political immorality, in the worst type it can assume, was epidemic among the statesmen of his faction, his patriotism and integrity remained without taint. It is certain that he had no share in the intrigues with James. It is certain that he resolutely opposed all attempts to tamper with the Act of Settlement. He expressed with great courage his disapprobation both of the conduct of Oxford and of the conduct of Bolingbroke, and he sought in a powerful pamphlet—one of the very best he ever wrote—to repair the mischief which their quarrels had inflicted on the common cause. But the manuscript unfortunately found its way into the hands of Bolingbroke, who, having his own purposes to serve, made in it certain alterations which were more calculated to benefit himself than his party; and Swift, justly annoyed, withdrew it from publication. Had this pamphlet, *Free Thoughts upon the present State of Affairs*, appeared a few weeks earlier, and had the policy prescribed in it been carried out,

---

[1] See in addition to the letters dated in these months, *Swift* (Scott), vol. xvi.; the letter to the Earl of Oxford, dated June 14, 1737 (Scott), xix. p. 158; and the *Inquiry into the Behaviour of the Queen's Last Ministry*. This appears to have been designed as a supplement to the *History of the Four Last Years*, and the two are probably fragments of Swift's design to write a history of the reign, abandoned when he failed to obtain the Royal Historiographership.

the ruin of the Tories would in all probability have
been averted. What Swift plainly foresaw was that
the Whigs, availing themselves of the dissensions
among the Tories, and identifying the Tories as a
party with the Jacobites, would, as a party, bring over
the Elector and carry out the Act of Settlement. He
proposed therefore to cut the ground from under the
Whigs by abolishing party distinctions, or rather by
enlarging the definition of what constituted a Tory, and
by narrowing the definition of what constituted a Whig.
There were, he says, two points on which 'a very
large majority of the kingdom appear perfectly hearty
and unanimous'; the first was loyalty to the Church of
England, the other was the security of the Protestant
Succession in the House of Hanover; and in this
party he recognises the Tories. The other party,
which he speaks of as 'the faction,' consisted of a
confederacy of the open and secret enemies of the
Church, of moderation men and of republicans; and
in this party he recognises the Whigs. Frankly attributing the disorganisation and anarchy of the Tories
to the ill-management and mutual dissensions of
Oxford and Bolingbroke, he points out that it is not
too late to retrieve the past. Let them rally round
them that 'very large majority,' the friends of the
Church and the friends of the Protestant Succession;
let there be no truce, no compromise, with 'the faction,'
which should be excluded from all civil and military
posts; let the army, and especially the Guards, be
under the closest surveillance; let them spare no pains
to counteract the slanders of their enemies at Herren-
hausen, and to reconcile themselves and their party
with the Elector. Had Swift known what we know

now, how deeply both Oxford and Bolingbroke were
implicated with the Pretender, he would not perhaps
have been surprised that his admonitions carried so
little weight.   On July 27 Oxford resigned, and the
reins of government were in the hands of Bolingbroke.

Nothing we know of Swift is more honourable to
him than his behaviour at this juncture. Of his two
friends, the one was at the summit of political greatness, the other was not merely under a cloud, but
ruined beyond possibility of redemption. Both sought
his presence. Bolingbroke, inviting him with eager
importunity to share his triumph, held out hopes at
once the most splendid and the most plausible. He
would undertake, he said, to reconcile him with the
Duchess of Somerset, he would introduce him to the
Queen, he would provide and provide amply for him
in the English Church. Oxford, pathetically appealing
to ancient friendship, had nothing to offer him but the
opportunity of proving that that friendship had been
sincere and disinterested. Without a moment's hesitation Swift chose the nobler course.

As he was on the point of setting out for Oxford's
country seat, he received a letter announcing the
death of Anne. It was an event which for some days
had been almost hourly expected, but its effect on
the Tories was the effect of sudden and unforeseen
calamity. It found them without resources, without
fixed plans, in the midst of internecine strife. Bolingbroke indeed continued to bluster about the miracles
which a little judicious management could still effect,
assured him that the Tories were not in despair, and
that the cry in a month might be that the Whigs

were a pack of Jacobites. And he hoped, he said, that his old friend would lose no time in assisting him 'to save the Constitution.' To this fustian Swift replied in a letter[1] written with great calmness, dignity, and good sense. He dwelt sadly on the efforts he had made to save from self-destruction the friends who had been so dear to him, and he spoke with some bitterness of the folly and infatuation which had made those efforts nugatory. In the present condition of affairs he was, he continued, unable to discern any favourable symptom. The wreck of the Tories was complete. All that remained for Bolingbroke to do was to maintain his post at the head of the Church party. 'You are,' he went on to say, 'still in the prime of life. You have sustained, it is true, a heavy defeat, but you will no doubt learn, like a prudent general, to profit from disaster.' He added in conclusion that he had a lively sense of the favours which his patron had purposed to confer on him, that he hoped before the end of the year to be again at his side, but that for the present he must, he feared, take leave of a scene which would, however, seldom be absent from his thoughts. And he took leave of that scene for ever. By the middle of August he was again in Dublin.

From this moment the biography of Swift assumes a new complexion. During the last few years circumstances had, in a manner, enabled him to escape from himself. Incessant activity had left him little time for gloomy reflection. If he was not among the Fathers of the Church, the position which he most coveted he had attained. His genius and force of

[1] Dated August 7, 1714 (Scott, xvi. p. 212).

character had extorted from society the homage which society is as a rule slow to pay to any but the opule and noble. In literary circles his pre-eminence was acknowledged. On politics the influence which he had exercised had been without parallel in the history of private men. Now all was changed. He found himself suddenly reduced to obscurity and impotence. He was no longer the confidant of great ministers, the companion of ambassadors and privy councillors, the pet of fine ladies, and the boon comrade of wits and poets. He was an exile, and an exile with little to do and with nothing to hope, in a place which was of all places in the world the most odious to him. The only society with which he could mingle was the society of inferiors. What followed, followed naturally. He became the prey of that constitutiona melancholy which had been his bane from childhood. The fierce and gloomy passions, which prosperous activity had for a while composed, again awoke. Each month as it passed by added to his irritation and wretchedness. Ill-health, the loss of friends, his own unpopularity, and, above all, the condition of the unhappy country in which his lot was cast, alternately maddened and depressed him.

CHAPTER VI

I

THE circumstances under which he entered on his new duties were sufficiently inauspicious. It was well known that he had been one of the chief supporters of the last Ministry, and that his preferment had been the price of his services. In Dublin, where the Whigs were as three to one, the downfall of the Tories had been hailed with savage glee. Indeed, of all the sects into which Irish politicians were divided and sub-divided, it may be questioned whether there was one which regarded with much favour the party to which Swift had attached himself. The victory gained by the Whigs was celebrated as such victories always were celebrated. On Swift's head broke in full force the storm of obloquy which was overwhelming his friends in England. Libels taunting him with Popery and Jacobitism freely circulated among the vulgar. He was hustled and pelted in the street. One mis-creant, an Irish nobleman, assaulted him with such ferocious violence that he presented a petition, which is still extant, appealing for protection to the House of Peers. For some months he went in fear of his life, and he never ventured to show himself even in the principal thoroughfares without an escort of armed

servants. And these were not his only troubles. He
was on bad terms with his Chapter ; he was on bad
terms with the Archbishop. He was in debt to his
predecessor for the deanery house. He was in
wretched health, and in still more wretched spirits.
His feelings found vent in a copy of verses, which are
inexpressibly sad and touching.

> Why should I repine
> To see my life so fast decline ?
> But why obscurely here alone,
> Where I am neither lov'd nor known ?
> My state of health none care to learn,
> My life is here no soul's concern,
> And those with whom I now converse
> Without a tear will tend my hearse.
> Remov'd from kind Arbuthnot's aid,
> Who knows his art but not his trade,
> Some formal visits, looks and words,
> Which mere humanity affords.
>
> .   .   .   .   .   .
>
> My life is now a burden grown
> To others, ere it be my own,
> Ye formal weepers for the sick,
> In your last offices be quick.[1]

Meanwhile, evil tidings were arriving by every
post from England. First came the news of the flight
of Bolingbroke ; then came the news of the impeachment and imprisonment of Oxford ; and lastly, the
still more incredible intelligence that Ormond had
declared for the Pretender, and was in France.
Under these stunning blows Swift acted as none but
men on whom Nature has been lavish of heroic
qualities are capable of acting. It was now plain
that all who had been in the confidence of the late
Ministry were in great danger, and that, unless they

[1] *Works*, x. p. 414.

were prepared to fare as their leaders had fared, it behoved them to walk warily. A vindictive faction in the flush of triumph is, as Swift well knew, in no mood for nice distinctions between guilt presumptive and guilt established. He was, moreover, well aware that rumour had already been busy with his name, and that his enemies were watching with malignant vigilance for anything which he might do or say to compromise himself. But all this was as nothing. Neither self-interest nor fear had any influence on his loyal and dauntless spirit. He wrote off to Oxford, not merely expressing his sympathy, but imploring permission to attend him in the Tower. 'It is the first time,' he said, ' that I ever solicited you in my own behalf, and if I am refused, it will be the first request you ever refused me.'[1] He braved the suspicions, nay more, the peril, to which a confidential correspondence with the families of Bolingbroke and Ormond, when the one had become the Secretary and the other the chief General of the Pretender, exposed him. We are told that, when the Ulster King-of-Arms attempted, on the attainder of the Duke, to remove the escutcheons of the Ormonds, which hung in St. Patrick's Cathedral, Swift sternly bade him begone, ' for as long as I am Dean,' he thundered out, ' I will never permit so gross an indignity to be offered to so noble a house.' It was not likely that he could act thus with impunity, and it appears from a letter of Archbishop King, dated May, 1715, and from one of his own letters to Atterbury, dated April, 1716, that he was twice in danger of arrest.

His conduct at this crisis was the more honourable

[1] Letter dated July 19, 1715.   Scott's *Swift*, xvi. p. 260.

to him as it sprang solely from the purest of
motives, from a chivalrous sense of what is due to
friends and benefactors, and especially to friends and
benefactors in misfortune.   Some writers have, it is
true, imputed his conduct, as hostile contemporaries
imputed it, to less worthy motives.   But it would be
mere waste of words to discuss their statements.
Nothing we know of Swift is more absolutely certain
than the fact that, so far from having any sympathy
with the Pretender, he always regarded him with
peculiar abhorrence.   He denounced him in his correspondence, he denounced him in his conversation, he
denounced him in his public writings.   'I always
professed,' he says in one of his familiar letters, 'to
be against the Pretender, because I look upon his
coming as a greater evil than we are likely to suffer
under the worst Whig Government that can be found.'
In the crisis of 1714, when it is not perhaps too much
to say that his pen might have turned the scale in
James's favour, he was among the most acrimonious
and vehement of anti-Jacobites.[1]   Indeed, his feelings
on this subject were so well known that both Oxford
and Bolingbroke studiously concealed from him their
negotiations with St. Germain's, and, as his *Historical Memoirs* show, he had never even a suspicion of
the intrigues the existence of which the *Stuart Papers*
have in our time placed beyond doubt.[2]

[1] See his remarks about the Pretender in his *Free Thoughts on
the present State of Affairs.*
[2] To the end of his life Swift contended that there was no design
on the part of Anne's last Ministry to bring in the Pretender; how
effectually Harley and Bolingbroke had concealed their intrigues from
him is clear from the Dean's letter to the Archbishop of Dublin,
Dec. 16, 1716. 'Had there been even the least overture or intent of

His pen, meanwhile, was not idle. In his letter to Oxford he had promised that, though the rage of faction had rendered contemporaries deaf and blind, future ages should at all events know the truth. With this view he drew up the *Memoirs relating to that Change which happened in the Queen's Ministry in the Year 1710*, a pamphlet in which, in a clear and temperate narrative, he explains the circumstances under which he had himself first engaged in politics, as well as the revolution which brought his party into power. On the completion of the *Memoirs*—they are dated on the manuscript October, 1714—he began the *Enquiry into the Behaviour of the Queen's Last Ministry*. This is a work of great interest and value. With a firm and impartial hand he traces the history of those fatal feuds which had cost himself and his friends so dear. He makes no attempt—and it is greatly to his honour—to palliate what was reprehensible in his own party; he makes no attempt to exaggerate what was reprehensible in their opponents. The prejudice of friendship is discernible perhaps in the portraits of Oxford, Bolingbroke, and Ormond, but it is a prejudice which extends no further than their personal characters. As public men, no more is assigned to them than is their due. They are as freely censured as their neighbours. Indeed, the

bringing in the Pretender, I think I must have been very stupid not to have picked out some discoveries or suspicions. And although I am not sure that I should have turned informer, yet I am certain I should have dropped some general cautions *and immediately have retired.*' See, too, in the second part of the *Enquiry into the Behaviour &c.*, where he again repeats more fully and emphatically what he here says in the letter to King (Scott, vi. 48-56, and compare also p. 15).

K

pamphlet is distinguished throughout by a spirit of candour not to be mistaken.

But his most elaborate contribution to contemporary history was a work which had, as we have seen, been completed [1] before he left London—the work which appears in his collected writings as the *Memoirs of the Last Four Years of the Queen*. It was commenced in 1712 at Windsor, about a year before the Peace with France was signed, and was, in effect, a vindication of the Treaty of Utrecht. Nothing he ever wrote seems to have given him so much satisfaction. He always described it as the best thing he had done, and it is certain that he expended more time and labour on it than he was in the habit of expending on any of his literary compositions. But the work, as it now appears, is so inferior to what might have been expected from Swift's account of it, that it has been sometimes doubted whether what we have is from the Dean's hand.[2] It was first given to the world under circumstances certainly suspicious. It was not published until thirteen years after his death; it was not printed from the original manuscripts; it was not edited by any member of his

---

[1] At the end of the published work this note is appended: 'It need hardly be observed that this history was left incomplete by the author'; but in the *Journal to Stella*, May 16, 1713, he says: 'I have just finished my *Treatise*, and must be ten days in correcting it.' The explanation, of course, is that the work under its present title is a misnomer. The portion which Swift completed was the *History of the Treaty of Utrecht*; he no doubt designed to continue it to the end of the reign.

[2] Macaulay, in some very amusing MS. notes scrawled on the margin of Orrery's *Remarks on Swift*, and preserved in the British Museum, makes short work of the book: 'Wretched stuff; and, I firmly believe, not Swift's.'

family, or by any one having authority from his executors. It was printed by an anonymous editor from
a copy surreptitiously taken by an anonymous friend.
And yet, surely, we need have no more doubt
of its genuineness than we have of the genuineness of *Gulliver's Travels*. One piece of evidence
alone is surely conclusive. In 1738 the original
manuscript was read by Erasmus Lewis, the second
Lord Oxford, and others, in conclave, with a view to
discussing the propriety of its publication. Their
opinion was that it contained several inaccuracies of
statement, and those inaccuracies Lewis, in a letter
to Swift—it may be found in Swift's correspondence [1]
—categorically pointed out. Now a reference to the
printed *Memoirs* will show that they contain the
identical errors detected by Lewis and his friends in
Swift's manuscript. Again, those portions in the
manuscript narrative which Lewis describes as most
entertaining and instructive are precisely those portions in the printed work which are undoubtedly best
entitled to that praise. And, to clamp this evidence,
there is in the British Museum an abstract of Swift's
original manuscript made in 1742, nearly three years
before the Dean's death, by Dr. Birch. A comparison of
this abstract with the work as printed in 1758 proves
conclusively that the manuscript abstracted by Birch
must have been a manuscript of the *History* then first
given to the world.[2] Nor is there anything improbable in the assertion of the editor—one Lucas—that

[1] Scott's *Swift*, xix. 218.

[2] For this interesting piece of evidence I am indebted to Mr.
Craik's *Life of Swift*, Appendix iii. p. 518. It was communicated to
him by Mr. Elwin.

he printed the work from a transcript of the original manuscript, for the original manuscript, as we know from Deane Swift, circulated freely among Swift's friends in Dublin. It is certain that Nugent, Dr. William King, and Orrery had perused that manuscript, and that they were alive when the printed work appeared; it is equally certain that none of them expressed any doubt of the genuineness of the printed *Memoirs*, though those *Memoirs* attracted so much attention that they were printed by instalments in the *Gentleman's Magazine*.

Swift's life during these years is reflected very faithfully in his correspondence. It was passed principally in the discharge of his clerical duties, which he performed with punctilious care; in improving the glebe of Laracor; in endeavouring to come to an understanding with the Archbishop on the one hand, and with his rebellious Chapter on the other; and in devising means for escaping from himself, and from the daily annoyances to which his position exposed him. 'I am,' he writes to Bolingbroke, 'forced into the most trifling amusements, to divert the vexation of former thoughts and present objects.' He gardened and sauntered; he turned over the Greek and Roman classics; he bandied nonsense with Sheridan and Esther Johnson; he went through a course of ecclesiastical history; he dabbled in mathematics. 'I live,' he writes to Pope, 'in the corner of a vast unfurnished house: my family consists of a steward, a groom, a helper in the stable, a footman, and an old maid, who are all at board wages, and when I do not dine abroad or make an entertainment, which last is very rare, I eat a mutton-pie and drink half a pint of

wine; my amusements are defending my small dominion against the Archbishop and endeavouring to
reduce my rebellious choir. *Perditur hæc inter misero
lux.'* Thus much the world saw; thus much he im-
parted with all the garrulity of Montaigne and
Walpole to the friends who exchanged letters with
him. But there were troubles—troubles which must
at this time have been weighing heavily on his mind
—which were little suspected by the world, and from
which he never raised the veil even to those who
knew him best.

II

Shortly after his arrival in London, in the autumn
of 1710, he had renewed his acquaintance with a lady
of the name of Vanhomrigh. Her husband, originally a merchant of Amsterdam, but subsequently the
holder of lucrative offices under the Government of
William III., had died some years before, leaving her
in easy circumstances, with a family of two sons and
two daughters. Her house was in Bury Street, St.
James's, within a few paces of Swift's lodgings. Mrs.
Vanhomrigh was fond—indeed, inordinately fond—
of society, and, as she was not only well connected
and hospitable, but the mother of two charming girls
in the bloom of youth, she had no difficulty in gratifying her whim. Among her male guests she could
number such distinguished men as Sir Andrew Foun-
taine. Among her female visitors were to be found
some of the most attractive and most accomplished
young women in England. There appears, indeed,
to have been no more pleasant lounge in London than
the little drawing-room in Bury Street. This Swift

soon discovered.   Within a few months he had come
to be regarded almost as a member of the family.
He took his coffee there of an afternoon; he dropped
in, as the humour took him, to breakfast or dinner;
his best gown and his best wig were kept there;
and when a friend sent him a flask of choice Florence
or a haunch of venison it was shared with his hospitable neighbours. With the young ladies, Miss Hester,
who had not yet completed her twentieth year, and
Miss Molly, who was a year or two younger, he was a
great favourite. No man thought more highly of the
moral and intellectual capacities of women than Swift,
and nothing gave him so much pleasure as superin-
tending their education.   What he had done for
Esther Johnson he now aspired to do for the Miss
Vanhomrighs, and, as he found his new pupils as
eager to receive as he was to impart instruction, he
became earnest in his pleasant task. So passed—
partly in the innocent frivolities of social gatherings,
and partly in the graver intercourse of teacher and
pupil—two happy years. But towards the end of
1712 Swift suddenly found, to his great embarrassment, that the elder of the two sisters had conceived a violent passion for him.   The unhappy girl,
who had, as she well knew, received no encouragement, struggled for a while, with maiden modesty, to
conceal her feelings. At this point it would have
been well, perhaps, if Swift had devised some means
of withdrawing.   But he probably judged all women
from the standard of Esther Johnson. She, too, had
at one time entertained feelings for him which it was
not in his power to return; but had, as soon as she
saw that reciprocity of passion was hopeless, cheer-

fully accepted friendship for love.   There was surely
no reason to suppose that Miss Vanhomrigh would
not consent to make the same compromise when she
was convinced that there was the same necessity.   All
that was needed was a clear understanding between
them.   That understanding would, as time went on, be
silently arrived at.   But he little knew the character
of the woman with whom he had to deal.   The less
her passion was encouraged the more it grew.   The
more eloquently he dilated on friendship, the more
rapturously she declaimed on love.   As he pleaded
for the mind, she pleaded for the heart.   So for some
months they continued to play at cross-purposes, each
perceiving, and each disregarding, the innuendoes of
the other.   At last the poor girl could bear her tortures
no longer, and, becoming lost to all sense of feminine
delicacy, threw herself at Swift's feet.

And now commenced the really culpable part of
his conduct.   He ought at once to have taken a decisive step.   He ought to have seen that there were
only two courses open to him : the one was to make
her his wife, the other was to take leave of her for
ever.   Unhappily, he did neither.   He merely proceeded to apply particularly what before he had stated
generally.   He continued to enlarge on the superiority
of friendship to love, and he went on to describe the
depth and sincerity of the friendship which he had
long felt for her; as for her passion—so ran his
reasoning—it was a passing whim—an unwelcome
intruder into the paradise of purer joys.   He could
not return it—no true philosopher would; he could
offer instead all that made human intercourse most
precious—devoted affection, gratitude, respect, esteem.

All this he contrived to convey in such a manner as
could not have inflicted a wound even on the most
sensitive pride. It was conveyed—perhaps conveyed
for the first time—in that exquisitely graceful and
original poem which has made the name of Hester
Vanhomrigh deathless. She could there read how
Venus, provoked by the complaints which were
daily reaching her about the degeneracy of the female
sex, resolved to retrieve the reputation of that sex;
how, with this object, she called into being a match-
less maid, who to every feminine virtue united every
feminine grace and charm; how, not content with
endowing her paragon with all that is proper to
woman, the goddess succeeded by a stratagem in inducing Pallas to bestow on her the choicest of the
virtues proper to man; how Pallas, angry at being
deceived, consoled herself with the reflection that a
being so endowed would be little likely to prove obe-
dient to the goddess who had created her; how
Vanessa—for such was the peerless creature's name—
did not for a while belie the expectations of Pallas,
but how at last she was attacked by treacherous
Cupid in Wisdom's very stronghold. The flattered
girl could then follow in a transparent allegory the
whole history of her relation with her friend, sketched
so delicately, and at the same time so humorously,
that it must have been impossible for her either to
take offence or to miss his meaning. How grievously
Swift had erred in thus temporising became every
day more apparent. It was in vain that he now
began to absent himself from Bury Street; in vain
that, as she grew more intemperate, he left her letters
unanswered; in vain that in his own letters he

showed, in a manner not to be mistaken, that he had
no ear for the language of love.

In the summer of 1714 occurred an event which
introduced further complications in this unhappy
business. Mrs. Vanhomrigh died, leaving her affairs
in a very embarrassed state. The daughters, who
appear to have been on bad terms with their brother,
applied for assistance to Swift; and Swift, who had
at this time left London, was thus again forced into
intimate relations with Hester. Nor was this all.
By the terms of her father's will she had become
possessed of some property near Dublin, and Swift
learned, to his intense mortification and perplexity,
that, as there was now nothing to detain her in
England, it was her intention to follow him to Ireland.
He at once wrote off, imploring her to be discreet,
and pointing out how easily such a relation as theirs
might be misinterpreted by censorious people. Dublin,
he said, was not a place for any freedom; everything
that happened there was known in a week, and everything that was known was exaggerated a hundredfold.
'If,' he added, 'you are in Ireland while I am there,
I shall see you very seldom.' But all was of no
avail, and a few weeks after his arrival in Dublin
Hester and her sister were in lodgings within a stone's
throw of the deanery.

Swift's position was now perplexing in the extreme.
By every tie but one which can bind man to woman he
was bound to Esther Johnson. For more than thirteen
years she had been a portion of his life. She had
been the partner of his most secret thoughts; she
had been his solace in gloom and sorrow; she had
been his nurse in sickness. In return for all this she

had claimed neither to bear his name nor to share
his fortune; she had been satisfied with his undivided
affection. As yet nothing had arisen to disturb their
sweet and placid intercourse. Indeed, he had been
so careful to abstain from anything which could
cause her uneasiness, that in his letters from London
he had never even referred to his intimacy with
Hester Vanhomrigh; and poor Stella, little suspect-
ing the presence of a rival, was now in the first joy
of having her idol again at her side. For awhile he
nursed the hope that Miss Vanhomrigh would, on
seeing that he absented himself from her society,
withdraw from Dublin. He was soon undeceived.
The more he left her to herself the more importunate
she became. The letters addressed by her at this
period to Swift have been preserved, and exhibit a
state of mind which it is both terrible and pitiable to
contemplate. ' It is impossible,' she writes in one of
her letters, ' to describe what I have suffered since I
saw you last. I am sure I could have borne the rack
much better than those killing, killing words of yours.
Sometimes I have resolved to die without seeing you
more, but those resolves, to your misfortune, did not
last long.' How deeply Swift was affected by all
this, and with what tenderness and delicacy he acted
under these most trying circumstances, is evident
from his reply to this letter :—

> I will see you in a day or two, and believe me it goes to my
> soul not to see you oftener. I will give you the best advice,
> countenance, and assistance I can. I would have been with
> you sooner if a thousand impediments had not prevented me. I
> did not imagine you had been under difficulties. I am sure my
> whole fortune should go to remove them. I cannot see you to-
> day, I fear, having affairs of my own place to do, but pray think

it not want of friendship or tenderness, which I will always continue to the utmost.

He did all in his power to recall her to reason. He implored her to remember that the world was censorious and that scandal was beginning to be busy with their names.

At last she left Dublin and removed to Celbridge. There, in seclusion, she continued to cherish her hopeless passion ; there Swift for some years regularly corresponded with her and occasionally visited her ; and there, in 1723, while still in the bloom of womanhood, she died.

This is a melancholy story, but it is a story little likely to lose in the telling, and peculiarly susceptible of prejudiced distortion. It behoves us, therefore, before passing judgment on Swift's conduct, to distinguish carefully between what has been asserted and what has been proved, between what rests on mere conjecture and what rests on authentic testimony. Now we may say at once that all that is certainly known of his connection with Hester Vanhomrigh is what may be gathered from the letters that passed between them, and from his own poem of *Cadenus and Vanessa*, and all that can be safely conjectured is that, when they finally parted, they parted abruptly and in anger. This exhausts the evidence on which we can fairly rely in judging Swift; but this is very far from exhausting the evidence on which the world has judged him. First came the almost incredibly malignant perversions of Orrery. Then came the loose and random gossip of Mrs. Pilkington and Thomas Sheridan. Out of these and similar materials Scott wove his dramatic narrative—not, indeed, with any prejudice against Swift, but doing him signal injustice by disseminating stories greatly calculated to prejudice others against him.   Thus he tells, and tells most impressively, a story which, if true, would justify us in believing the very worst of Swift.   Hester Vanhomrigh—so the story runs—having discovered his intimacy with Stella, wrote to her, requesting to know the nature of her connection with Swift.   Stella, indignant that such a question should be put to her, placed the letter in Swift's hands.   Swift instantly rode off in a paroxysm of fury to Celbridge, and, abruptly entering the room where Miss Vanhomrigh was sitting, flung the letter angrily on the table, and then, without saying a word, remounted his horse and galloped back to Dublin. From that moment he was a stranger to her.   In a few weeks Vanessa was in her grave.

The authority cited for this anecdote is Sheridan,[1] who wrote nearly sixty years after the event he narrates, who is confessedly among the most in-accurate and uncritical of Swift's biographers, whose habit of grossly exaggerating whatever he described is notorious, and who has been more than once suspected of enlivening his pages with deliberate fabrications. In the present case, however, he had contented him-self with embellishment; for the story had been already told, first by Orrery, in whose hands it had assumed an entirely different form, and secondly by Hawkesworth, who merely copied what he found in Orrery.   What Orrery says is that Vanessa wrote, not to Stella, but to Swift; and that the object of her letter was, not to ascertain the nature of Swift's con-

---

[1] *Life of Swift*, pp. 330–1; *Remarks*, p. 113.

nection with her rival, but to ascertain his intentions with regard to herself—in other words, to insist on knowing whether it was his intention to make her his wife. Why the letter, which he describes as a very tender one—it would be interesting to know how he could have seen it—should have had such an effect on Swift he has not condescended to explain. But Orrery's whole story is not only in itself monstrously improbable, but it rests on his own unsupported testimony; and on the value of Orrery's unsupported testimony it is scarcely necessary to comment.

Such is the evidence in support of one of the gravest of the charges which have been brought against Swift with respect to Vanessa. Again, Scott asserts, still following Sheridan, that, on hearing of Miss Vanhomrigh's death, Swift 'retreated in an agony of self-reproach and remorse into the South of Ireland, where he spent two months, without the place of his abode being known to any one.' Nothing can be more untrue. A reference to his correspondence at this period will show that he had long intended to take what he calls a southern journey, that many of his friends were acquainted with his movements, and that, so far from wishing to bury himself in solitude, he was extremely vexed that a clergyman, who had promised to be his companion, disappointed him at the last moment.[1] That Miss Vanhomrigh's death deeply distressed him is likely enough; that it excited in him any such emotions as Scott and Sheridan describe requires better proof than evidence which, on the only point on which it is capable of being tested, turns out to be false.

[1] Letter to Robert Cope, June 1723, *Works*, xvi. 440.

To pass, however, from what is apocryphal to what is authentic. A careful study of the letters which passed between Swift and Vanessa [1] must satisfy anyone that Swift's conduct throughout was far less culpable than it would at first sight seem to have been. It resolves itself, in fact, into one great error. As soon as he discovered that he had inspired a passion which he was unable to return, his intercourse with Miss Vanhomrigh should have immediately ceased. All that followed, followed as the result of that error. And yet that error was, as his poem and correspondence clearly show, a mere error of judgment. Had he been aware that, by continuing the intimacy, he was pursuing a course which would be fatal to the girl's happiness, he was either under the spell of a libertine passion or he was a man of a nature inconceivably callous and brutal. That he was no libertine is admitted even by those who have taken the least favourable view of his conduct; that he was neither callous nor brutal, but, on the contrary, a man preeminently distinguished by humanity and tenderness, is admitted by no one more emphatically than by Miss Vanhomrigh herself.

The truth is that he recognised no essential distinction between the affection which exists between man and man, and the affection which exists between man and woman. He knew, indeed, that in the latter case it frequently becomes complicated with passion, but such a complication he regarded as purely accidental. It was a mere excrescence which, without the nutrition of sympathetic folly, would wither up and perish. It was a fault of the heart, which the head would and should correct.

[1] The correspondence is printed by Scott, xix. 393–454.

Hence he saw no necessity for breaking off a friendship which he valued.   Hence the indifference, the
easy jocularity, with which, after the first emotion of
surprise was over, he persistently treated the poor
girl's rhapsodies.   Time passed on, and before he
could discover his error it was too late to repair it.
From the moment of Mrs. Vanhomrigh's death he
was, in truth, involved in a labyrinth, out of which it
was not merely difficult, but simply impossible, to
extricate himself.   If he attempted, as he twice did
attempt, to take the step to which duty pointed, en-
treaties, which would have melted a heart far more
obdurate than his, instantly recalled him.   Could he
leave a miserable girl—such is the burden of the first
appeal which was made to him—to struggle alone
with 'a wretch of a brother, cunning executors, and
importunate creditors'?   'Pray what,' she asks, 'can
be wrong in seeing and advising an unhappy young
woman?'   'All I beg is that you will for once counterfeit, since you can't do otherwise, that indulgent
friend you once were, till I get the better of these
difficulties.'   He assists her; he visits her; he sees
her safely through her difficulties; and he again with-
draws.   Upon that she breaks out into hysterical
raving, informs him that she had been on the point
of destroying herself, and appeals to him in the most
piteous terms to renew his visits.   To this he replies
in the letter which has been already quoted, and he
grants the favour so importunately and indelicately
extorted.   It is remarkable that throughout the whole
correspondence she makes no attempt to conceal the
fact that she is forcing herself upon him, frankly admitting over and over again that there had been

nothing either in his actions or in his words to justify
her conduct.   Search as we may, however carefully, for
any indications of a belief, or even of a hint on her
part, that she had been deceived or misled, nothing of
the kind is to be found.   From beginning to end it is
the same story—on the woman's side, blind, uncontrollable passion—on the man's side, perplexity, com-
miseration, undeviating kindness.   ' Believe me,' she
says at the commencement of one of her letters, 'it is
with the utmost regret that I now complain to you,
because I know your good nature that you cannot see
any human creature miserable without being sensibly
touched; yet what can I do?   I must unload my
heart.'   But she was not always, it may be added, in
the melting mood.   Occasionally she expressed herself in very different language.   It is easy to conceive
Swift's embarrassment on having the following mis-
sive handed in to him while entertaining a party of
friends at the deanery :—

> I believe you thought I only rallied when I told you the
> other night that I would pester you with letters.   Once more I
> advise you, if you have any regard for your own quiet, to alter
> your behaviour quickly,—

that is, to visit her more frequently, though he had
already told her that scandal was beginning to be
busy with their names—

> for I have too much spirit to sit down contented with this
> treatment.   Pray think calmly of it!   Is it not better to come
> of yourself than to be brought by force, and that perhaps when
> you have the most agreeable engagement in the world [an allu-
> sion probably to Esther Johnson], for when I undertake any-
> thing, I don't love to do it by halves.

In a letter written not long afterwards he complains bitterly of the embarrassment which one of her communications had caused. 'I received your letter,' he writes, ' when some company was with me on Saturday, and it put me into such confusion, that I could not tell what to do.' His patience was often, no doubt, severely tried, and his irritation appears occasionally to have found sharp expression. But it is clear from his letters that until within a few months of Vanessa's death he studied in every way to soothe and cheer her. What finally parted them we have now no means of knowing. That they parted in anger and were never afterwards reconciled seems certain. It is possible that the habits of intemperance to which Miss Vanhomrigh latterly gave way [1] may have led to some action or some expression which Swift could neither pardon nor forget.

Far be it from any man to speak a harsh or disrespectful word of this unhappy woman. Never, perhaps, has the grave closed over a sadder or more truly tragical life. It is a story which no man of sensibility could possibly follow without deep emotion. But such emotion should not be permitted to blind us to justice and truth. No protest can be too strong against the course adopted by writers like Jeffrey and Thackeray in treating of this portion of Swift's life. They assume that the measure of Vanessa's frenzy is the measure of Swift's culpability. They argue that, because she was infatuated, he was inhuman. They print long extracts from her ravings, and then ask, with indignation, whether there could be two opinions about the man whose conduct had wrought such

[1] Delany, pp. 123-4.

L

wretchedness.   Nor is it surprising that they should
have carried their point.   The world knows that,
when women address men in such language as Vanessa
addresses Swift, they are not as a rule taking the
initiative ; that, if feminine passion is strong, feminine
delicacy is stronger; and that nothing is more improbable than that a young and eminently attractive
woman should, for twelve years, continue, without the
smallest encouragement, to force her love on a man
who, though double her age, was still in the prime of
life.   And yet this was most assuredly the case.
Vanessa is most sincerely to be pitied, but there is
nothing in Swift's conduct to justify the charges which
hostile biographers have brought against him.

> Condemn you him for that the maid did love him ?
> So may you blame some fair and crystal river
> For that some melancholic distracted woman
> Hath drown'd herself in 't.

But it is only right to say that those who have
judged him thus harshly have proceeded on an assumption which would, if correct, have greatly modified
this view of the question.   If Swift was the husband
of Esther Johnson, it may be admitted, without the
smallest hesitation, that his conduct was all that his
enemies would represent.   It was at once cruel and
mean; it was at once cowardly and treacherous ; it
was at once lying and hypocritical.   In that case
every visit he paid, every letter he wrote, to Miss Vanhomrigh subsequent to 1716 was derogatory to him.
We may go further.   In that case, we are justified in
believing the very worst of him, not only in his relations with Stella and Vanessa, but in his relations with
men and the world.   In that case, there is not ambi-

guous action, either in his public or in his private
career, which does not become pregnant with suspicion. For, in that case, he stands convicted of having
passed half his life in systematically practising, and
in compelling the woman he loved to practise systematically, the two vices which of all vices he professed to hold in the deepest abhorrence. Those who
know anything of Swift know with what loathing he
always shrank from anything bearing the remotest
resemblance to duplicity and falsehood. As a political
pamphleteer he might, like his brother-penmen, allow
himself licence, but in the ordinary intercourse of
life it was his habit to exact and assume absolute
sincerity. It was the virtue, indeed, on which he
ostentatiously prided himself; it was the virtue by
which, in the opinion of those who were intimate
with him, he was most distinguished. 'Dr. Swift
may be described,' observed Bolingbroke on one occasion, 'as a hypocrite reversed.' He was never known
to tell an untruth.

In discussing, therefore, the question of his supposed marriage, the point at issue is not simply
whether he was the husband of Esther Johnson, but
whether we are to believe him capable of acting in a
manner wholly inconsistent with his principles and
his reputation—in other words, whether we are to
believe that a man, whose scrupulous veracity and
whose repugnance to falsehood in any form were proverbial, would, with the object of concealing what
there was surely no adequate motive for concealing,
deliberately devise the subtlest and most elaborate
system of hypocrisy ever yet exposed to the world.
It is scarcely necessary to say that the documents

bearing on Swift's relations with Esther Johnson are very voluminous, and, from a biographical point of view, of unusual value. We have the verses which he was accustomed to send to her on the anniversary of her birthday. We have the *Journal* addressed to her during his residence in London. We have allusions to her in his most secret memoranda. We have the letters written in agony to Worral, Stopford, and Sheridan, when he expected that every post would bring him news of her death. We have the prayers which he offered up at her bedside during her last hours; and we have the whole history of his acquaintance with her, written with his own hand while she was lying unburied in her coffin—a history intended for no eye but his own. Now, from the beginning to the end of these documents, there is not one line which could by any possibility be tortured into an indication that she was his wife. Throughout the language is the same. He addresses her as the ' kindest and wisest of his friends.' He described her in his *Memoir* as 'the truest, most virtuous and valuable friend that I, or perhaps any other person, was ever blessed with.' In all his letters he alludes to her in similar terms. In the Diary at Holyhead she is his ' dearest friend.' At her bedside, when the end was hourly expected, he prays for her as his ' dear and useful friend.' ' There is not,' he writes to Dr. Stopford on the occasion of Stella's fatal illness, ' a greater folly than that of entering into too strict and particular friendship, with the loss of which a man must be absolutely miserable, but especially at an age when it is too late to engage in a new friendship; besides, this was a person of my own rearing and instructing from childhood; but, pardon me, I know

not what I am saying, but, believe me, that violent
friendship is much more lasting and engaging than
violent love.' If Stella was his wife, could hypocrisy
go further ? [1]   It is certain that he not only led all
who were acquainted with him to believe that he was
unmarried, but, whenever he spoke of wedlock, he
spoke of it as a thing utterly alien to his tastes and
inclinations. 'I never yet,' he once said to a gentleman who was speaking to him about marriage, 'saw
the woman I would wish to make my wife.' It would
be easy to multiply instances, both in his correspondence and in his recorded conversation, in which, if
he was even formally a married man, he went out of
his way to indulge in unnecessary hypocrisy. What,
again, could be more improbable than that Esther
Johnson, a woman of distinguished piety, nay, a
woman whose detestation of falsehood formed, as
Swift has himself told us, one of her chief attrac-
tions, would, when on the point of death, preface her
will with a wholly gratuitous lie ? For not only

[1] Is it credible that a man could have addressed a woman who
had, if the theory of the marriage is true, been his wife for four years,
in lines like these—lines, we may add, intended for no eyes but her
own ?—

> Thou, Stella, wert no longer young
> When first for thee my harp was strung
> Without one word of Cupid's darts,
> Of killing eyes or bleeding hearts.
> With friendship and esteem possess'd
> I ne'er admitted love a guest.
> In all the habitudes of life,
> The friend, the mistress, and the wife,
> Variety we still pursue,
> In pleasure seek for something new;
> But his pursuits are at an end
> Whom Stella chooses for a friend.

is that will signed with her maiden name, but in
the first clause she describes herself as an unmarried
woman.

The external evidence against the marriage appears
equally conclusive. If there was any person entitled
to speak with authority on the subject, that person
was assuredly Mrs. Dingley. For twenty-nine years,
from the commencement, that is to say, of Swift's
intimate connection with Stella till the day of Stella's
death, she had been her inseparable companion, her
friend and confidant. She had shared the same
lodgings with her; it was understood that Swift and
Esther were to have no secrets apart from her.
When they met, they met in her presence; what they
wrote, passed, by Swift's special request, through her
hands. Now it is well known that Mrs. Dingley
was convinced that no marriage had ever taken place.
The whole story was, she said, an idle tale. Two of
Stella's executors, Dr. Corbet and Mr. Rochford, distinctly stated that no suspicion of a marriage had
ever even crossed their minds, though they had seen
the Dean and Esther together a thousand times.
Swift's housekeeper, Mrs. Brent, a shrewd and obser-
vant woman, who resided at the deanery during the
whole period of her master's intimacy with Miss
Johnson, was satisfied that there had been no marriage. So said Mrs. Ridgeway, who succeeded her as
housekeeper, and who watched over the Dean in his
declining years. But no testimony could carry greater
weight than that of Dr. John Lyon. He was one of
Swift's most intimate friends, and, when the state of
the Dean's health was such that it had become necessary to place him under surveillance, Lyon was the

person selected to undertake the duty. He lived with him at the deanery; he had full control over his papers; he was consequently brought into contact with all who corresponded with him, and with all who visited him. He had thus at his command every contemporary source of information. Not long after the story was first circulated, he set to work to ascertain, if possible, the truth. The result of his investigations was to convince him that there was absolutely no foundation for it but popular gossip, unsupported by a particle of evidence.

Such is the testimony against the marriage. Let us now briefly review the evidence in its favour. The first writer who mentions it is Orrery, and his words are these : ' Stella was the concealed but undoubted wife of Dr. Swift, and if my informations are right, she was married to him in the year 1716 by Dr. Ash, then Bishop of Clogher.' [1] On this we need merely remark that he offers no proof whatever of what he asserts, though he must have known well enough that what he asserted was contrary to current tradition; that in thus expressing himself he was guilty of gross inconsistency, as he had nine years before maintained the opposite opinion ; [2] and that there is every reason to believe that he resorted to this fiction, as he resorted to other fictions, with the simple object of seasoning his narrative with the piquant scandal in which he notoriously delighted. The next deponent is Delany,[3] whose independent testi-

[1] *Remarks*, p. 22.

[2] See his letter to Deane Swift, dated Dec. 4, 1742 ; Scott, xix. 336.

[3] *Observations on Orrery's Remarks*, p. 52 *seqq.*

mony would undoubtedly have carried great weight with
it. But Delany simply follows Orrery, without explaining his reason for doing so, without bringing forward
anything in proof of what Orrery had stated, and
without contributing a single fact on his own authority. Then comes Deane Swift.[1] All that he con-
tributes to the question is simply the statement that
he was thoroughly persuaded that Swift was married
to Stella in or about 1716. But he gives no explanation of what induced his persuasion, and admits that
there was no evidence at all of the marriage. And,
unsatisfactory as his testimony is, it is rendered
more so by the fact that some years before he had,
in a letter to Lord Orrery, stated that to many the
marriage seemed based only ' on a buzz and rumours.' [2]
Such was the story in its first stage. In 1780 a new
particular was added, and a new authority cited.
The new particular was that the marriage took place
in the garden; the new authority was Dr. Samuel
Madden, and the narrator was Dr. Johnson. Of
Madden it may suffice to say that there is no proof
that he was acquainted either with Swift himself or
with any member of Swift's circle; that in temper and
blood he was half French, half Irish; and that as a
writer he is chiefly known as the author of a work
wilder and more absurd than the wildest and most
absurd of Whiston's prophecies or Asgill's paradoxes.
On the value of the unsupported testimony of such a
person there is surely no necessity for commenting.
Next comes Sheridan's account, which, as it adds an
incident very much to Swift's discredit, it is necessary

---

[1] *Essay on the Life and Writings of Swift*, p. 92 *seqq.*
[2] *Orrery Papers*, quoted by Mr. Craik.

to examine with some care. The substance of it is this :—that, at the earnest solicitation of Stella, Swift consented to marry her ; that the marriage ceremony was performed without witnesses, and on two conditions—first, that they should continue to live separately ; and secondly, that their union should remain a secret ; that for some years these conditions were observed, but that on her death-bed Stella implored Swift to acknowledge her as his wife ; that to this request Swift made no reply, but, turning on his heel, left the room, and never afterwards saw her. The first part of this story he professes to have derived from Mrs. Sican, the second part from his father. We have no right to charge Sheridan with deliberate falsehood, but his whole account of Swift's relations with Miss Johnson teems with inconsistencies and improbabilities so glaring that it is impossible to place the smallest confidence in what he says. He here tells us that the marriage had been kept a profound secret ; in another place he tells us that Stella had herself communicated it to Miss Vanhomrigh. He admits that the only unequivocal proof of the marriage is the evidence of Dr. Sheridan, and yet in his account of the marriage he cites as his authority, not Dr. Sheridan, but Mrs. Sican. But a single circumstance is, perhaps, quite sufficient to prove the utterly untrustworthy character of his assertions. He informs us, on the authority of his father, that Stella was so enraged by Swift's refusal to acknowledge her as his wife, that to spite and annoy him she bequeathed her fortune to a public charity. A reference to Swift's correspondence[1] will show that it was in accordance

---

[1] See Swift's letter to Worral, dated July 15, 1726.

with his wishes that she thus disposed of her property.
A reference to the will itself will show that, so far
from expressing ill-will towards him, she left him her
strong box and all her papers. Nor is this all. His
statement is flatly contradicted both by Delany and
by Deane Swift. Delany tells us that he had been
informed by a friend that Swift had earnestly desired
to acknowledge the marriage, but that Stella had
wished it to remain a secret. Deane Swift assured
Orrery, on the authority of Mrs. Whiteway, that Stella
had told Sheridan ' that Swift had offered to declare
the marriage to the world, but that she had refused.'
Again, Sheridan asserts that his father, Dr. Sheridan,
was present during the supposed conversation between
Swift and Stella. Mrs. Whiteway, on the contrary,
assured Deane Swift that Dr. Sheridan was not present
on that occasion.[1]

This brings us to the last deponent whose evidence
is worth consideration. In 1789 Mr. Monck-Berkeley[2]
brought forward the authority of a Mrs. Hearne, who
was, it seems, a niece of Esther Johnson, to prove
that the Dean had made Stella his wife. As nothing,
however, is known of the history of Mrs. Hearne, and
as she cited nothing in corroboration of her statement,
except vaguely that it was a tradition among her
relatives—a tradition which was, of course, just as likely
to have had its origin from the narratives of Orrery
and Delany as in any authentic communication—no
importance whatever can be attached to it. But the
evidence on which Monck-Berkeley chiefly relied was

---

[1] For Sheridan's narrative, see section vi. of his *Life of Swift*.
[2] See Monck-Berkeley's *Inquiry into the Life of Dean Swift*, prefixed to his *Literary Relics*, xxvi.-xxix.

not that of Mrs. Hearne. ' I was,' he says, ' informed
by the relict of Bishop Berkeley that her husband had
assured her of the truth of Swift's marriage, as the
Bishop of Clogher, who had performed the ceremony,
had himself communicated the circumstance to him.'
If this could be depended on, it would, of course, settle
the question ; but, unfortunately for Monck-Berkeley,
and for Monck-Berkeley's adherents, it can be conclusively proved that no such communication could
have taken place.   In 1715, a year before the supposed
marriage was solemnised, Berkeley was in Italy, where
he remained till 1721.   Between 1716 and 1717 it is
certain that the Bishop of Clogher never left Ireland,
and at the end of 1717 he died.   As for the testimony
on which Scott lays so much stress—the story, that
is to say, about Mrs. Whiteway having heard Swift
mutter to Stella that ' if she wished, it should be
owned,' and of having heard Stella sigh back to Swift
that ' it was too late '—it need only be observed, first,
that it was communicated about seventy years after
the supposed words had been spoken, not by the son
of Mrs. Whiteway, who, had he known of it or had he
attached the smallest importance to it, would have
inserted it in his *Memoirs of Swift*, but by her
grandson, Theophilus Swift, who was the laughing-
stock of all who knew him ; [1] secondly, it was admitted
that those words, and that those words only, had been
heard, and that consequently there was nothing to
indicate either that the words themselves, or that the

[1] Those who would understand what Theophilus Swift was would
do well to turn to *The Touch-stone of Truth uniting Mr. Swift's
late Correspondence with the Rev. Doctor Dobbin and his Family*.
Such another fool probably never existed out of fiction.

conversation of which they formed a portion, had any reference to the marriage.

How, then, stands the case? Even thus. Against the marriage we have the fact that there is no documentary evidence of its having been solemnised; that, so far from there being any evidence of it deducible from the conduct of Swift and Stella, Orrery himself admits that it would be difficult, if not impossible, to prove that they had ever been alone together during their whole lives. We have the fact that Esther Johnson, at a time when there could have been no possible motive for falsehood, emphatically asserted that she was unmarried: the fact that Swift led every one to believe that he was unmarried: the fact that Esther Johnson's bosom friend and inseparable companion was satisfied that there had been no marriage: the fact that two of Swift's housekeepers, two of Stella's executors, and Dr. Lyon, were satisfied that there had been no marriage. It is easy to say that all that has been advanced merely proves that the marriage was a secret, and that the secret was well kept. But that is no answer. The question must be argued on evidence; and it is incumbent on those who insist, in the teeth of such evidence as has been adduced, that a marriage was solemnised, to produce evidence as satisfactory. This they have failed to do. Till they have done so, let us decline to charge Swift with mendacity and hypocrisy, and to convict him of having acted both meanly and treacherously in his dealings with the two women whose names will for all time be bound up with his. In itself it matters not two straws to any one whether Swift was or was not the husband of Stella. But the point of importance is this. If he was the husband of Stella, his conduct to Miss Vanhomrigh admits of no defence—it was unmanly and dishonourable. If he was not married to Stella, the fate of her rival leaves no stain on his memory. Moral courage in a man's relations with men is, it is true, quite compatible with moral cowardice in his relations with women, but that this deplorable anomaly finds illustration in Swift is at present mere assumption. However, it is too late now to reverse, or even to modify, the verdict of the world. The story of Stella and Vanessa soon passed from essayists and biographers to novelists and poets. Not long after Swift's death appeared, dedicated to the Countess of Pembroke, a wretched fiction entitled *The Amours and Intrigues of a certain Irish Dean.* Chaufepié, in his supplements to Bayle's *Dictionary*, scattered, in an article on Swift, the traditions of Orrery, Delany, and Deane Swift broadcast over Europe. The romance arrested Lessing, who founded on it his famous domestic drama *Miss Sara Sampson.* Then it was consecrated by the genius of Goethe, and his *Stella* made it a household word wherever German was spoken. It has formed the plot of more than one romance in French. It is now going the round of Mr. Mudie's readers in a three-volume novel.

CHAPTER VII

IRISH POLITICS

I

' NOTHING has convinced me so much that I am of a little subaltern spirit, *inopis atque pusilli animi*, as to reflect how I am forced into the most trifling amusements to divert the vexation of former thoughts and present objects.' So wrote Swift to Bolingbroke at the end of 1719. And reason, indeed, were his old enemies soon to have for exclaiming with the Roman poet :

Utinam his potius nugis tota illa dedisset
Tempora sævitiæ !

With the new year his diversion took another turn. In the spring he began to direct his attention seriously to Irish affairs. In the summer appeared the pamphlet which opened the war with England. It was entitled *A Proposal for the Universal Use of Irish Manufactures*, and its ostensible object was to induce the people of Ireland to rely entirely, so far at least as house furniture and wearing apparel were concerned, on their own industry and on their own produce, and to close their markets against everything wearable which should be imported from England. In the first part of this proposal there was nothing new.

It was merely the embodiment of a resolution which had been repeatedly passed by the Irish House of Commons, and passed without opposition from the Crown. It may be doubted whether even the second part of the proposal, audacious though it undoubtedly was, would in itself have provoked the English Government to retaliate. But the ostensible object of the pamphlet, as it requires very little penetration to see, was by no means its only or indeed its chief object. In effect it was a bitter protest against the inhumanity and injustice which had since 1665 characterised the Irish policy of England; and it was an appeal to Ireland to assert her independence in the only way in which fortune had as yet enabled her to assert it. Both as a protest and as an appeal, the pamphlet was equally justified. Even now, on recalling those cruel statutes which completed between 1665 and 1699 the annihilation of Irish trade, it is impossible not to feel something of the indignation which burned in Swift. In 1660 there was every prospect that in a few years Ireland might become a happy and prosperous country. Her natural advantages were great. In no regions within the compass of the British Isles was the soil more fertile. As pasture land she was indeed to the modern world what Argos was to the ancient. She was not without navigable rivers; the ports and harbours with which Nature had bountifully provided her were the envy of every maritime nation in Europe; and her geographical position was eminently propitious to commercial enterprise. For the first time in her history she was at peace. The aborigines had at last succumbed to the Englishry. A race of sturdy and industrious colonists were rapidly changing the face of the country. Agriculture was thriving. A remunerative trade in live cattle and in miscellaneous farm produce had been opened with England; a still more remunerative trade in manufactured wool was holding out prospects still more promising. There were even hopes of an extensive mercantile connection with the colonies. But the dawn of this fair day was soon overcast. Impelled partly by jealousy, partly by that short-sighted selfishness which was, in former days, so unhappily conspicuous in her commercial relations with subject states, and partly in accordance with the principles ordinarily regulating her colonial policy, England proceeded to the systematic destruction of Irish commerce and of Irish industrial art. First came the two statutes forbidding the importation of live cattle and farm produce into England, and Ireland was at once deprived of her chief source of revenue. Then came the statutes which annihilated her colonial trade. Crushing and terrible though these blows were, she still, however, continued to struggle on, crippled and dispirited indeed, but not entirely without heart. But in 1699 was enacted the statute which completed her ruin. By this she was prohibited from seeking any vent for her raw and manufactured wool except in England and Wales, where the duties imposed on both these commodities were so heavy as virtually to exclude them from the market. The immediate result of this atrocious measure was to turn flourishing villages into deserts, and to throw between twenty and thirty thousand able-bodied and industrious artisans on public charity. The ultimate result of all these measures was the complete paralysis of opera-

tive energy, the emigration of the only class who were
of benefit to the community, and the commencement of a period of unprecedented wretchedness and
degradation.[1]

The condition of Ireland between 1700 and 1750
was in truth such as no historian, who was not prepared to have his narrative laid aside with disgust
and incredulity, would venture to depict. If analogy
is to be sought for it, it must be sought in the scenes
through which, in the frightful fiction of Monti, the
disembodied spirit of Bassville was condemned to
roam. In a time of peace the unhappy island suffered all the most terrible calamities which follow in
the train of war. Famine succeeding famine deci-
mated the provincial villages and depopulated whole
regions. Travellers have described how their way
has lain through districts strewn like a battlefield
with unburied corpses, which lay some in ditches,
some on the roadside, and some on heaps of offal, the
prey of dogs and carrion birds.[2] 'I have seen,' says a
writer quoted by Mr. Lecky,[3] 'the helpless orphan
exposed on the dunghill, and the hungry infant sucking

---

[1] See *The Present Miserable State of Ireland*, in a letter from a
gentleman in Dublin—attributed to Swift and printed in the Appendix
to Scott's *Swift*, vol. i. lxxxix. *seqq*. The chief tracts and letters of
Swift bearing on Irish affairs are, in addition to the *Proposal* and the
Drapier Letters, *Two Letters on Subjects Relative to Ireland*, Scott,
vol. vii.; *The Story of an Injured Lady*, id.; *A Short View of the
State of Ireland*, id.; *Maxims controlled in Ireland*, id.; *A Letter
to the Archbishop of Dublin concerning the Weavers*, id.; *Answer
to a Paper called a Memorial*, id.; *A Modest Proposal*, id.; *Letter
to Peterborough*, Scott, xvii. 68; Sermon ix. *On the Causes of the
Wretched Condition of Ireland*.

[2] Burdy's *Life of Skelton*, p. 333.

[3] *History of England in the Eighteenth Century*, ii. 219.

at the breast of the already expired servant.' Even
when there was no actual famine, the food of the rustic
vulgar was often such as our domestic animals would
reject with disgust. Their ordinary fare was buttermilk and potatoes, and when these failed they were
at the mercy of fortune. Frequently the pot of the
wretched cottier contained nothing but the product
of the marsh and the waste ground. The flesh of a
horse which had died in harness, the flesh of woodland
vermin, even when corruption had begun to do its
revolting work, were devoured voraciously. Burdy [1]
tells us that these famishing savages would surreptitiously bleed the cattle which they had not the
courage to steal, and, boiling the blood with sorrel,
convert the sickening mixture into food. Epidemic
diseases, and all the loathsome maladies which were
the natural inheritance of men whose food was the
food of hogs and jackals, whose dwellings were
scarcely distinguishable from dunghills, and whose
personal habits were filthy even to beastliness, raged
with a fury rarely witnessed in Western latitudes.
Not less deplorable was the spectacle presented by
the country itself. ' Whoever took a journey through
Ireland,' says Swift, ' would be apt to imagine himself
travelling in Lapland or Iceland.' In the south, in
the east, and in the west, stretched vast tracks of
land untilled and unpeopled, mere waste and solitude.
Even where Nature had been most bounteous, the
traveller might wander for miles without finding
a single habitation, without meeting a single human
being, without beholding a single trace of human
culture. Many of the churches were roofless, the

[1] *Life of Skelton*, p. 385.

walls still gaping with the breaches which the cannon of Cromwell had made in them. Almost all the old seats of the nobility were in ruins. In the villages and country towns every object on which the eye rested told the same lamentable story.

Much of this misery was undoubtedly to be attributed to the inhabitants themselves. For the aborigines Swift could scarcely find terms sufficiently strong to express his contempt. He always, indeed, denied their title to the denomination of Irishmen, and nothing enraged him more than the persistency with which the English Government confounded, under the common name of Irish, the natives and the Englishry. He regarded it, and perhaps justly, as a manœuvre employed to thwart and baffle his efforts to place Ireland on a footing of equality with England.[1] But there was little to choose between them. It was distinction without difference. If the Celt had been exterminated, Celtic infiltration had done its work. Never had co-operation and concord been more necessary, but never had civil and religious dissension raged with greater fury than it was raging now. Feuds in religion, feuds in politics, feuds which had their origin in private differences, and feuds which had descended as a cursed heirloom from father to child, rankled in their hearts and inflamed their blood. There was the old enmity between the aborigines and the English; there was a deadly feud between the Catholics and the Protestants; there was a feud not less deadly between the Episcopalians and the Nonconformists; while the war between Whig and Tory

---

[1] See particularly his letter to Peterborough giving an account of what he had submitted to Walpole (Scott's *Swift*, xvii. 68).

was prosecuted with a ferocity and malignity scarcely human. 'There is hardly a Whig in Ireland,' wrote Swift to Sheridan, 'who would allow a potato and buttermilk to a reputed Tory.' But this was not all. The principal landowners resided in England, leaving as their lieutenants a class of men known in Irish history as Middlemen. It may be doubted whether, since the days of the Roman Publicans, oppression and rapacity had ever assumed a shape so odious as they assumed in these men. The Middleman was, as a rule, entirely destitute of education ; his tastes were low, his habits debauched and recklessly extravagant. Long familiarity with such scenes as have been described had rendered him not merely indifferent to human suffering, but ruthless and brutal. All the tenancies held under him were at rack-rent, and with the extraction of that rent, or what was, in kind, equivalent to that rent, began and ended his relations with his tenants. As many of those tenants were little better than impecunious serfs, often insolvent and always in arrears, it was only by keeping a wary eye on their movements, and by pouncing with seasonable avidity on anything of which they might happen to become possessed, either by the labour of their hands or by some accident of fortune, that he could turn them to account. Sometimes the produce of the potato-plot became his prey, sometimes their agricultural tools ; not unfrequently he would seize everything which belonged to them, and, driving them with their wives and children, often under circumstances of revolting cruelty, out of their cabins, send them to perish of cold and hunger in the open country.

Nor were the Irish provincial gentry in any way

superior to the Middlemen. Swift, indeed, regarded
them with still greater detestation. As public men,
they were chiefly remarkable for their savage oppression of the clergy, for the mercilessness with which
they exacted their rack-rents from the tenantry, and
for the mean ingenuity with which they contrived to
make capital out of the miseries of their country. In
private life they were dissolute, litigious, and arrogant,
and their vices would comprehend some of the worst
vices incident to man—inhuman cruelty, tyranny in
its most repulsive aspects, brutal appetites forcibly
gratified, or gratified under circumstances scarcely
less atrocious, and an ostentatious lawlessness which
revelled unchecked either by civil authority or by
religion.

But, whatever degree of culpability may attach
itself to the inhabitants of Ireland, there can be no
question that the English Government were in the
main responsible for the existence of this hell. It
requires very little sagacity to see that the miseries
of Ireland flowed naturally and inevitably from the
paralysis of national industry, from the alienation of
the national revenue, from the complete dislocation of
the machinery of government, and from the almost
total absence, so far at least as the masses were concerned, of the influence of civilising culture and religion. Reference has already been made to the statutes which annihilated the trade and prostrated the
industrial energy of the country. Equally iniquitous
and oppressive was the alienation of the revenue. On
that revenue had been quartered the parasites and
mistresses of succeeding generations of English kings.
Almost all the most remunerative public posts were

sinecures in the possession of men who resided in
England.   Indeed, some of these sinecurists had never
set foot on Irish earth.   But nothing was more derogatory to England than the scandalous condition of
the Protestant hierarchy.   On that body depended not
only the spiritual welfare but the education of the
multitude, and their responsibility was the greater in
consequence of the inhibitions which had been laid
by the Legislature on the Catholic priesthood.   But
the Protestant clergy were, as a class, a scandal to
Christendom.   Many of the bishops would have disgraced the hierarchy of Henry III.   Their ignorance,
their apathy, their nepotism, were proverbial.   It was
not uncommon for them to abandon even the semblance of their sacred character, and to live the life
of jovial country squires, their palaces ringing with
revelry, their dioceses mere anarchy.   If their sees
were not to their taste, they resided elsewhere.   The
Bishop of Down, for example, settled at Hammersmith,
where he lived for twenty years without having once
during the whole of that time set foot in his diocese.[1]
That there were a few noble exceptions must in justice
be admitted.   No churchman could pronounce the
names of Berkeley, King, and Synge without reverence.   But the virtues of these illustrious prelates
had little influence either on their degenerate peers
or on the inferior clergy.   Of this body it would not
be too much to say that no section of the demoralised
society of which they formed a part was more demoralised or so completely despicable.   Here and there
indeed might be found a priest who resided among his

---

[1] See for all this Lecky's *History of England in the Eighteenth
Century* (ii. 231–235), and the authorities quoted by him.

parishioners, and who performed conscientiously the duties of his profession. Such a priest was Skelton, and such a priest was Jackson, but Skelton and Jackson were to the general body of the minor clergy what Dr. Primrose was to Trulliber, or what the parson in the *Canterbury Tales* is to the parson in *Peregrine Pickle*.

Few men could have contemplated unmoved the spectacle of a country in such a condition as this. Its effect on Swift was to excite emotions which in ordinary men are seldom excited save by personal injuries. It fevered his blood, it broke his rest, it drove him at times half-frantic with furious indignation, it sunk him at times in abysses of sullen despondency. He brooded over it in solitude ; it is his constant theme in his correspondence ; it was his constant topic in conversation. He spoke of it as eating his flesh and exhausting his spirits. For a while he cherished the hope that these evils, vast and complicated though they were, were not beyond remedy. And this remedy lay, he thought, not in appealing to the justice and humanity of the English Government, for such an appeal he knew would be vain, but in appealing to the Irish themselves, to the landed gentry, to the middlemen, to the manufacturers, to the clergy. Throughout his object was twofold—the internal reformation of the kingdom, and the establishment of the principle that Ireland ought either to be autonomous or on a footing of exact political equality with the mother-country.

His first pamphlet, the *Proposal for the Universal Use of Irish Manufactures*, is a masterpiece. Addressed, in what it insinuates, to the passions, and in what it directly asserts, to the reason, it is at once an inflammatory harangue and a manual of sober counsel. In a few plain paragraphs the secret of Ireland's wretchedness is laid bare, how far it is in her power to alleviate that wretchedness is demonstrated, and the step which ought immediately to be taken is pointed out. In the proposal that she should close her markets against English goods and draw entirely on her own manufactures there was nothing treasonable or even disrespectful to England. It was no more than she had a perfect right to do; it was no more than the English Government would probably have permitted her to do. But the pamphlet had another side. Though there is not perhaps a sentence in it which could, so far as the mere words are concerned, have been challenged as either inflammatory or insulting, the whole piece is in effect a fierce and bitter commentary on the tyranny of the mother-country, and an appeal to Ireland to strike, if not for independence, at least for indemnity. The pamphlet, though it appeared, as almost all Swift's pamphlets did appear, anonymously, instantly attracted attention. The English Government became alarmed. The work was pronounced to be 'seditious, factious, and virulent,' and the attention of Whitshed, then Chief Justice of Ireland, was directed to it. Whitshed, who had little sympathy with Irish agitation, and who was probably acting on instructions from England, proceeded at once to extreme measures. The pamphlet was laid before the Grand Jury of the county and the city. The printer was arrested. The trial came on, and a disgraceful scene ensued. The jury acquitted the prisoner. The Chief Justice refused to accept the

verdict, and the jury were sent back to reconsider
their decision. Again they found the man not guilty,
and again Whitshed declined to record the verdict.
Nine times was this odious farce repeated, until the
wretched men, worn out by physical fatigue, left the
case by special verdict in the hands of the judge. But
Whitshed's iniquitous triumph was merely nominal,
for his conduct had excited such disgust that it was
deemed advisable to put off the trial of the verdict.
Successive postponements terminated at last in the
Lord Lieutenant granting a *nolle prosequi*. Such a
concession to popular feeling the English Government
had never before made. It was a victory on which the
Irish justly congratulated themselves. It was a victory
destined, indeed, to form a new era in their history.

Nothing we know of Swift illustrates more
strikingly his tact and sagacity as a political leader
than his conduct at this juncture. A less skilful
strategist would, in the elation of triumph, have been
impatient for new triumphs, would have lost no time
in pressing eagerly forward, and would thus have
forced on a crisis when a crisis was premature. But
Swift saw that affairs were at that stage when the
wisest course is to leave them to themselves. The
fire had been kindled—it might be safely trusted to
spread; the leaven of dissatisfaction and resistance
was seething—it was best to leave it to ferment. Up
to a certain point the course of revolution is determined by human agency, but in all revolutions there
is a point at which human agency is powerless, and
the reins are in the hands of Fortune. At such crises
occur those apparently insignificant accidents, the
effects of which are so strangely disproportionate to

the character of the accidents themselves, and which
are to political communities what the spark is to
combustible explosives. Such a crisis had not as yet
arrived in the struggle between England and Ireland,
but for such a crisis—and he saw it was maturing—
Swift deemed it expedient to wait.

He employed the interval in serving Ireland in
another way. The mania for commercial adventures,
which originating in Law's Mississippi Scheme had
culminated in the South Sea Bubble, was now in-
vading Dublin. Among other schemes, a project was
formed for establishing a National Bank, and was
regarded with favour by some of the leading citizens
and many of the petty tradesmen in Dublin. But
Swift saw that an institution eminently useful, and
indeed necessary, in a prosperous community could
only end in ruin and mischief in a community where
stock is incommensurate with credit. He determined,
therefore, to oppose the scheme ; and ridicule was his
weapon. Two pamphlets bearing the signature of
Thomas Hope were soon in circulation. Introducing,
by an *Essay on English Bubbles*, a project for establishing a Swearer's Bank, Mr. Hope proposes to raise
a revenue by enforcing the Act against profane
language. The fine for swearing was, he reminds his
readers, one shilling, and of the two million who made
up the population of Ireland one-half might be fairly
computed as swearing souls. Of these it might be
safely assumed that five thousand were gentlemen,
everyone of whom could afford an oath a day. This
would yield a yearly produce of 1,825,000 oaths,
which, at a shilling each, would amount annually to
91,250*l.* Twenty-five thousand a year might be

expected from the farmers, who, if reckoned at 10,000, would surely be equal to the annual expenditure of 500,000 oaths. Provision for a sufficient number of informers would constitute, no doubt, a serious item in the expenses of the Bank, but, allowing for them and for all other necessary deductions, there would remain from these and other sources a clear yearly sum of 100,000*l.*, 'which,' says Mr. Hope, 'may very justly claim a million subscription.' As the projector's motives are purely patriotic, and as his scheme is designed solely for the benefit of the nation, he proposes that the Bank should be erected on parliamentary security. And, 'to take away all jealousy of any private view of the undertaker, he assures the world that he is now in a garret, in a very thin waistcoat, studying the public good; having given an undeniable pledge of his love to his country by pawning his cloak in order to defray the expense of the press.'

Swift's satire was effective. The project for a National Bank was rejected by the House of Commons in the ensuing Session.

These pamphlets were succeeded a few months afterwards by a little piece in which the extraordinary versatility of Swift's genius is very strikingly and very amusingly illustrated. The streets of Dublin had for several years been infested with gangs of marauders, whose depredations and violence made them the terror of the citizens. A man who ventured out unarmed at night carried, it was said, his life in his hands. Scarce a week passed without some gross outrage. At such a pitch, indeed, had their lawlessness and audacity arrived, that it had become perilous

even in broad daylight to walk in any but the most
frequented thoroughfares. Conspicuous among these
miscreants was one Ebenezer Elliston. The fellow
had long succeeded in eluding the police, but had
recently been captured and publicly executed. In
itself, however, the execution would probably have
had very little effect, for the class to which Elliston
belonged is, as a rule, either too sanguine or too
obtuse to take warning from example. But on the
very day of the execution appeared, in the form of a
broadsheet, an announcement which carried terror
and dismay into every rookery in Dublin. This was
the *Last Speech and Dying Words of Ebenezer
Elliston*, published, as was stated on the title-page,
by his own desire, and for the public good. In it he
not only solemnly exhorted his brother-bandits to
amend their lives, and to avoid the fate which had
most righteously overtaken himself, and would in the
end inevitably overtake them, but he informed them
that, having resolved to atone in some measure for
his own crimes against God and society, he had
thought it his duty to do what in him lay to assist
the Government in suppressing the crimes of others.
'For that purpose, I have,' he said, 'left with an
honest man the names of all my wicked brethren, the
present places of their abode, with a short account of
the chief crimes they have committed. I have likewise set down the names of those we call our setters,
of the wicked houses we frequent, and of those who
receive and buy our stolen goods.' He then goes on
to say that the person with whom the paper had been
deposited would, on hearing of the arrest of any rogue
whose name was mentioned in it, place the document

in the hands of the Government. 'And of this,' he
adds, 'I hereby give my companions fair and public
warning, and hope they will take it.' As Elliston
was known to be a man of education, and as the
information displayed in the piece was such as it
seemed scarcely possible that any one who was not in
the secrets of Elliston's fraternity could possess, the
genuineness of the confession was never for a moment
doubted. Its effect was, we are told, immediately
apparent. Brigandism lost heart ; many of the leading bandits quitted the city ; and the Dean was enabled to boast that Dublin enjoyed, for a time at least,
almost complete immunity from the most formidable
of social pests.

And now arrived, suddenly and unexpectedly, that
crisis in the struggle with England which Swift had
with judicious patience been so long awaiting. For
some years there had been a great scarcity of copper
money, and the deficiency had led to the circulation
of debased and counterfeit coins on a very large
scale. Accordingly, in the spring of 1722, a memorial was presented to the Lords of the Treasury,
stating the grievance and petitioning for a remedy.
The petition was considered, and the memorialists
were informed that measures would be immediately
taken for remedying the evil. Such courteous alacrity
had not been usual with the English Government in
dealing with Irish grievances, and excited, not un-
naturally, some surprise. But it was soon explained.
In a few weeks intelligence reached Dublin that a
patent had been granted to a person of the name of
Wood, empowering him to coin as his exclusive right
108,000*l.* worth of farthings and halfpence for circula-

tion in Ireland. As less than a third of that sum in
halfpence and farthings would have sufficed, and more
than sufficed, for what was needed, the announcement
was received with astonishment. And astonishment
soon passed into indignation. For it appeared on
inquiry that the patent had been granted without
consulting the Irish Privy Council or any Irish official,
nay, even without consulting the Lord Lieutenant,
though he was then residing in London. It appeared,
on further inquiry, that the whole transaction had
been a disgraceful job, and that the person to whom
the patent had been conceded was a mere adventurer,
whose sole care was to make the grant sufficiently
remunerative to indemnify himself for a heavy bribe
which he had paid for obtaining it, and to fill his own
pockets. The inference was obvious. As the profits
of the man would be in proportion to the quantity of
copper coin turned out by him, and in proportion to
the inferiority of the metal employed in the manufacture, his first object would be the indefinite multi-
plication of his coinage, and his second object would
be its debasement. In August the Commissioners of
the Revenue addressed a letter to the Secretary of the
Lord Lieutenant, respectfully appealing against the
patent. This was succeeded by a second letter,
directed to the Lords Commissioners of the Treasury,
informing them that the money was not needed. But
to these letters no attention was paid. Meanwhile
the mint of Wood was hard at work. Several cargoes
of the coins had already been imported and were in
circulation at the ports. Each week brought with it
a fresh influx. The tradespeople, well aware of the
prejudice against the coins, were in the greatest per-

plexity. If they accepted them, they accepted what might very possibly turn to dross in their hands; if they refused them, they must either lose custom or receive payment in a coinage no longer current.

In August, 1723, the Lord Lieutenant arrived, and a few weeks afterwards Parliament met. The greatest excitement prevailed in both Houses. Opinions were divided; but it was resolved at last to appeal against the patent. On September 23 an Address to the King was voted by the Commons. The Lords followed with a similar Address on the 28th. It was asserted that Wood had been guilty of fraud and deceit; that he had infringed the terms of the patent, both in the quantity and in the quality of the coin; and that the circulation of his coinage would be highly prejudicial to the revenue, and destructive to the commerce of Ireland. Walpole had the good sense to see that these Addresses could not with safety be treated as the previous appeals had been treated, and the two Houses were informed, in courteous and conciliatory terms, that the matter would receive His Majesty's most careful consideration. And the promise was kept. A Committee of the Privy Council was specially convened. Their sittings extended over many weeks, and it is abundantly clear that they performed their duties with scrupulous conscientiousness. Walpole now hoped, and hoped not without reason, that Ireland would be pacified, or that, at the worst, a compromise, which would save the Ministry from the humiliation of having to withdraw the patent, could be arranged. But, before the Committee could arrive at any conclusion, an event had occurred which dashed all these hopes to the ground.

Up to this point Swift appears to have remained
passive, though it is highly probable that he had contributed largely to the pasquinade and broadsheet
literature which had never ceased, since the announcement of Wood's patent, to pour forth each week from
the public press.   He was well aware that, of all the
expedients which can be devised for keeping up
popular irritation, and for impressing on the will of
many the will of one, these trifles are the most efficacious.   They had served his turn before, and nothing
is less likely than that he neglected them now.   It is
certain that after the publication of the first Drapier
Letter he was a voluminous contributor to what he
has himself designated as Grub Street literature.
However that may be, he commenced in the summer
of 1724 that famous series of Letters which, if they
are to be estimated by the effect they produced, must
be allowed the first place in political literature.   The
opening Letter is a model of the art which lies in the
concealment of art.   There cannot be the smallest
doubt that Swift designed from the very beginning to
proceed from the discomfiture of Wood to the resuscita-
tion of Ireland, and on in regular progression to the
vindication of Irish independence.   But of this there
is no indication in the first Letter.   It is simply an
appeal purporting to emanate from one M. B., a
draper, or, as Swift chooses to spell it, drapier, of
Dublin, to the lower and middle classes, calling on
them to have nothing to do with the farthings and
halfpence of Wood.   'Brethren, friends, countrymen,
and fellow-subjects,' so runs the opening sentence,
'what I intend now to say to you is, next to your
duty to God, and the care of your salvation, of the

greatest concern to yourselves and your children, your bread and clothing and every common necessary of life entirely depend upon it.' In a style pitched studiously in the lowest key, and with the sort of reasoning that comes home to the dullest and most illiterate of the vulgar, the Drapier then points out to his countrymen that the value of money is determined by its intrinsic value; that the intrinsic value of Wood's coins was at least six parts in seven below sterling; and that the man who was fool enough to accept payment in them must to a certainty lose more than tenpence in every shilling. 'If,' he said, 'you accept the money, the kingdom is undone, and every poor man in it is undone.' The halfpence would run about like the plague and destroy every one who laid his hand upon them. 'Therefore, my friends, stand to it one and all; refuse this filthy trash.' On the monstrous exaggerations and palpable sophistry by which these assertions were supported it would be mere waste of words to comment. The object which Swift sought to attain was an object the legitimacy of which admits of no question, and, if he sought its attainment by the only means which fortune had placed at his disposal, who can blame him? It will not be disputed that the concession of the patent had been a scandalous job; that in conferring it without consulting the Irish Government England had been guilty of grossly insulting the subjects of that Government; that the profits which Wood anticipated were such as could scarcely be compatible with a strict adherence to the terms of his contract; and that, as a matter of fact, some of his coins were, in spite of the risk incurred by detection,

N

found on examination to be below the stipulated value.[1]

The publication of the Letter was as well-timed as the skill with which it was written was consummate. It appeared at a moment when the social and political atmosphere was in the highest possible state of inflammability, and ready at any moment to burst into flame. It was the spark which ignited it, and the explosion was terrific. From Cork to Londonderry, from Galway to Dublin, Ireland was in a blaze. The feuds which had for years been raging between party and party, between sect and sect, between caste and caste, were suspended, and the whole country responded as one man to the appeal of the Drapier. For the first time in Irish history the Celt and the Saxon had a common bond. For once the Whig joined hand with the Tory. For once the same sentiment animated the Episcopalian and the Papist, the Presbyterian and the New Lighter, the Hanoverian and the Jacobite.[2]

On August 4 appeared a second Letter from the Drapier. In substance it is like the first, partly a philippic and partly an appeal, but it is a philippic infinitely more savage and scathing, it is an appeal in a higher and more passionate strain. This Letter was addressed to Harding, the printer, in consequence

---

[1] That Sir Isaac Newton tested the coins and found them satisfactory is nothing to the point, for the samples tested by him were only those struck between March, 1723, and March, 1724, which were never uttered in Ireland (Monck Mason, *Annals*, p. 340). There were, in fact, four varieties struck. Ruding (*Annals of the Coinage*, iii. 476) says that, if the coinage was uniformly of the same kind as the worst samples, the loss to Ireland would have been 82,000*l*.

[2] Boulter to the Duke of Newcastle, *Letters*, i. 7.

of a paragraph which had three days before appeared
in his newspaper. The paragraph was to the effect
that the Privy Council, whose decision had not as
yet been officially announced, had in their Report recommended a compromise. The report of Sir Isaac
Newton, who, as Master of the Mint, had been in-
structed to test the coins, had, it was stated, been
favourable to Wood. Wood, therefore, was to retain
the right of mintage, but, in deference to public feeling in Ireland, the amount of the sum to be coined
by him was to be reduced from a hundred and eight
thousand pounds to forty thousand. The justice and
reasonableness of this proposal—a proposal which had
emanated from Wood himself—must have been as
obvious then as it is obvious now. But Swift saw at
once that, if the compromise were accepted, the victory,
though nominally on the side of Ireland, would in
reality be on the side of England. In essence England had conceded nothing. Wood still retained his
obnoxious prerogative; England still assumed the
right of conferring that prerogative. A particular
evil had been lightened, but the greater evil, the evil
principle, remained. Nor was this all. Nothing can
be more certain than that it was Swift's design
from the very beginning to make the controversy with
Wood the basis of far more extensive operations.[1] It

[1] The letter which he addressed to Lord Carteret in April, 1724,
just after Carteret had been appointed Lord Lieutenant, might at first
sight seem to favour the view that his chief object was what it
appeared to be, the withdrawal of the obnoxious coin. But the letter
was evidently written to ingratiate himself, or at least to bring himself into correspondence, with Carteret, in whom he had many
reasons for supposing that he might find a coadjutor in the general
cause of Irish reform. He must have known perfectly well that no

had furnished him with the means of waking Ireland
from long lethargy into fiery life.   He looked to it to
furnish him with the means of elevating her from
servitude to independence, from ignominy to honour.
His only fear was lest the spirit which he had kindled
should burn itself out or be prematurely quenched.
And of this he must have felt that there was some
danger, when it was announced that England had
given way much more than it was expected she would
give way, and much more than she had ever given
way before.   In his second Letter, therefore, written
to prepare his readers for the official announcement
of the Report, he treats the proffered compromise
with indignant disdain, and, with a skill which would
have done honour to Demosthenes, tears the whole
case of his opponents into shreds before they had had
the opportunity of unfolding it.   The patent has been
reduced to forty thousand pounds.   Of what avail is
that ?   If there was not one farthing of copper change
in the whole of Ireland, five-and-twenty thousand
pounds' worth would amply suffice.   The coins have
been tested at the Royal Mint, and it has been pronounced by the assayers that Wood has fulfilled his
contract.   What has been tested ?   A dozen or two
selected for the purpose by Wood.   And what contract has he fulfilled—with whom has it been made ?
With the Parliament or people of Ireland ?   But they
detest, abhor, reject it as fraudulent and corrupt.
Then he goes on to deal with the proposals which
Wood, fearing that his patent might be altogether
withdrawn, had himself offered : namely, that he

private application from a private man would at that moment carry
any weight with it in a matter of public policy.

would not coin more than the seventeen thousand pounds which he had already coined unless the exigencies of trade required it ; that he would be willing to take manufactures in exchange for his coin ; and that he would not oblige anyone to receive more than fivepence halfpenny at one payment.

'Good God!' exclaims the Drapier, 'who are this wretch's advisers? Who are his supporters, abetters, encouragers, or sharers? Mr. Wood will oblige me to take fivepence halfpenny of his brass in every payment. And I will shoot Mr. Wood and his deputies, like highwaymen or housebreakers, if they dare to force one farthing of their coin on me in the payment of a hundred pounds. It is no loss of honour to submit to the lion, but who with the figure of a man can think with patience of being devoured alive by a rat?'

He then proceeds to recommend the tactics which have been practised so effectually in our own day. 'Let us mark and observe those who presume to offer these halfpence in payment. Let their names and places of abode be made public, that every one may beware of them as betrayers of their country and confederates with Mr. Wood.'

A few days afterwards the Report arrived, and a third Letter, with the now famous signature attached to it, followed almost immediately. It was addressed to the nobility and gentry, as its predecessors had been addressed to the lower and middle classes. In effect it repeats, but repeats more emphatically and at greater length, what he had commented on in the second Letter—the mendacity and impudence of Wood, and of the witnesses who had, in the inquiry before the Privy Council, borne testimony in Wood's favour ; the cruelty and illegality of the patent; the scandalous circumstances under which it had been obtained ; the still more scandalous circumstances under which it had been executed ; the intrinsic worthlessness of the coins ; the tyranny and injustice of the mother-country. But the matter which forms the staple of the Letter is not the matter which gives the Letter its distinctive character. It is here that we catch for the first time unmistakable glimpses of Swift's ultimate design. The words of the fourteenth paragraph could have left the English Government in little doubt of the turn which the controversy was about to take. ' Were not the people of Ireland,' asks the Drapier, ' born as free as those of England ? How have they perfected their freedom ? Are not they subjects of the same King ? Am I a freeman in England, and do I become a slave in six hours by crossing the Channel ? ' In another passage he adverts to some of the principal political grievances of the kingdom, sarcastically remarking that a people whose loyalty had been proof against so many attempts to shake it was surely entitled to as much consideration on the part of the Crown as a people whose loyalty had not always been above suspicion. The remark was as pointed as it was just. The events of 1715 and 1722 had left a deep stain on the loyalty of England, but Ireland had never wavered in her fidelity to the House of Hanover.

But it was not simply in the character of the Drapier that Swift was scattering his firebrands. In every form which political literature can assume, from ribald songs roared out to thieves and harlots over their gin, to satires, lampoons, and disquisitions which infected with the popular madness the Common Room of Trinity and the drawing-rooms of College

Green and Grafton Street, he sought to fan tumult
into rebellion.[1] He even brought the matter into the
pulpit. In a sermon which Burke afterwards described as 'containing the best motives to patriotism
which were ever delivered in so small a compass,' the
Dean called on his brethren to remember that next to
their duty to their Creator came their duty to themselves and to their fellow-citizens, and that, as duty and
religion bound them to resist what was evil and mischievous, so duty and religion bound them to be as
one man against Wood and Wood's upholders.[2]

Meanwhile meetings were held, clubs were
formed, petitions and addresses came pouring in.
The Grand Jury and the inhabitants of the Liberty
of St. Patrick's drew up a resolution formally announcing that they would neither receive nor tender
payment in Wood's coins. The butchers passed a
resolution to the same effect; the brewers followed;
and at last the very newsboys, or, as they were then
called, the 'flying stationers,' issued a manifesto
against the coins. Nor was it in the capital only that
these bold proceedings were taking place. In many
of the provincial towns similar resolutions were
passed, and the excitement in Cork and Waterford
was uncontrollable.

It was now apparent even to Walpole that some
decisive step must be taken. The Duke of Grafton,
whose want of tact, whose fretful and choleric temper,
and whose haughty and unconciliating manners,
rendered him peculiarly ill-fitted for his position, was
recalled, and the Minister appointed to succeed him

[1] For samples of these see Scott's *Swift*, vii. 295-304; x. 468-489.
[2] Sermon xii.—*On Doing Good*.

was Carteret. The appointment justly excited great surprise. Walpole and Carteret had long been in open enmity. During several sessions it had been Carteret's chief object to perplex and annoy his rival; and he was suspected, and suspected with reason, of having fomented the disturbances which he was now being sent out to quell. With the Lord Chancellor Midleton, and with the Lord Chancellor's relatives the Brodricks, he had certainly been in friendly communication; and of all the opponents of the patent, Midleton and the Brodricks had, next to Swift, been the most pertinacious. Coxe tell us that it was Carteret who informed Alan Brodrick of the secret arrangement between Wood and the Duchess of Kendal with regard to the profits of the patent, a scandal which the malcontents had turned to great account.[1] Thus in a private capacity he had been in league with those whom in his official capacity he was bound to regard as opponents.

In this singular position Carteret landed in Ireland towards the end of October, with general instructions and with ample powers. He was to soothe or coerce, to yield or resist, as the exigencies of the crisis demanded. If on inquiry it should seem expedient to suspend the patent, the patent was to be suspended; if he thought it desirable to go further and withdraw it altogether, it was to be withdrawn. But he had scarcely time to take the oaths before new and alarming complications arose. On October 23 appeared the fourth Drapier Letter. In this discourse Swift threw off all disguise. The question of the

---

[1] *Memoirs of Walpole*, i. 222.

patent is here subordinated to the far more important question of the nature of the relations between
Ireland and England. Contemptuously dismissing a
recent protest of Wood as 'the last howl of a dog who
had been dissected alive,' he goes on to assert that
the Royal Prerogative, the power on which, during the
whole struggle with Wood, so much stress had been
laid, was as limited in Ireland as it was in the
mother-country. He comments bitterly on the so-
called dependency of Ireland, 'as if the people of
Ireland are in some sort of slavery or dependence
different from those of England.' Dependent they
are, but they are dependent in the same sense, and in
the same sense only, as the people of England are
dependent—dependent on a monarchy common to
both. True it unhappily is, that the Parliaments of
England have sometimes assumed the power of binding Ireland by laws enacted by themselves, but it has
been in defiance of justice, in defiance of reason, in
defiance of the opposition of 'the greatest patriots
and best Whigs in England.' He denounces the injustice of filling all posts of trust and emolument with
Englishmen, instead of conferring them, as they ought
to be conferred, on Irishmen. But the remedy, he
said, was in their own hands; and in two sentences,
which vibrated through the whole kingdom, he suggested it: 'By the laws of God, of nature, of nations,
and of your country, you are and ought to be as free
a people as your brethren in England.' Again: 'All
government without the consent of the governed is
the very definition of slavery'—'though,' he added,
with bitter sarcasm, 'eleven men well armed will
certainly subdue one single man in his shirt.' It

was impossible for the Lord Lieutenant to allow this
to pass. A Proclamation was issued describing the
Letter as wicked and malicious, and offering a reward
of three hundred pounds to any one who would discover the author. Harding, the printer of it, was
arrested and thrown into prison.

Up to this point Swift had, as an individual, kept
studiously in the background. He now came prominently forward. A day or two before the Proclamation he addressed, it would seem privately, a letter
to the Lord Chancellor Midleton, vindicating the
Drapier, and urging the importance of resisting to
the utmost the imposition of Wood's coinage.[1] On the
day succeeding the Proclamation he presented himself
at the levee of the Lord Lieutenant, and, forcing his
way into the presence of Carteret, sternly upbraided
him with what he had done. ' Your Excellency has,'
he thundered out with a voice and manner which
struck the whole assembly dumb with amazement,
' given us a noble specimen of what this devoted
nation has to hope for from your government.' He
then burst out into a torrent of invectives against the
Proclamation, the arrest of Harding, and the protection given to the patent. To a man in Carteret's
position such a scene must have been sufficiently
embarrassing. But he was too accomplished a diplomatist to betray either surprise or anger. He listened
with great composure and urbanity to all Swift had
to say, and then with a bow and a smile gave him his
answer in an exquisitely felicitous quotation from
Virgil :—

---

[1] This is printed by Scott as the sixth Drapier Letter, but he has
put it out of its place ; it should succeed in order the fourth.

Res dura et regni novitas me talia cogunt
Moliri.

So terminated this strange interview.

And now the struggle with England reached its climax; the Bill against Harding was about to be presented to the Grand Jury. On its rejection hung the hopes of the patriots; on its acceptation hung the hopes of the Government. In an admirable address Swift calmly and solemnly explained to his fellow-citizens the momentous issues which some of them would shortly be called upon to try.[1] The important day arrived. What followed was what every one anticipated would follow—the Bill was thrown out. But the Chief Justice Whitshed, acting as he had acted on a former occasion, concluded a scene which would have disgraced Scroggs by dissolving the jury. This insane measure served only to swell the triumph of the patriots. Another jury was immediately summoned. The Bill against Harding was again ignored, and, to complete the discomfiture of the Government, the rejection of the Bill was coupled with a formal vindication of the Drapier. From this moment the battle was virtually won—the Drapier had triumphed, and Swift ruled Ireland. But nine troubled months had yet to pass before victory definitely declared itself. In the interval the voice of the Drapier was heard once more. Swift's object in the sixth Letter, which was addressed to Lord Molesworth, appears to have been twofold—to urge again the necessity of standing firm against the coinage, and to bring into prominence, though with cautious insinuation, all that had in the former

[1] *Seasonable Advice to the Grand Jury.*

Letters been advanced on the general question of Ireland's rights and England's duties. The struggle between dignity and expediency was a severe one. At last England yielded. 'I have His Majesty's commands to acquaint you that an entire end is put to the patent formerly granted to Mr. Wood' were the words in which, at the commencement of the autumn session of 1725, the Viceroy announced to Ireland that the greatest victory she had ever won had been gained.

The public joy knew no bounds. In a few hours Dublin presented the appearance of a vast jubilee. In a few days there was scarcely a town or a village in Ireland which was not beside itself with exultation. The whole island rang with the praises of the Drapier. It was the Drapier, they cried, who had saved them, it was the Drapier who had taught them to be patriots. Had Swift rescued the country from some overwhelming calamity, had he done all and more than all that the Œdipus of story is fabled to have done for the city of Amphion, popular gratitude could not have gone further. Medals were struck in his honour. A club, the professed object of which was to perpetuate his fame, was formed. His portrait stamped on medallions, or woven on handkerchiefs, was the ornament most cherished by both sexes. When he appeared in the streets all heads were uncovered. If for the first time he visited a town, it was usual for the Corporation to receive him with public honours. Each year, as his birthday came round, it was celebrated with tumultuous festivity. 'He became,' says Orrery, 'the idol of the people of Ireland to a degree of devotion that in the most superstitious country

scarcely any idol ever attained.' 'Spirit of Swift!'
exclaimed Grattan on that memorable day when he
brought forward his Declaration of Legislative Independence, 'Spirit of Swift! your genius has prevailed; Ireland is now a nation.' Even now no true
Irishman ever pronounces his name without reverence.

II

But it was not as a political agitator only that
Swift sought to attain his object. Nothing, he believed, contributed more to the degradation and
wretchedness of the country than the state of the
Church. As a churchman his own convictions and
principles had never wavered. From the very first
he had attached himself to the High Church party;
from the very first he had regarded the Low Church
party not merely with suspicion but with abhorrence.
Their latitudinarian opinions, the indulgence with
which they were inclined to treat the Nonconformists,
their close alliance with the clique of the Castle, their
readiness on every occasion to play into the hands of
that clique, and to sacrifice the interests of the Church
to the interests of a faction largely composed of men
at open enmity with the Church—all this he had
long beheld with indignation and alarm. On arriving
in Ireland he found himself in the midst of this obnoxious party. For a while, however, he contented
himself with standing aloof and remaining passive.
But between 1714 and 1720 it became clearly apparent that it was the intention of the Whig Ministry
in England to make the Church of Ireland subser-
vient to the English Government. This was to be

accomplished by the gradual elimination of all High Churchmen and of all natives from offices of trust and emolument. Regularly, as each see or as each deanery fell vacant, it was conferred on some member of the Low Church party in England, selected not because he possessed any moral or intellectual qualification for the post, but because his patrons could depend on his obsequious compliance with their designs. Against this system of preferment, and against the whole body of those who thus obtained preferment, Swift waged incessant war. If they endeavoured to aggrandise themselves, if they essayed in any way to oppress the inferior clergy, or to extend the bounds of episcopal authority, he was in the arena in a moment. Thus in 1723 he opposed an attempt to enlarge the power of the bishops in letting leases.[1] Thus in 1733 he succeeded in inducing the Lower House to throw out the Residence Bill and the Division Bill.[2] Individually and as a body they were the constant theme now of his contemptuous mockery and now of his furious abuse. They are

> Pastors of the ravenous breed,
> Who come to fleece the flocks and not to feed,

' Anti-Christian rooks,' ' new Iscariots,' and the like. But he could not be said to agree with those who blamed the Court for these appointments. Excellent and moral men had, he was satisfied, been selected to fill every vacancy. ' But it unfortunately and uni-

---

[1] See the tract *Some Arguments against enlarging the Power of Bishops in letting Leases*, Scott, viii. 417.

[2] See the two tracts, *On the Bill for the Clergy residing on their Livings*, and *Considerations upon two Bills sent down from the House of Lords*, &c., Scott, ix. 5 and 13.

formly happened that, as these worthy divines crossed
Hounslow Heath on their road to Ireland to take
possession of their bishopricks, they have been regularly robbed and murdered by the highwaymen fre-
quenting that common, who seize upon their robes and
patents, come over to Ireland, and are consecrated
bishops in their stead.' The hatred which Swift bore
to the Whig hierarchy of Ireland is perfectly explicable on political and ecclesiastical grounds, but we
may perhaps suspect that feelings less creditable to
him entered into its composition. It was hardly in
human nature—it was certainly not in his nature—to
forget that men, immeasurably his inferiors in parts
and character, had outstripped him in the race of
honour.

While he was thus defending the Church from
enemies from within—for such he considered these
prelates—he was equally indefatigable in defending
her from enemies from without. It was owing to his
efforts that the Modus Bill—a Bill which would, by
commuting the tithe upon hemp and flax for a fixed
sum, have benefited the laity at the expense of the
clergy—was defeated.[1] It was an attempt on the
part of the Commons and the landlords to rob the
Church of the tithe of agistment that inspired the
last and most furious of his satires. But nothing
excited his indignation more than the indulgence
extended to the Nonconformists. Of all the enemies
of the Established Church they were, in his eyes, the
most odious and the most formidable. It was no secret
that the largest and most influential sect among them

[1] See the tract *Some Reasons Against the Bill for settling the
Tithe of Hemp and Flax by a Modus*, Scott, ix. 29.

aimed at nothing less than the subversion of Episco-
pacy. In numbers these sectaries already equalled the
Episcopalian Protestants; in activity and zeal they
were far superior to them. Indeed, Swift firmly believed that it was the Test Act, and the Test Act only,
which stood between the Church and her destroyers.
But the Whigs argued that the danger came not from
the Nonconformists but from the Papists. The
struggle, they said, lay not between Protestantism
and Protestantism, but between Protestantism and
Roman Catholicism ; and the extension of indulgences
to the sectaries would, they thought, have the effect
of uniting the Protestants, without distinction of sect,
against the common enemy. To this Swift replied
that there was little to fear from the Papists. The
Papists had been reduced to unimportance and impotence by the Penal Laws ; they were as inconsiderable
in point of power as women and children. Popery
was, no doubt, a more portentous monster than Pres-
byterianism, as a lion is stronger and larger than a
cat ; but, he adds in one of those happy and witty
illustrations with which his pamphlets abound, ' if a
man were to have his choice, either a lion at his foot
bound fast with three or four chains, his teeth drawn,
and his claws pared to the quick, or an angry cat in
full liberty at his throat, he would take no long time
to determine.' For this reason he not only opposed
all attempts to repeal the Test Act, but all attempts
to relax its stringency. And the pamphlets and
verses produced by him in the course of this long
controversy are among the ablest and most entertaining of his minor writings.[1]

[1] To this question I shall have to return, but it may be well to

Not less strenuous were his attempts to awaken in the Church itself the spirit of resistance and reform. Among the Bishops there was a small minority by no means favourably disposed towards the policy of England. The Toleration Act of 1719 had alarmed them. The obvious intention of the English Government to degrade the Irish Church into a mere instrument of political dominion had disgusted them. With this section, at the head of which was King, Archbishop of Dublin, Swift coalesced, and out of this section he laboured to construct a party which should combat the Nonconformists on the one hand and the Hanoverian Hierarchy on the other, which should protest against the systematic exclusion of the Irish clergy from remunerative preferment—which should inaugurate a national Church.

Meanwhile he was doing all in his power to raise the character and improve the condition of the inferior clergy. It was with this object that he wrote in 1720 his admirable *Letter to a Young Clergyman*, and if into the *Essay on the Fates of Clergymen*, drawing on his own bitter experience, he infused more sarcasm than admonition, he gave his brethren much salutary advice. He was a friend, an adviser, an advocate, on whom they could always depend. He defended them against the Bishops; he fought for them against the

enumerate here the chief tracts of Swift on this subject: *The Presbyterian's Plea of Merit, A Narrative of the several Attempts which the Dissenters of Ireland have made for a Repeal of the Test Act, The Advantages proposed by Repealing the Sacramental Test impartially Considered, Queries concerning the Sacramental Test, Reasons humbly Offered to the Parliament of Ireland for Repealing the Test.*

landlords. Many of them owed what preferment they possessed to his generous importunity.[1]

It is melancholy to turn from Swift's public to his private life. We open his correspondence, and we find abundant proof that, so far from having derived any gratification either from his recent triumph or from the discharge of duty, he continued to be, what in truth he had long been, the most wretched, the most discontented, the most solitary of men. The very name of the country for which he had done so much was odious to him. He scarcely ever referred either to the Englishry or to the native Irish but with some epithet indicative of loathing and contempt. In the English rule he saw the embodiment of all that is most detestable in power ; in the condition of his compatriots, the embodiment of all that is most despicable in submission. 'I am sitting,' he writes in one of his letters, ' like a toad in the corner of my great house, with a perfect hatred of all public actions and persons.' Though his active benevolence never slumbered, and though he still felt, he says, affection for particular individuals, his feelings towards humanity in general were those of a man in whom misanthropy was beginning to border on monomania. He also complains of his broken health, of his sleepless nights, of his solitude in the midst of acquaintances, of his enforced residence in a country which he abhorred, of his banish-

---

[1] See particularly his letter to Lady Betty Germaine, June 15, 1736, and to Carteret, July, 1725. In the interests of the Irish clergy he did all in his power to counteract the policy of Boulter in conferring the Church patronage on Englishmen. He was not aware how powerless Carteret, who would always have favoured Swift's nominees, really was.

ment from those in whose society he had found the
burden of existence less intolerable. 'I very well
know,' he writes to Pope, 'to whom I would give the
first places in my friendship, but they are not in the
way. I am condemned to another scene, and therefore I distribute it in pennyworths to those about me
who displease me least.' He would do the same, he
said, to his fellow-prisoners, if he were condemned to
jail.

Among those 'who displeased him least' was a lazy,
good-natured, scholarly, and accomplished Irishman
named Sheridan. They rode and walked together; they
read the Greek and Latin poets together; they bandied
nonsense in verse and prose, and became at last inseparable companions. Poor Sheridan, who had a large
family, was always in difficulties. He had set up a
private school in Dublin, but his improvidence and
slovenly habits had prevented him from doing justice
to his great abilities as a teacher, and he had got
heavily into debt. Then Swift had induced the Lord
Primate Lindsay to offer him the richly endowed
school of Armagh, but this offer Sheridan most fool-
ishly declined. At last, again through Swift's recommendation, Carteret appointed him one of the Lord
Lieutenant's Chaplains, and presented him with a small
living near Cork. And now all seemed well. He
went up to Cork to be inducted into the living, and,
good-naturedly undertaking to preach for a brother-
clergyman, without observing that the day on which
he was preaching was the anniversary of the accession
of the House of Hanover, the unhappy man chose for
his text, 'Sufficient unto the day is the evil thereof.'
The congregation were amazed   one Richard Tighe,

a zealous Hanoverian, hurried immediately off to
Dublin, reported the matter to the Lord Lieutenant,
and Sheridan's name was struck off the list of the
Royal Chaplains.[1]

In his vacations Sheridan was in the habit of
retiring with his family to a small country house
which he possessed at Quilca, about seven miles from
Kells. This house he placed at the disposal of Swift,
and here, generally accompanied by Mrs. Dingley and
Stella, Swift frequently resided. Of the life he led
here, and of the house and its occupants, he has left a
most amusing description. He began in April, 1724,
*The Blunders, Deficiencies, and Distresses of Quilca,
to be continued if due encouragement be given.* It
forms, as Scott observes, no bad supplement to Swift's
pictures of Ireland.

---

[1] Swift vowed that he would make Tighe smart for this, and never
ceased to persecute him, whether alive or dead, with satire. And he
kept his vow. Of his lampoons, among the bitterest and more
scathing are those on Tighe. See *Mad Mullinix and Timothy, Tim
and the Fables, Tom and Dick, Clad all in White, Dick a Maggot,
Dick's Variety,* &c. (Scott's *Swift*, vol. x.).

CHAPTER VIII

VISIT TO ENGLAND

FOR some time his old friends had been importuning him to pay a visit to England. Though Atterbury was in exile, and death had removed Oxford, Parnell, and Prior, the Scriblerus Club could still muster a goodly company. Bolingbroke, after many vicissitudes, was again on English soil. Pope, who had achieved a reputation second to no poet in Europe, had settled at Twickenham, and was gradually gathering round him that splendid society on which his genius has shed additional lustre. Arbuthnot,

> Social, cheerful, and serene,
> And just as rich as when he served a queen,

had lost nothing of the wit, the humour, the wisdom, the humanity, which had sixteen years before won the hearts of all who knew him. And not less importunate were those many other friends in whose mansions he had been a welcome guest when he sat each week among the Brethren. But it was long before he could make up his mind to cross the Channel, and it was not till the spring of 1726 that he found himself once more in London.

During this visit occurred two memorable events: the interview with Walpole, and the publication of

Gulliver's Travels. No incident in Swift's biography has been so grossly misrepresented as his connection with Walpole. It was whispered at the time that he had sold himself to the Court, and that the price of his apostasy was to be high ecclesiastical preferment. It was subsequently reported that he had merely offered to turn renegade; for that Walpole, having discovered from an intercepted letter that he was playing a double part, declined to have any dealings with him.[1] Chesterfield confidently asserted that

---

[1] A very circumstantial version of this story is given in a letter dated April 23, 1806, from Edward Roberts, Deputy Clerk of the Pells, to his son Barrè Charles Roberts, which is so curious that I will transcribe it: 'You ask me about the anecdote which Sir Edward Walpole told me he was privy to respecting his father and Swift. Lord Peterborough, the common friend of both these personages, persuaded Sir Robert to take Swift into his favour and to promote him in England, urging that Swift had seen the folly of his adherence to Tory principles, and was become a Whig and a friend to the reigning family and to Sir Robert's administration; that he found himself buried alive in Ireland and wished to pass his remaining days with English preferment on English ground. After frequent importunities Sir Robert consented to see Swift: he came from Ireland and was brought by Lord Peterborough to dine at Chelsea. His manner was very captivating and full of respect to Sir Robert, and completely imposing on Lord Chesterfield. After dinner Sir Robert retired to his closet and sent for Lord Peterborough, who entered full of joy at Swift's demeanour. This was soon done away with. Sir Robert said: "You see, my lord, how highly I stand in the Dean's favour." "Yes," replied Lord Peterborough, "and I am confident he means as he speaks." Sir Robert proceeded: "In my situation, assailed as I am by secret enemies, I hold it my duty, and for the King's benefit, to watch correspondence. This letter I caused to be stopped at the post-office and read it." It was a letter of Swift, I think, to Arbuthnot, saying that Sir Robert had consented to receive him, that he knew that, as no flattery was too gross for Sir Robert, he should receive plenty, and added that he should soon have the rascal in his clutches. . . . I mentioned this remark to old Sheridan, who was outrageous at hearing it. I mentioned Sheridan's disbelief to Sir Edward, who was

Swift had offered his services to the Ministry, and that Walpole had rejected the offer.[1] Now the facts of the case are simply these. Shortly after the Dean's arrival in London, Walpole, who was probably acquainted with him, and who was certainly acquainted with many of his friends, invited him with other guests to a dinner party at Chelsea. It chanced that not long before a libel had appeared, in which the character of the First Minister had been very severely handled. And that libel Walpole had attributed, but attributed erroneously, to Gay. Poor Gay had in consequence not only made an enemy of Walpole, but, what was still more serious, had lost caste at Leicester House. It was, therefore, with an allusion to Gay's misadventure that Swift took occasion to observe at Walpole's table that, 'when great Ministers heard an ill thing of a private person who expected some favour, although they were afterwards convinced that the person was innocent, yet they would never be reconciled.'[2] The words were ambiguous, though Walpole was probably well aware that when Swift uttered them he was referring not to himself but to Gay. He affected, however, to believe that Swift was referring to himself, and he appears to have circulated a

almost equally outrageous, and applied in my hearing to his brother Horace to confirm it. But Horace, for reasons best known to himself, had a convenient want of recollection.'—*Letters and Miscellaneous Papers*, by Barrè Charles Roberts, Student of Christchurch. See also Colton's *Lacon*, dxxx.

[1] Communicated to Sheridan by Clarke, one of the Fellows of Trinity College, who said he had it from Chesterfield.—*Life of Swift*, p. 258.

[2] See Swift's account of this in his letter to Lady Betty Germaine, Jan. 8, 173$\frac{3}{4}$ (Scott, xviii. 127).

report that the Dean had been apologising—in other
words, had been currying favour with him. It is just
possible, of course, that Walpole may for the moment
have misinterpreted Swift's meaning. If he did so,
he was soon undeceived. At the end of April, Swift
had a second interview. It had been granted at the
request of Peterborough, and it was granted that
Swift might have an opportunity of discussing the
affairs of Ireland. What passed on this occasion is
partly a matter of certainty and partly a matter of
conjecture almost as conclusive as certainty.[1] That
Walpole frankly communicated his views with regard
to the relations between England and Ireland; that
these views were diametrically opposed to Swift's;
that Swift, seeing that debate was useless, said very
much less than he designed to say; and that the two
men parted, if not exactly in enmity, at least with
no friendly feelings, we know definitely from Swift's
correspondence. What seem to place it beyond doubt
that Walpole sought in the course of the interview to deal with Swift as he was in the habit of
dealing with men whom it was his policy to conciliate,
are two passages in Swift's correspondence. ' I have
had,' he writes to Sheridan,[2] ' the fairest offer made
me of a settlement here that one can imagine, within
twelve miles of London, and in the midst of my
friends; but I am too old for new schemes, and especially such as would bridle me in my freedom.' Again,
he says in a letter to Stopford,[3] referring to the see
of Cloyne, that it was not offered him, and would not

---

[1] See, for what passed at this interview, Swift to Peterborough,
April 28, 1726 (Scott, xvii. 68).

[2] July 8, 1726.　　　　　　　　　[3] July 20, 1726.

have been accepted by him 'except under conditions which would never have been granted;' adding, 'I absolutely broke with the First Minister, and have never seen him since.' The inference is obvious. Walpole, well aware of Swift's wish to settle in England, was disposed to turn that wish to account. In all probability he offered what Swift mentions to Sheridan without imposing conditions other than those implied conditions which men who accept favours from others spontaneously hold to be binding. It was no doubt hinted at the same time, vaguely but intelligibly, that higher preferment was in reserve if higher preferment should be earned ; and to this Swift probably refers when he speaks of conditions which would never have been granted. But, whatever interpretation may be placed on Swift's words, whatever obscurity may still cloud this much-discussed passage in his life, one thing is clear : he never for a moment allowed self-interest to weigh against duty and principle. It was as the representative advocate of Irish reform that he sought an interview with Walpole. It was because Walpole declined to move in Irish reform that he broke with him and saw him no more.

Meanwhile he was putting the finishing touches to that immortal satire, the fame of which has thrown all his other writings into the shade. At what precise time he commenced the composition of *Gulliver* is not known. It was originally designed to form a portion of the work projected by the Scriblerus Club in 1714 ; and, if it was not commenced then, it was in all probability commenced shortly afterwards. He had certainly made some progress in it

as early as the winter of 1721, for we find allusion
to it in a letter of Bolingbroke's dated January, 1721,
and in a letter of Miss Vanhomrigh's, undated, but
written probably about the same time. There can be
little doubt, therefore, that the work was far advanced
before his visit to Quilca at the end of 1724, and we
know from his correspondence that during that visit—a
visit which extended over the greater part of a year—
the manuscript was seldom out of his hands. Between
that date and the date of publication it appears to
have undergone repeated revisions. Many passages,
for example, must almost certainly have been inserted
during his residence in England. Indeed, I am inclined to suspect that it was to his residence in
England that the satire owed much of its local colour-
ing. Nor is it at all surprising that *Gulliver* should
have occupied Swift's thoughts for many years, and
should have been the result of patient and protracted
labour. It would be easy to point to fictions which
in wealth of imagination and fancy, in humour, in
wit, in originality, would suffer nothing from comparison with Swift's masterpiece. Such in ancient
times would be the *Birds* and the *True Art of Writing
History*; such, in later times, would be the romances
of Rabelais and Cervantes. But what distinguishes
Swift's satire from all other works of the same
class is not merely its comprehensiveness and intensity, but its exact and elaborate propriety. The
skill with which every incident, nay, almost every
allusion, in a narrative as rich in incident as the
Travels of Pinto, and as minutely particular as the
Journal of the Plague, is invested with satirical significance, is little short of marvellous. From the com-

mencement to the end there is nothing superfluous, and there is nothing irrelevant. The merest trifle has its point. Where the satire is not general, it is personal and local; where the analogies are not to be found in the vices and follies common to all ages, they are to be found in the social and political history of Swift's own time. But the fiction has been framed with such nice ingenuity, that the allegory blends what is ephemeral with what is universal; and a satire which is on the one hand as wide as humanity, is on the other hand as local and particular as the *History of John Bull* or *The Satyre Menippée*. Regarded simply as a romance, the work is not less finished. De Morgan has pointed out the scrupulous accuracy with which in the two first voyages the scale of proportions is adjusted and maintained. So artfully, he observes, has Swift guarded against the possibility of discrepancy, that he has taken care to baffle mathematical scrutiny by avoiding any statement which would furnish a standard for exact calculation. And this minute diligence, this subtle skill, is manifest in the delineation of the hero Gulliver, who is not merely the ironical embodiment of Swift himself, but a portrait as true to life as Bowling or Trunnion—in the style, which is at once a parody of the style of the old voyagers, and a style in itself of a high order of intrinsic excellence—in the fine and delicate touches, which give to incidents, in themselves monstrously extravagant, so much verisimilitude, that as we follow the story we are almost cheated into believing it. In all works of a similar kind every incident is, as Scott well observes, a new demand upon the patience and credulity of the reader. In Swift's

romance, as soon as the first shock of incredulity
is over, the process of illusion is uninterrupted.   If
the premises of the fiction be once granted, if the
existence of Lilliput and Brobdingnag, of Laputa and
Balnibarbi, be postulated, we have before us a narrative as logical as it is consistent and plausible.   No
writer, indeed, has excelled, or perhaps equalled, Swift
in the art of what Aristotle describes as ' deception '—
the art, that is to say, of inducing false inference.
When, says that great critic, one thing is observed to
be constantly accompanied or followed by another,
men are apt to conclude that if the latter is or has
happened, the former must also be or must have
happened.   For, knowing the latter to be true, the
mind is betrayed into the false inference that the first
is true also.[1]   Indeed, the skill with which Swift has
by a thousand minute strokes contrived to invest the
whole work with the semblance of authenticity is
inimitable.   De Foe himself is not a greater master
of the art of realistic effect.

That in the plot of his ingenious story Swift
was largely indebted to preceding writers cannot be
disputed.   The resemblances which exist between
passages in *Gulliver* and passages in works with
which Swift is known to have been conversant are
too close to be mere coincidences.   There can be no
doubt, for example, that the Academy of Lagado was
suggested by the diversions of the courtiers of Queen
Quintessence in the fifth book of *Pantagruel*; that the

---

[1] Οἴονται γὰρ ἄνθρωποι, ὅταν τουδὶ ὄντος τοδὶ ᾖ, ἢ γινομένου γίνηται,
εἰ τὸ ὕστερόν ἐστι, καὶ τὸ πρότερον εἶναι ἢ γίνεσθαι· τοῦτο δέ ἐστι ψεῦδος.
διὸ δή, ἂν τὸ πρῶτον ψεῦδος, ἄλλο δ', ὃ τούτου ὄντος ἀνάγκη εἶναι ἢ
γενέσθαι ἢ προσθεῖναι· διὰ γὰρ τὸ τοῦτο εἰδέναι ἀληθὲς ὄν, παραλογίζεται
ἡμῶν ἡ ψυχὴ καὶ τὸ πρῶτον ὡς ὄν.—*Poetics*, xxiv.

attack of the Lilliputians on Gulliver is the counterpart of the attack of the Pygmies on Hercules in the
second book of the *Imagines* of Philostratus ; that the
scenes with the ghosts in Glubbdubdrib are modelled
on Lucian ; that in the *Voyage to Laputa* the romances
of Cyrano de Bergerac were laid under contribution ; and that in the *Voyage to the Houyhnhnms* he
drew both on the *Arabian Nights* and on Goodwin's
Voyage of Domingo Gonsalez. It is very likely that
the Houyhnhnms were suggested by the forty-fifth
chapter of Solinus, and that several strokes for the
Yahoos were borrowed from the *Travels* of Sir Thomas
Herbert. In his characteristic contention of the superiority of the natural animal to the natural man he
has been anticipated by Lucian, whose remarks form
an excellent commentary not only on the *Voyage to
the Houyhnhnms* but on the poetical supplement of
the *Voyage*, the *Beasts' Confession.* ' Tell me,' says
Micyllus to the Cock, ' when you were a dog, a horse,
a fish, or a frog, how did you like that life ? ' ' Everyone of these lives,' is the reply, ' is much more quiet
than that of man, as the life of animals is within
the bound of natural desires and needs, for among
them you could never see a usurious horse, or a back-
biting frog, or a sophistical jay, or a *gourmet* gnat, or
a pimping cock.' [1] It is certain that Swift was, like
Sterne, a diligent student of curious and recondite literature, and that, like Sterne, he was in the habit of turning that knowledge to account. Of this we have a
remarkable illustration in the *Voyage to Brobdingnag.*
Few readers who know anything of nautical science have
not been surprised at the minuteness and accuracy of the
technical knowledge displayed by Swift in his account

[1] *Gallus*, xxvii.

of the manœuvres of Gulliver's crew in the storm off the Moluccas. It is curious that Scott, who ought to have known better, describes the passage as merely a farrago of sea-terms put together at random. Now the whole of this passage was taken nearly verbatim from a work then probably circulating only among naval students, and in our time one of the rarest known to bibliographers. This was Samuel Sturmy's *Mariner's Magazine*, published at London in 1679, a copy of which may be found in the British Museum.[1]

---

[1] As this most curious appropriation, to which my attention was directed by a slip in a scrap-book in the British Museum (Press mark 1881. C. 3), has wholly escaped Swift's biographers and critics, and has not, so far as I know, travelled beyond the scrap-book, I will transcribe the original and the copy, giving them in parallel columns :—

SWIFT.	STURMY.
Gulliver, pp. 108, 109.	*Mariner's Magazine*, pp. 15, 16, 1684.
'Finding it was likely to overblow, we took in our sprit sail, and stood by to hand the fore sail; but, making foul weather, we looked the guns were all fast, and handed the mizen.	'It is like to overblow, take in your sprit sail, stand by to hand the fore sail. . . . We make foul weather, look the guns be all fast, come hand the mizen.
'The ship lay very broad off, so we thought it better spooning before the sea than trying or hulling.	'The ship lies very broad off; it is better spooning before the sea than trying or hulling.
'We reefed the fore-sail and set him, and hauled aft the fore-sheet; the helm was hard aweather.	'Go reef the foresail and set him; hawl aft the fore-sheet. The helm is hard aweather.
'We belayed the fore downhaul, but the sail was split, and we hauled down the yard, and got the sail into the ship, and unbound all the things clear of it.	'Belay the fore down haul. The sail is split: go hawl down the yard and get the sail into the ship and unbind all things clear of it.

But to suppose that these appropriations and reminiscences detract in any way from the essential originality of the work would be as absurd as to tax Shakespeare with stealing *Antony and Cleopatra* from Plutarch, or *Macbeth* from Holinshed. What Swift borrowed was what Shakespeare borrowed, and what the creative artists of all ages have never scrupled to borrow—incidents and hints. The description from Sturmy is to the *Voyage to Brobdingnag* precisely what the progress of Cleopatra in North's *Plutarch* is to the drama of *Antony and Cleopatra*. Indeed, the sum of Swift's obligations to the writers who have been mentioned would, though

SWIFT.	STURMY.
'It was a very fierce storm: the sea broke strange and dangerous.	'A very fierce storm. The sea breaks strange and dangerous.
'We hauled off upon the lanyard of the whip-staff, and helped the man at the helm.	'Stand by to haul off above the lanyard of the whip staff and help the man at the helm.
'We could not get down our topmast, but let all stand, because she scudded before the sea very well, and we knew that, the topmast being aloft, the ship was the wholesomer and made better way through the sea, seeing we had sea-room. . . .	'Shall we get down our topmasts? No, let all stand: she scuds before the sea very well: the topmast being aloft the ship is the wholesomest and maketh better way through the sea, seeing we hav sea room.
'We got the starboard tacks aboard, we cast off our weatherbraces and lifts; we set-in the leebraces and hauled forward by the weather-bowlings, and hauled them tight, and belayed them, and hauled over the mizen-tack to windward, and kept her full and by as near as she would lie.'	'Get the starboard tacks aboard, cast off our weather braces and lifts; set in the lee braces and hawl them taught and belaye them and hawl over the mizen tacks to windward and keep her full and by as near as she would lie.'

considerable, be found on examination to be infinitely less than the obligations of the most original of poets to the novelists of Italy and to the works of contemporaries.

Much has been said about Swift's object in writing *Gulliver*. That object he has himself explained. It was to vex the world. It was to embody in allegory the hatred and disdain with which he personally regarded all nations, all professions, all communities, and especially man, as man in essence is. The key to it is to be found in the sentiments with which his correspondence abounds—in such a sentence as this in a letter to Pope : 'I have ever hated all nations, professions, and communities : and all my love is toward individuals. . . I hate and detest that animal called man, although I heartily love John, Peter, Thomas, and so forth.'[1] Again, to Sheridan : ' You should think and deal with every man as a villain, without calling him so, or flying from him, or valuing him less.'[2] But he was resolved, he said, to laugh and to cry ' *Vive la bagatelle !* ' as long as he lived, and the laugh and the jest are embodied in *Gulliver*. It had no moral, no social, no philosophical purpose. It was the mere ebullition of cynicism and misanthropy —a savage *jeu d'esprit*. And as such wise men will regard it. But there have never been wanting—there probably never will be wanting—critics to place it on a much higher footing. In their eyes it is, as a satire, as an estimate of humanity, and as a criticism of life, as reasonable as it is just. ' *Gulliver*,' says Hazlitt, ' is an attempt to tear off the mask of imposture from the world, to strip empty pride and grandeur of the

[1] To Pope, Sept. 29, 1725.   [2] Letter dated Sept. 11, 1725.

imposing air which external circumstances throw
around them. And nothing,' he adds, ' but imposture
has a right to complain of it.' The answer to this is
obvious. Where satire has a moral purpose it is dis-
criminating. It is levelled, not at defects and infirmities which are essential and in nature unremovable,
but at defects and infirmities which are unessen-
tial, and therefore corrigible. If its immediate object
is to punish, its ultimate object is to amend. But
this is not the spirit of *Gulliver*. Take the Yahoos.
Nothing can be plainer than that these odious and
repulsive creatures were designed to be types, not of
man, as man when brutalised and degenerate may
become, but of man as man is naturally constituted.
Take the Struldbrugs. What end could possibly be
attained by so shocking an exposure of human infirmities ? Juvenal has, it is true, left us a similar
delineation; but Juvenal's object was, by teaching
men to distinguish between what is desirable and
what is not desirable, to guide them to a cheerful and
elevated philosophy. Swift's design began and ended
in cynical mockery. Again, in the *Voyage to Laputa*,
though the local satire—the satire, for example, on
the projectors—is pointed and just, the general satire
is in the highest degree extravagant and absurd. No
one would dispute that intellectual energy may, like
the passions, be abused and perverted, and no one
would dispute that its abuse and perversion are fair
game for the satirist. The inutility of such energy,
when misapplied, is, however, no criterion of its utility
when properly directed. But Swift makes no distinction. He assumes that, whatever form that energy
may take, or to whatever purpose it may be directed,

P

it is equally futile and equally contemptible. He thus contrives—and contrives most dishonestly—to represent the mathematical and mechanical sciences as despicable and ridiculous, medicine as mere charlatanry, and experimental philosophy as an idle and silly delusion—in a word, to pour contempt on those pursuits and faculties on which the intellectual supremacy of man is based. Not less sophistical and disingenuous is the device employed by him in the *Voyage to the Houyhnhnms* for dethroning his kind from their moral supremacy. We here find him assigning to beasts the qualities characteristic of men, and assigning to men the qualities characteristic of beasts, that men may by comparison with beasts be degraded, and that beasts may by comparison with men be exalted. In the brutal passages ridiculing the construction of the human body the satire glances from the creature to the Creator, and is in truth as impious as it is absurd. It is when we compare a work like this with such works as the *Apologie de Raimond Sebond* [1] and the *Essay on Man* that its real character becomes at once apparent. The aim both of Montaigne and of Pope was, like that of Swift, to mortify human pride, to show how little, how despicable, how helpless a creature is man. But their exposure of human infirmities and human errors rested on no ' basis of misanthropy.' It was a means to an end—and a noble end. Montaigne's object was to teach us that all is vain but faith and grace, and that we are to live not by the senses and the reason

---

[1] It is curious that none of Pope's commentators should have noticed how greatly he was indebted to this remarkable Essay. Swift has also drawn on it.

but by the spirit. He humbled man that he might exalt him. Pope's object was to teach us the secret of success and happiness by teaching us to know ourselves, and to know our place in the scheme of creation. If he rebuked man's pride, he never forgot man's dignity. If he reminded us that we are below angels, he reminded us that we are above brutes.

But it is necessary to distinguish. What applies to the last two Voyages does not as a rule apply to the first two. In the *Voyage to Lilliput* the satire, which is more local and personal than in any other portion of the work, is, as a rule, as just as it is temperate. If we catch the note of the later strain, it is only in subdued tones here and there. The humour is exquisite, and, though pungent, often playful, and seldom flavoured with the bitterness so characteristic of what follows. In the next Voyage another chord is struck. The satire becomes more general, and has gathered intensity and vehemence. It is here for the first time that the *saeva indignatio* begins to find expression, that the misanthrope declares himself. But the warfare is legitimate, and if it be vengeance it is justice. Nothing could be more admirable than the conversation between Gulliver and the King of Brobdingnag, who appears to represent Swift's ideal of a patriot king, or than the description of the constitution, habits, and customs of Brobdingnag. Many passages recall and might have been suggested by More's inimitable romance. If the work be regarded merely as a satire, it is not perhaps too much to say that in condensed and sustained power it has neither equal nor second among human productions. But it

P 2

is a satire the philosophy and morality of which will not for a moment bear serious examination.

The work appeared anonymously early in November, 1726. It became instantly popular. Within a week the first edition was exhausted. A second edition speedily followed, but before the second was ready pirated copies of the first were in circulation in Ireland, and the work was traversing Great Britain in all directions in the columns of a weekly journal. No one has, I think, noticed that *Gulliver* was reprinted in successive instalments in a contemporary newspaper called *Parker's Penny Post*, between November 28, 1726, and the following spring—a sufficient indication of the opinion formed of it by those who are best acquainted with the popular taste, and probably the first occasion on which the weekly press was applied to such a purpose. In France it was read with avidity, and a few weeks after its appearance portions of it were twice dramatised.[1]

But, though the work appealed to all, it appealed in different ways. By the multitude it was read, as it is read in the nurseries and playrooms of our more enlightened age, with wondering credulity. But the avidity with which it was devoured by readers to whom the allegory was nothing and the story everything was equalled by the avidity with which it was devoured by readers to whom the allegory was supreme and the story purely subordinate. At Court and in political circles it was read and quoted as no satire since *Hudibras* had been. To them Flimnap and Munobi, Skyresh Bolgolam and

---

[1] Lady Bolingbroke to Swift, in a letter undated, but apparently written about February 17$\frac{2\cdot6}{2\cdot7}$.

Reldresal, the Tramecksan and Slamecksan, the Big-endians and Little-endians, the Sardrals and the Nardacs, the two Frelocks and Mully Ully Gue, were what the caricatures of Gilray were, fifty years later, to the Court of George III. The circumstances which led to the flight of Gulliver from Lilliput, and the account given of the natives of Tribnia, must have come home with peculiar force and pungency to readers who could remember the proceedings which led to the imprisonment of Harley and the flight of Bolingbroke and Ormond, and in whose memories the trial of Atterbury was still fresh. To us the schemes propounded in the Academy of Lagado have no more point than the schemes which occupied the courtiers of Queen Entelechy; but how pregnant, how pertinent, how exquisite must the satire have appeared to readers who were still smarting from the Bubble-mania, who had been shareholders in the Society for Transmuting Quicksilver into Malleable Metal, or in the Society for Extracting Silver from Lead!

Nor was the satire in its broader aspect less keenly relished. Aristotle has observed that the measure of a man's moral degradation may be held to be complete when he sees nothing derogatory in joining in the gibe against himself. And what is true of an individual is assuredly true of an age. At no period distinguished by generosity of sentiment, by humanity, by decency, by any of the nobler and finer qualities of mankind, could such satire as the satire of which the greater part of *Gulliver* is the embodiment have been universally applauded. Yet so it was. The men and women of those times appear to have seen nothing objectionable in an apologue which would

scarcely have passed without protest in the Rome of
Petronius. The Queen and the Princess of Wales were
in raptures with it.   One noble lady facetiously identified herself with the Yahoos ; another declared that
her whole life had been lost in caressing the worse part
of mankind, and in treating the best as her foes.   And
so surely could Swift rely on the most disgusting
passages of his work being to the taste of the ladies
of the Court, that in a private letter to one of the
Maids of Honour he not only referred facetiously to
one of its most indecent passages, but added to the
indecency.   Here and there, indeed, a reader might
be found who was of opinion that the satire was too
strongly flavoured with misanthropy,[1] but such readers
were altogether in the minority.   It is remarkable
that even Arbuthnot, though he objected to Laputa,
expressed no dissatisfaction with the *Voyage to the
Houyhnhnms*.

Nearly three months before the publication of
Gulliver Swift had quitted London for Dublin.   His
departure had been hastened by the terrible news
that the calamity which of all calamities he dreaded
most was imminent.   The health of Miss Johnson
had long been failing, and had latterly afforded matter
for grave anxiety.   Shortly after Swift's arrival in
England alarming symptoms had begun to develop
themselves.   For a while, however, his friends in
Dublin had mercifully concealed the worst, and for a
while his fears were not unmingled with hope.   At
last he knew the worst.   She was on the point of
death.   His grief was such as absolutely to unnerve
and unman him.   The letters written at this time to

---

[1] See Young, *Conjectures on Original Composition*.

Sheridan, Worral, and Stopford[1] exhibit a state of mind
pitiable in the extreme. 'Ever since I left you,' he
writes, ' my heart has been so sunk that I have not
been the same man nor ever shall be again, but drag on
a wretched life till it shall please God to call me away.'
And again, when he expected to hear that she had
passed away : ' Judge in what a temper I write this.
. . . I have been long weary of the world, and shall for
my small remainder of years be weary of life, having
for ever lost that conversation which could only make
it tolerable.' But the blow was not to fall yet. Esther
Johnson rallied, and Swift again visited England.

He arrived in London with impaired health and
with a mind ill at ease. Nor was the life on which
he now entered at all calculated to remedy the mischief. His great work appeared. His popularity and
fame were at their height, and he soon found that he
had to pay the full price for his position. Neither
friends nor strangers allowed him any peace. At
Twickenham Pope teased him to death about the
corrected edition of *Gulliver* and about the third
volume of the *Miscellanies*. Gay, busy with the
Beggar's Opera, sought anxiously to profit from his
criticism ; and, if tradition is to be trusted, the drama
which owed its existence to Swift's suggestion owes
to his pen two of its most famous songs.[2] In London
and at Dawley he was subjected to persecutions of
another kind. Peterborough and Harcourt were eager
to negotiate an understanding with Walpole. Bolingbroke and Pulteney sought to engage him in active

[1] Letters between July 8 and July 26, 1726.
[2] The song beginning ' Through all the employments of life,' and
that beginning ' Since laws were made for every degree.'

co-operation with the Opposition. The Opposition were now high in hope. The death of the King could be no remote event; and it was confidently believed that with the accession of the Prince of Wales the supremacy of Walpole would be at an end and that the Ministry would be reconstructed. The person who was popularly supposed to direct the counsels of the Prince was Mrs. Howard, the declared enemy of Walpole, the staunch ally of the faction opposed to him. That Swift shared in some measure the hopes of his friends is very likely. With Mrs. Howard he was on terms of close intimacy. Before his arrival in England he had frequently corresponded with her. During his residence in England he regularly visited her. At Leicester House he had been received with marked favour, and the Princess had gone out of her way to pay him attention. He had thus ample reason for supposing that, if affairs took the turn which his friends anticipated, the prize which had twice before eluded him would again be within his grasp. He said, indeed, that he was too old to enter into new schemes, and we know from his correspondence how greatly ill-health and private anxieties were depressing him. But his pen was not idle. To contribute to the downfall of a minister whose treatment of him had not been very different from the treatment for which he had eighteen years before made Godolphin and Somers pay so heavy a price must have been a congenial task. At the suggestion of Bolingbroke he began a letter to the *Craftsman*, in which he significantly reminded Walpole that it was a grievous mistake in a great minister to neglect or despise, much more to irritate, men of genius and

learning.[1] Suddenly—far more suddenly than was
expected—occurred the event on which so much depended. On June 10 the King died. Swift remained
in London during that period of intense excitement
which intervened between the preferment of Sir
Spencer Compton and the re-establishment of Walpole.
He kissed the hands of the new King and the new
Queen, made a scathing attack on the tottering
minister's character and conduct,[2] saw in a few days
that all was over, and then hurried off, sick and
weary, to bury himself, first in Pope's study at
Twickenham, and then at Lord Oxford's country seat
at Wimpole. At the end of September he abruptly
quitted England for ever.

Of his last days on this side of the Channel a
singularly interesting record has within the last few
years come to light. On arriving at Holyhead he
found himself too late for the Dublin packet. Unfavourable weather set in, and he was detained for
upwards of a week in what was then the most com-
fortless of British seaports. During that week he
amused himself with scribbling verses and with keeping a diary. The manuscript of this diary came into
the possession of the late Mr. Forster, and is preserved in the Dyce and Forster Library at South Kensington. It was edited and published by the present
writer in the *Gentleman's Magazine* for June, 1882,
and it has since been printed by Mr. Craik.[3] Its
records are of no interest in themselves, but are

---

[1] *Letter to the Writer of the Occasional Paper* (*Works*, x. 329).

[2] To this period almost certainly belongs the attack on Walpole
in the *Account of the Court and Empire of Japan* (*Works*, x. 337).

[3] *Life of Swift*, Appendix IX.

curiously illustrative of the temper and habits of
Swift. He gives a full account of all that occurred
to him since leaving Chester on September 22, entering with minute particularity into every detail of his
daily experience, what he ate and drank, what he
saw, where he walked, what he dreamt, and 'all this
to divert thinking.' In reading the journal it is impossible not to be struck with its resemblance to the
diary kept by Byron at Ravenna. In both there is
the same contrast between what appears on the surface and what is beneath. In both cases the same
listless wretchedness takes refuge in the same laborious
trifling. Both are the soliloquies of men who are as
weary of themselves as they are weary of the world,
and who clutch desperately at every expedient for
escaping reflection and for killing time, sometimes by
investing trifles with adventitious importance, sometimes by indulging half-ironically in a sort of humorous self-analysis, sometimes by dallying lazily with idle
fancies.

The death of Esther Johnson, in January, 1728,
dissolved the only tie which bound Swift to life. It
had been long expected, but when the end came it
must have come suddenly, for, though in Dublin, he
was not with her. With pathetic minuteness he
has himself recorded the circumstances under which
he heard of his irreparable loss. It was late in the
evening of Sunday, January 28. The guests who
were in the habit of assembling weekly at the
deanery on that evening were round him, and it was
nearly midnight before he could be alone with his
sorrow. How that sad night was passed was known
to none until he had himself been laid in the grave.

Then was found among his papers that most touching memorial of his grief and love—the *Memoir and Character of Esther Johnson*. Firmly and calmly had the desolate old man met the calamity which a few months before he had described himself as not daring to contemplate. That night he commenced the narrative which tells the story of her in whose coffin was buried all that made existence tolerable to him. And regularly as each night came round he appears to have resumed his task. There is something almost ghastly in the contrast between the smooth and icy flow of the chronicle itself and the terribly pathetic significance of the parentheses which mark the stages in its composition. 'This,' he writes on the night of the 30th, ' is the night of the funeral, which my sickness will not suffer me to attend. It is now nine o'clock, and I am removed into another compartment that I may not see the light in the church, which is just over the window of my bed-chamber.' Sorrow and despair have many voices, but seldom have they found expression so affecting as in those calm and simple words. It is said that her name was never afterwards known to pass his lips. When, seventeen years later, his own coffin had been laid beside hers, his executors found in his desk a lock of hair with four words written on the paper which wrapped it. The hair was Stella's; the words, 'Only a woman's hair.'

Se non piangi, di che pianger suoli ?

CHAPTER IX

LIFE IN IRELAND—LAST DAYS AND DEATH

I

THE biography of Swift from the death of Esther Johnson to the hour in which his own eyes closed on the world is a tragedy sadder and more awful than any of those pathetic fictions which appal and melt us on the stage of Sophocles and Shakespeare. The distressing malady under which he laboured never for long relaxed its grasp, and when the paroxysms were not actually on him the daily and hourly dread of their return was scarcely less agonising. In that malady he thought he discerned the gradual but inevitable approach of a calamity which is of all the calamities incident to man the most frightful to contemplate. Over his spirits hung the cloud of profound and settled melancholy. His wretchedness was without respite and without alloy. When he was not under the spell of dull, dumb misery, he was on the rack of furious passions.

> Sense of intolerable wrong,
> And whom he scorned, those only strong;
> Thirst of revenge, the powerless will
> Still baffled and yet burning still,
> For aye entempesting anew
> The unfathomable hell within.

His writings and correspondence exhibit a mind perpetually oscillating between unutterable despair and demoniac rage, between a misanthropy bitterer and more savage than that which tore the heart of Timon, and a sympathy with suffering humanity as acute and sensitive as that which vibrated in Rousseau and Shelley.

It was not until the accession of George II. that Swift fully realised the hopelessness of effecting any reform in Ireland. His second interview with Walpole had convinced him that, so long as that minister was at the head of affairs, the policy of England would remain unchanged, that a deaf ear would be turned to all appeals, all protests, all suggestions. The new reign would, he had hoped, have placed the reins of government in new hands. It had, on the contrary, confirmed the supremacy of Walpole, and the fate of Ireland was sealed. But what enraged him most was the consciousness that his efforts to awaken in the Irish themselves the spirit of resistance and reform had wholly failed. None of his proposals had been carried out, none of his warnings had been heeded. All was as all had been before. An ignoble rabble of sycophants and slaves still grovelled at the feet of Power. Corruption and iniquity pervaded the whole public service; the two Houses still swarmed with the tools of oppression ; and the country, which his genius and energy had for a moment galvanised into life, had again sunk torpid and inert into the degradation in which he had found her. In the provinces was raging one of the most frightful famines ever known in the annals of the peasantry. Never, perhaps, in the whole course of her melancholy history

was the condition of Ireland more deplorable than at
the beginning of 1729.[1]   All this worked like poison
in Swift's blood, and, like the cleaving mischief of the
fable, tortured him without intermission till torture
ceased to be possible.   But the savage indignation
which the spectacle of English misgovernment excited
in him was now fully equalled by the disdain and
loathing with which he regarded the sufferers themselves.   Towards the aborigines his feelings had never
been other than those of repulsion and contempt,
mingled with the sort of pity which the humane feel
for the sufferings of the inferior animals.   As a
politician he looked upon them pretty much as
Prospero looked upon Caliban, or as a Spartan legis-
lator looked upon the Helots.   On the regeneration
of the Englishry depended, in his opinion, the regeneration of the whole island.   It was in their interests
that he had laboured.   It was on their co-operation
that he had relied.   It was to them that he had
appealed.   And he had found them as frivolous, as
impracticable, as despicable, as their compatriots.
The hatred with which Swift in his latter years
regarded Ireland and its inhabitants recalls in its intensity and bitterness the hatred with which Juvenal
appears to have regarded the people of Egypt and
Dante the people of the Val d'Arno.   It resembled a
consuming passion.   It overflowed, we are told, in his
conversation, it glows at white heat in his writings,
it flames out in his correspondence.   'It is time for
me,' he says in one place, 'to have done with the
world, and not die here in a rage, like a poisoned rat
in a hole.'   He is 'in a cursed, oppressed, miserable

[1] See Boulter's letters between November, 1728, and October, 1729.

country, not made so by nature, but by the slavish, hellish principles of an execrable prevailing faction.' He is surrounded ' by slaves and knaves and fools,' in a country which is 'a wretched dirty dog-hole; a prison, but good enough to die in.' Man 'he hates more than a toad, a viper, a wasp, a stork, a fox, or any other that you will please to add.' He is ' worn out with years and sickness and rage against all public proceedings; ' and ' what has sunk his spirits more than years and sickness is reflecting on the most execrable corruptions that run through every branch of public management.' 'My flesh and bones,' he furiously exclaims in another letter, ' are to be carried to Holyhead, for I will not lie in a country of slaves.'

His serious writings during the whole of the period between the death of Stella and the time at which he sank into fatuity have one note—rage and despair. In *A Short View of the State of Ireland*, published in the middle of 1727, he again drew the attention of England to the horrors and calamities for which she was responsible. But the words he sowed he was sowing, as he well knew, on the wind. Then his pleas and his protests clothed themselves in the ghastly irony of the *Modest Proposal*, and England answered that she appreciated the humour and enjoyed the joke. Next he turned furiously on his old enemies the Bishops. In 1731 two Bills had been brought forward—one for the purpose of enforcing clerical residence and compelling the clergy to build houses upon their glebes, the other for subdividing large livings into as many portions as the Bishops should advise. It is not easy to see what was mischievous or unreasonable in these proposals. But

Swift, tearing them to pieces in two savage pamphlets,[1]
denounced them as designed to enslave and beggar
the clergy, and as having taken their birth from Hell.
Nor did the Bishops escape without castigation.   The
fathers of the Church have seldom stood in such a
pillory as we find them standing in *Judas* and in
The Irish Bishops.[2]   From the Bishops he turned to
the Dissenters.   Any indulgence to the Dissenters,
any attempt to relax the stringency of the Test Act,
had even in his calmer days brought him instantly
into the arena.   But his hostility was now inflamed
by other causes; his opposition had new motives.
The Government were almost pledged to indulgence,
the Whig Bishops to a man were in favour of it.   In
resisting such a measure he would therefore be annoy-
ing and embarrassing his political enemies, and have
at the same time the peculiar satisfaction of assuming
the championship of the Church against its natural
defenders.   Between 1731 and 1734 measures were
taken for introducing a Bill, and a memorial was
drawn up for presentation to the Privy Council.[3]
Then Swift opened fire.   He began by reprinting his
Presbyterian Plea of Merit, and went on to produce
his *Narrative of the Several Attempts which have been
made for a Repeal of the Sacramental Test,* following it
up next year by his bitterly ironical *Advantages Proposed by Repealing the Sacramental Test.*   This was succeeded by his *Queries concerning the Sacramental Test*
and his *Reasons humbly offered to the Parliament of*

---

[1] *On the Bill for the Clergy Residing on their Livings* (Scott,
ix. 5), and *Considerations upon the Two Bills* (Id. p. 13).

[2] Scott, x. 268, and xiv. 525.

[3] For all this see Boulter's *Letters,* ii. 85–90.

*Ireland for Repealing the Sacramental Test in Favour
of the Catholics.* The contempt and ridicule which he
poured on the unfortunate sectaries and their advocates
lost no point when embodied in verse.[1] His efforts
had been successful, and a large majority in the Irish
House of Commons were firm for the Test Act. He
now fought the battle of the Church on another field—
against the landlords and against the Parliament.
Towards the close of 1733 a Bill had been presented
in the Commons for the encouragement of the linen
manufacture, containing a clause for limiting, by a
modus, the tithe payable on flax and hemp. As flax
was the staple commodity of Ireland, the proposed
commutation would have affected seriously the in-
comes of the inferior clergy, entailing a loss of two
parts in three of the legal tithe. Swift therefore
opposed the Bill in a most powerful pamphlet,[2] and
joined with others in a petition presented to the
House of Commons. The result was a compromise,
and a compromise which was not satisfactory. And
now began his war with the Irish House of Commons.
There appears at this time to have been a determined
attempt on the part of the landlords to resist the
claims of the clergy. The contest centred on the
tithe of pasturage, or, as it was technically called,
the tithe of agistment. It was resisted on all sides.
Several suits instituted by defrauded clergymen were
pending in the Court of Exchequer. The burdens
of this tithe fell principally on the great graziers

[1] See the poem *Brother Protestants and Fellow Christians*
(Scott, x. 532).
[2] *Some Reasons against the Bill for settling the Tythe of Hemp
and Flax by a Modus* (Scott, x. 29).

Q

and the great landlords, many of whom had a seat
in the House of Commons. At their instigation
resolutions were passed against the claims for the
purpose of intimidating the clergy from instituting
suits and the courts of law from deliberating upon
them. Of the illegality and gross injustice of such
proceedings there could be no question. A more
flagrant opposition of power to right could scarcely
be conceived. By these persecutions many of the
clergy were all but ruined. A very cruel case came
prominently into public notice. A Mr. Throp, who
had refused to surrender to the patron of his living,
one Colonel Waller, some of its most important
rights, was so harassed and broken by lawsuits,
assaults, and arrests, that his health sank under
them and he died. Upon that his brother presented a petition to Parliament, stating the case
against the Colonel, and praying that the House,
considering the atrocity of Waller's conduct, would,
though Waller was a member of their body, waive
their privilege, and allow proceedings by arrest to
be taken against him. Swift, already exasperated
beyond measure by the action of the Commons in
the agistment matter, now stepped in. He drew up
a short statement of Throp's case which so provoked
Waller that he offered a reward of ten guineas to
any one who would discover the author. Meanwhile,
the petition had been considered and unanimously
rejected by the House. To say that the philippic
in which Swift's vengeance found expression has
neither equal nor second in the literature of invective and satire would be but feeble testimony to its
appalling power. The *Legion Club* stands alone—

alone alike in the spirit that animates it and as a
masterpiece of art. It seems to boil, a blasting
flood of filth and vitriol, out of some hellish fountain. So devilish is the malignity infusing it, so
maniacal the fury of the scorn and hatred, that it
would not have been surprising if the inspiration
had overpowered the artist. But the execution is
perfect. Nothing could be constructed with more
exquisite ingenuity than the framework, nothing more
elaborately finished than the details. The skill
with which he selects, and in selecting concentrates,
all those images and associations which could
deform, degrade, and defile—the malicious tact with
which, in gibbeting individuals, he seizes on what
could be turned to most account against them in
their persons, or in their public or private life, till
every couplet has the sting of a hornet—the delibera-
tion with which he gradually unfolds his horrible
and loathsome panorama—the climax in the pinch
of snuff and the parting curse, ' May their God—
the devil—confound them ! '—all show that the most
terrible of satirists was one of the most finished and
patient of artists.

II

But these controversies did not occupy the whole of
Swift's time. The extraordinary activity of his mind,
and his habit of occupying himself in writing that he
might escape from himself and, in his own words,
divert thinking, resulted in the production of an
immense number of compositions both in verse and
in prose. Indeed, the mere enumeration of the pieces

composed by him between 1727 and 1737 would
occupy several pages. The greater part of these are
trifles, which have been piously collected by his editors,
but which were hardly worth preserving. But the list
contains also some of his best poems and two of the
best of his non-political minor prose writings. In the
autumn of 1731 he told his friends Gay and the
Duchess of Queensberry that he was engaged on a
work which was to reduce the whole politeness, wit,
humour, and style of England into one short system
for the use of all persons of quality, and particularly
the Maids of Honour. This was the *Art of Polite
Conversation*. With an irony the acrimony of which is
very characteristic of his temper in his later days, but
hardly appropriate to the trifles on which it is here
employed, he ridicules the frivolities and affectations
then characteristic of conversation in modish society.
With the *Directions to Servants*, a part of the same
scheme, he took immense pains, kept it by him, and
added to it year by year. When the manuscript
had passed out of his hands he was anxious for its
recovery that it might not be lost, for he thought the
work 'useful as well as humorous.' Of its humour there
can be no question; its usefulness may be doubted.
It is the most striking illustration to be found in his
works of one of his characteristics—his habit of
observing and noting with minute accuracy all that
passed round him. The work has some happy touches,
but the general effect is tedious, and by its incomple-
tion literature has sustained no great loss. To one
portion of it special interest belongs. The Directions
to the Footman gave Fielding the idea of Jonathan
Wild.

Of the poems, the verses *On the Death of Dr. Swift*,
the *Grand Question Debated*, the *Rhapsody on Poetry*,
the *Directions for Making a Birthday Song*, the
*Epistle to a Lady who desired the Author to write
some Verses upon her in the Heroic Style*, and the
Day of Judgment, are incomparably the best. But,
with the exception of the first and the last, they were
mere trifles, thrown off occasionally, as scores of others
were, listlessly, to kill time. ‘I would not give three
pence,’ he writes to his friend Barber, ‘for all I read,
or write, or think, in the compass of a year.’ They
stand in the same relation to the man himself as his
frivolities at Market Hill or at Howth Castle, transitory
gleams on an abyss of gloom, straws on a boiling
torrent. It is not to these poems, it is to poems of
another class, and to his correspondence, that we
must turn if we would raise the veil of his inner life.
In these poems—and they extend over the whole of
this period—he found a vent for the passions which
the turn of a mood or the smallest provocation
instantly awoke. In them his misanthropy, his
hatred of individuals, his rage, his pessimism, flamed
out unrestrained. Of some of these poems it would
be no exaggeration to say that nothing so purely dia-
bolical had ever before emanated from man. There
are passages in the satirists of antiquity which are—
in mere indecency perhaps—as shameless and brutal.
A misanthropy almost as bitter flavours the satire in
which Juvenal depicts the feud between the Ombites
and the Tentyrites. The invectives of Junius and the
libels of Pope not unfrequently exhibit a malignity
scarcely human; and if the Mephistopheles of fable
could be clothed in flesh, his mockery would probably

be the mockery of Voltaire and Heine.   But the later
satire of Swift stands alone.   It is the very alcohol of
hatred and contempt.   Its intensity is the intensity
of monomania, whether its object be an individual, a
sect, or mankind.   To find any parallel to such pieces
as the *Ladies' Dressing Room*, *Cassinus and Peter*,
On Corinna, *Strephon and Chloe*, *A Love Poem*,
the *Place of the Damned*, the *Beasts' Confession*,
and the *Legion Club*, we must go to the speeches in
which the depraved and diseased mind of Lear runs
riot in obscenity and rage.   But it was when his satire
was directed against particular individuals that it
became most inhuman and most noisome.   Such, for
example, would be the attack on Walpole in the *Epistle
to Gay*, the attack on Allen in *Traulus*, the libels
on Bellesworth, and the libels on Tighe.   To provoke
the hostility of Swift was, in truth, like rousing the
energies of a skunk and a polecat.   It was to engage
in a contest the issue of which was certain—to be
compelled to beat an ignominious retreat, cruelly
lacerated, and half suffocated with filth.

But, if the sufferings entailed on him by passions
like these were great, if the *inordinatus animus*
brought its tortures, we have only to turn to his
correspondence to see how black were the clouds that
had settled over his life.   There is something inexpressibly pathetic in the way in which he clings to
the old scenes, to the old associations, to the old
friends.   Sheridan, Acheson, Delany, were shadows to
him.   He never took them to his heart; he never
admitted them into his confidence.   It is only when
he is writing to Pope, to Peterborough, to Gay, to
Arbuthnot, to Barber, to Bolingbroke, that he seems

to be himself. But one by one all sank out of his life. In December, 1732, death removed Gay. In October, 1734, Arbuthnot followed. The acuteness with which he felt these losses and the inexpressible wretchedness of his life during all these years are sufficiently testified by his letters to those to whom he opened his mind freely. That he never woke without finding life a more insignificant thing than it was the day before—that it was not a farce but a ridiculous tragedy—that he thought of death not, as he once did, every day, but every minute—that he never took up his pen in any cause without saying to himself a thousand times *non est tanti*—this is the strain from first to last.

But Swift's private miseries, his fierce or gloomy moods, his feuds, his controversies, his contempt for those he served, his contempt for those who assisted him, never suspended or even interrupted his benevolent activity. The most savage of misanthropes was in practice the most indefatigable of philanthropists. No city ever owed more to a private man than Dublin owed to Swift. We have already seen how in 1720 he defeated, or at least contributed to defeat, a scheme which would in all probability have involved hundreds of her citizens in beggary, and how successfully he grappled with one of the most formidable pests which infest great cities. His proposal to provide beggars with badges did much to abate another nuisance scarcely less mischievous and troublesome;[1] and his *Considerations about Maintaining the*

[1] See his *Proposal for giving Badges to the Beggars in all the Parishes of Dublin* (Scott, vii. 581).

Poor,[1] which was probably interrupted by ill-health, shows with what anxious attention he had studied the subject. His care, indeed, extended to every department of civic economy, from the direction of municipal and parliamentary elections[2] to the regulation of the coal traffic.[3]

It may be said of Dr. Swift, writes one who knew him well, that he literally followed the example of his Master, and went about doing good.[4] His private charity, though judicious, was boundless. He never, we are told, went about without a pocketful of coins, which he distributed among the indigent and sick. His severe frugality, which fools mistook for avarice, arose solely from his determination to devote his money to the noblest uses to which money can be applied. If he denied himself and his guests super-fluities, it was that he might provide the needy with necessaries and posterity with St. Patrick's Hospital. He established a fund for charitable loans to the industrious poor; he was acquainted with every beggar within the liberties of St. Patrick's, many of whom were in receipt of a small pension from him. His correspondence teems with instances of his kindness. Indeed, no one who deserved assistance or needed advice ever applied to him in vain. And he had his reward. If as the Drapier he commanded the homage and gratitude of all Ireland, as the Dean he was the idol of the people of Dublin. He

[1] *Works*, vii. 576.
[2] See his *Considerations . . . on the Choice of a Recorder* (Scott, vii. 561), and *Advice to the Freemen of Dublin* (Id. p. 553).
[3] See his *Letters upon the Use of Irish Coal*, and Scott, p. 408 *seqq.*
[4] Delany, *Observations*, p. 261.

called them his subjects, and they were proud of the title. 'I know by experience' (wrote Carteret just after he resigned the Lord Lieutenancy) 'how much the city of Dublin thinks itself under your protection, and how strictly they used to obey all orders fulminated from the sovereignty of St. Patrick's.' On the last occasion on which he took part in public affairs the Primate Boulter, whose proposal for diminishing the value of gold coin he had opposed, charged him at an entertainment of the Lord Mayor's with inflaming the populace against him. 'I inflame them!' replied Swift; 'had I lifted my finger they would have torn you to pieces.' In his war with England and with that party in Dublin which was in the English interest he was not unfrequently threatened with violence; but the mere rumour that the Dean was in danger was sufficient to rally round him a bodyguard so formidable that he had little to fear either from the law or from private malice. It is said that Walpole was once on the point of despatching a messenger with a warrant to arrest the Dean and bring him over to England. But on a gentleman, who knew Swift's position better than the minister, asking significantly what army was to accompany the messenger, and whether the Government had ten thousand men to spare, Walpole very wisely took the hint and the matter dropped.

But to Swift all this was nothing. Sick of himself, sick of the world, fully aware of the awful fate which was impending over him—he saw it, says Lyon, as plainly as men foresee a coming shower—he longed only, he prayed only, for death. It was his constant habit—it had been so for years—to take leave of one

of the few friends whom he admitted to his intimacy,
and who was accustomed to visit him two or three
times a week, with the words, 'Well, God bless you,
good night to you, but I hope I shall never see you
again.'[1] At the end of 1737 it became apparent to
his friends, and it becomes painfully apparent in his
correspondence, that his mind was rapidly failing.
The deafness and giddiness which had before visited
him intermittently now rarely left him. His memory
was so impaired that he was scarcely able to converse.
It was only with the greatest difficulty that he could
express himself on paper. 'I am so stupid and confounded,' he writes to Mrs. Whiteway in July, 1740,
'that I cannot express the mortification I am under
both in body and mind. All I can say is I am not in
torture, but I daily and hourly expect it. I am sure
my days will be very few, few and miserable they must
be.' Few they were not to be. More than five years
of agony and degradation were before him. As his intellect decayed his irritability and ferocity increased.
On the slightest provocation he would break out into
paroxysms of frantic rage. At last he lost completely
all self-command. His reason gave way, and he
ceased to be responsible either for his words or for his
actions.[2] In March, 1742, guardians were appointed
for him by the Court of Chancery. On August 12 in
the same year, at the petition of the Rev. John Grattan
and the Rev. James King, a Writ *De Lunatic*

---

[1] Sheridan, p. 391.

[2] In the Hardwicke MSS. quoted by Harris, *Life of Hardwicke*,
ii. 21, a very painful detail of Swift's madness is given, which sufficiently explains why Mrs. Whiteway could not be in attendance on
him.

Inquirendo was issued, reciting 'that the Dean of St. Patrick's hath for these nine months past been gradually failing in his memory, and that he is incapable of transacting any business or managing, conducting, or taking care either of his estate or person.' On August 17 a Commission was appointed; a jury was empanelled, and their report corroborated the statement of the petitioners.[1] Into a particular account of Swift's last years it would be almost agony to enter. Nothing in the recorded history of humanity, nothing that the imagination of man has conceived, can transcend in horror and pathos the accounts which have come down to us of the closing scenes of his life. His memory was gone, his reason was gone; he recognised no friend; he was below his own Struldbrugs. Day after day he paced his chamber, as a wild beast paces its cage, taking his food as he walked, but refusing to touch it as long as any one remained in the room. During the autumn of 1742 his state was horrible and pitiable beyond expression. At last, after suffering unspeakable tortures from one of the most agonising maladies known to surgery, he sank into the torpor of imbecility. By the mercy of Providence it generally happens that man so degraded is unconscious of his degradation. But this mercy was withheld from Swift. On one occasion he was found gazing at his image in a pier-glass and muttering piteously over and over again, 'Poor old man!' On another he exclaimed, frequently repeating it, 'I am what I am.'

[1] These melancholy documents, the originals or copies of which are in the Forster Collection at the South Kensington Museum, have only recently come to light, and are printed for the first time in the second Appendix to this volume.

'He never talked nonsense,' says Deane Swift, 'nor said a foolish thing.' In this deplorable condition he continued for two years, and then maintained unbroken silence till death released him from calamity. He expired at three o'clock on the afternoon of Saturday, October 19, 1745. Three days afterwards his coffin was laid at midnight beside the coffin of Esther Johnson in the south nave of St. Patrick's Cathedral.

CHAPTER X

CHARACTERISTICS

I

THE characteristics of this extraordinary man, so far as they revealed themselves practically in action and conduct, and reflectively in his writings, have in the preceding pages been sufficiently illustrated. We have now to consider him critically, to analyse and, if possible, to account for his idiosyncrasies, and to examine his claims to a place among English classics. But the critic of Swift has no easy task. He is confronted on the very threshold of his inquiry with a problem perplexing enough in itself, but perplexed still further by the efforts which have been made to solve it. From Swift's own day to the present it has been assumed that many of the essential peculiarities of his temper and genius are to be referred to constitutional disease, or were, at all events, considerably modified by it; that in early youth were sown the seeds of a malady which, developing ultimately into insanity, tainted his whole life and affected throughout, both directly and indirectly, much of his work. We now know, and know with certainty, that this was not the case. The distressing complaints which caused him so much inconvenience and suffering, and of which he speaks so frequently in his correspondence, had not,

as he himself supposed, any connection with the calamity which befell him in his later days.   They neither
impaired nor perverted his mental powers.   They had
no more effect on the brain than an attack of bron-
chitis or a fit of the gout would have had.   My readers
will, I trust, forgive me for entering into medical
details, but until the erroneous views which have been
so long prevalent on the subject of Swift's disease
have been dispelled, erroneous views will continue to
be prevalent on more important points.   He can
never, as a subject of physiological study, be approached properly.   He can never, as a critic of man
and life, be correctly estimated.   The history of his
case is briefly this.   In his twenty-third year he
became subject to fits of giddiness ; in his twenty-
eighth year, or, according to another account, before
he had completed his twentieth year, he was attacked
by fits of deafness.   The first disorder he attributed
primarily to a surfeit of green fruit ; the origin of the
second he ascribed to a common cold.   The giddiness
was occasionally attended with sickness, the deafness
with ringing in the ears, and both with extreme depression.   The attacks were periodic and paroxysmal,
increasing in frequency and severity as life advanced.
As old age drew on, his giddiness and deafness became
more constant and intense ; he grew morbidly irritable ; he lost all control over his temper, his intellect
became abnormally enfeebled, his memory at times
almost totally failed him.   But it was not until he
had completed his seventy-fourth year that he exhi-
bited what seemed to be symptoms of insanity.   In
1742 what appeared to be an attack of acute mania—
though it was mania without delusion, and may

perhaps have been merely the frenzied expression of excruciating physical pain, occasioned by a tumour in the eye—was succeeded by absolute fatuity. In this state, broken, however, as we have seen, by occasional gleams of sensibility and reason, he remained till death. The autopsy revealed water on the brain—the common result, it may be added, of cerebral atrophy.

That a disease presenting such symptoms as these should have originated from a surfeit of fruit and a common cold was a theory that may have passed unchallenged in the infancy of medical science, but was not likely to find favour in more enlightened times. Accordingly, at the beginning of this century, an eminent physician, Dr. Beddoes,[1] came forward with another hypothesis. He entertained no doubt that the disease was homogeneous and progressive, and, connecting its primary symptoms with other peculiarities of Swift's conduct and writings, he ascribed their origin to a cause very derogatory to the moral character of the sufferer. Scott, justly indignant that such an aspersion should have been cast on the Dean's memory, took occasion in his *Life of Swift* to comment very severely on Beddoes's remarks.[2] But Scott, unfortunately, had no means of refuting them. Medical science was silent; and Swift, ludicrous to relate, has been held up in more than one publication as an appalling illustration of the effects of profligate indulgence. At last, in 1846, Sir William Wilde came to the rescue. In an essay in the *Dublin Quarterly Journal of Medical Science*, afterwards published in a volume entitled *The Closing Years of Dean Swift's Life*, he reinvestigated with the minutest care the whole

[1] *Hygeia*, Essay ix.   [2] P. 28, *note.*

case. In the first place, he made the important discovery that Swift had undoubtedly had a stroke of paralysis. This was a circumstance which had not been recorded by any of the biographers, but which a plaster cast, taken from the mask applied to the face after death, placed beyond doubt. Wilde boldly contended that there was no proof at all that Swift was ever insane in the sense in which the word is usually understood—nay, that previous to 1742 he showed no symptoms whatever of mental disease 'beyond the ordinary decay of nature.' The deplorable condition into which he subsequently sank Wilde attributed not to insanity, or to imbecility, but to paralysis of the muscles by which the mechanism of speech is produced, and to loss of memory, the result in all probability of subarachnoid effusion. But what Wilde failed to understand was the nature of the original disease—in other words, the cause of the giddiness and deafness which, whatever may have been their connection with the graver symptoms of the case, undoubtedly preceded and ushered them in. And it is here that Dr. Bucknill comes to our assistance. In his opinion the life-long malady of Swift is to be identified with a malady which medical science has only recently recognised, ' Labyrinthine Vertigo,' or, as it is sometimes called, in honour of the eminent pathologist who discovered it, ' Ménière's Disease.'[1] To this are to be attributed all the symptoms which were supposed by Swift himself to have originated from a surfeit of fruit or a chill, which Beddoes attributed to profligate habits, and which Sir William Wilde was

---

[1] See *Brain* for January, 1882, and letter printed in Appendix I. of this volume.

unable satisfactorily to account for. It was a purely physical and local disorder, which in no way affected the intellect, and which, had it run its course uncomplicated, would probably have ended merely in complete deafness. But on this disorder supervened, between 1738 and 1742, dementia, with hemiplegia and aphasia ; the dementia arising from general decay of the brain occasioned by age and degeneration, the hemiplegia and aphasia resulting from disease of a particular part of the brain, probably the third left frontal convolution. Thus the insanity, or, to speak more accurately, the fatuity, of Swift was not, as he himself and his biographers after him have supposed, the gradual development of years, but was partly the effect of senile decay and partly the effect of a local lesion.

The truth is that a mind saner than Swift's, a mind of stouter and stonger fabric, a mind in which the reason, the pure reason, sate enthroned more securely, has never existed. From first to last, so long as he continued in possession of his faculties, it was his distinguishing characteristic ; it was his standard ; it was his touchstone ; it remained unshaken and unimpaired, a fortress of rock on which the turbulent chaos of his furious passions broke harmlessly.

The chief peculiarity of Swift's temper lay in the coexistence not merely of opposite qualities but of opposite natures. The union of a hard, cold, logical intellect with a heart of almost feminine tenderness is no uncommon anomaly. But the anomaly which Swift presents is not an anomaly of this kind. In acute susceptibility to sensuous and emotional

R

impression he resembled Rousseau and Shelley. His nervous organisation was quite as exquisite, his sensibility as keen, his perceptions as nice. He was as dependent on human sympathy and on human affection; he was as passionately moved by what men less finely tempered regard with composure. The sight of a fellow-creature in distress or pain, the spectacle of an unjust or cruel action, a fancied slight conveyed in a word or look, an offensive or disagreeable object, were to him, as to them, little less than torture. Thus on the sensuous and emotional side he had the temperament of the poet and the enthusiast. But Nature had not completed what she had begun. She had bestowed on him the *cor cordium*; she had endowed him with 'the love of love' and 'the hate of hate'; she had been lavish of the gifts which are the poet's most painful inheritance; but from all else, from all that constitutes the poet's solaces, the poet's charm, the poet's power, she had excluded him. Utterly devoid of a sense of the beautiful, of the beautiful in nature, in the human form, in morals, in art, in philosophy, he neither sought it nor recognised it when seen. Its representation in concrete form is always perverted by him into the grotesque and ugly. As a critic and philosopher he has only one criterion—plain good sense in the one case, practical utility in the other. Of any perception of the ideal, of any sympathy with effort or tendency to aspire to it, he was as destitute as Sancho Panza and Falstaff. On no class of people have the shafts of his contemptuous raillery fallen thicker than on those who would seek for finer bread than is made of flour, and on the originators of Utopian schemes. His own ideal of life began and ended, as he himself frankly admitted, with the attainment of worldly success.[1] Of transcendental imagination, nay, of the transcendental instinct, he had nothing. He never appears to have had even a glimpse of those truths which lie outside the scope of the senses and the reason, and which find their expression in poetry and in sentimental religion. He never refers to them as embodied in the first without ridicule and contempt, nor as embodied in the second without coldly resolving them into compulsory dogmas. 'Violent zeal for Truth,' he observes, 'has a hundred to one odds to be either petulancy, ambition, or pride.'[2] If he does not deny the divine element in man and in the world, it is only because it forms an article of the creed which for other reasons he thought it expedient to uphold. But what he did not deny he either ignored or obscured. A conception of human nature and of human life more inconsistent than his with any theory of divinity either within man or without it would be impossible to find, even in the writings of professed atheists. 'Miserable mortals!' he exclaims in his *Thoughts on Religion*, 'can we contribute to the honour and glory of God? I could wish that expression were struck out of our prayer-books.' His whole conception of religion appears to have been almost purely political. What Fielding puts into the mouth of

---

[1] 'All my endeavours, from a boy, to distinguish myself were only for the want of a great title and fortune, that I might be used like a lord by those who have an opinion of my parts, whether right or wrong it is no great matter; and so the reputation of wit and great learning does the office of a blue ribbon or of a coach and six horses.' (Letter to Bolingbroke, April 5, 1829.)

[2] *Thoughts on Religion* (*Works*, viii. 173).

Thwackum is literally descriptive of Swift's attitude: 'When I mention religion I mean the Christian religion; and not only the Christian religion, but the Protestant; and not only the Protestant, but the Church of England.' He makes no distinction between Deists and Nonconformists, between Roman Catholics and Infidels. They are all equally denounced, and regarded as equally excluded from the pale of what constitutes 'religion.' And what constitutes religion has been prescribed by the State. To that every man should be compelled to adhere. In relation to its essence and apart from its accidents he never contemplates it. 'Religion,' he insists, 'supposes Heaven and Hell, the Word of God, and Sacraments.'[1] He complains bitterly that men should be allowed a freedom in religious matters which they are not allowed in political; that a citizen who prefers a commonwealth to monarchy, and who should endeavour to establish one, would be punished with the utmost rigour of the law, but that a citizen who prefers Nonconformity to Episcopalianism is at perfect liberty to choose the one instead of the other.[2] So completely are the spiritual and essential elements of religion subordinated to its political and temporal utility, that he contends boldly that the truth or falsehood of the fundamental opinions on which the creed of the Christian rests are of comparatively little moment compared with the mischief involved in questioning them; that it is not requisite for a man to believe what he professes; and that it matters little what doubts and scruples he may have, provided

---

[1] *Advice to a Young Poet* (*Works*, ix. 392).
[2] *Thoughts on Religion* (*Id.* viii. 176).

he keeps them to himself.[1] A man may be allowed, he observes elsewhere in reference to this subject, to keep poisons in his closet, but not to vend them about for cordials.[2] If, as has been sometimes supposed, he depicts his ideal man in the King of Brobdingnag, and his ideal of human excellence in the Houyhnhnms, it is remarkable that religion has no place in the education and life of either. The virtues of the former are those of pure stoicism; the virtues of the latter are summed up in friendship, benevolence, temperance, industry, and cleanliness.

It is, of course, impossible to say, but it is very doubtful whether Swift's own opinions inclined certainly towards belief in the promises of Christianity, or even in a future state. The balance of probability is decidedly adverse to the first supposition, and wavers very uncertainly in favour of the second. His attitude towards the metaphysics of Christianity is always the same; he never dwells on them, and whenever it is possible he avoids them. In his sermon on the Trinity he speaks of his theme as 'a subject which probably I should not have chosen if I had not been invited to it.' Rigidly orthodox, he repeats over and over again that what the Church teaches is no matter for argument and question, but must be accepted implicitly and in its integrity. Episcopal Protestant Christianity supplies as a coercive moral agency what no system of morality apart from it is able to supply; it must, therefore, be retained, and if it is not retained

---

[1] *Thoughts on Religion* (*Works*, viii. 174).
[2] *Gulliver's Travels—Voyage to Brobdingnag.*

with all its dogmas it ceases to be Christianity.[1]   This
is his note throughout in apology as in exegesis.
Without unction, without fervour, without sentiment,
he leaves us with the impression that he neither
sought nor found in the Gospel which he accepted and
delivered so faithfully anything that illuminated or
anything that cheered.   Of its power as a source of
consolation in sorrow he was well aware.   'Take
courage from Christianity,' he writes to Mrs. Whiteway, 'which will assist you when humanity fails.'
But he took from it, or seems to have taken from it,
little courage himself.   It is mournfully apparent that
no ray from the creed of faith and hope pierced the
gloom of that long night which descended on the
winter of his life.

Assuming, as a churchman, the truth of Christianity, he was bound also, as a churchman, to assume
the existence of a future state.   But the evidence for
supposing that it formed any article of his personal
belief is very slight.   In his *Thoughts on Religion* he
makes no reference to it, but observes of death that a
thing so natural, so necessary, and so universal could
not have been designed by Providence as an evil to
mankind.   In his sermons he never dwells on it.   In
his letters of consolation in bereavement he wrote, of
course, as propriety dictated that a clergyman should
write.   And yet even here his expressions are frequently very guarded and sometimes ambiguous.
'Religion regards life,' he writes to Mrs. Moore on
the death of her daughter, 'only as a preparation
for a better, which you are taught to be certain that

---

[1] See Sermons, *passim*, but particularly that on the Testimony of
Conscience.

so innocent a person is now in possession of.'[1] He would, he said to Pope, exchange youth for advanced old age, if he could be as secure of a better life as Mrs. Pope deemed herself.[2] 'If,' he remarked when his mother died, 'the way to Heaven be through piety, truth, justice and charity, she is there.' In his reflections on the death of Esther Johnson he makes no reference to immortality. In the prayers which he offered for her in her last illness he expresses a hope that she 'may be received into everlasting habitations,' but there is nothing to indicate that he felt the smallest confidence in the realisation of such hopes. His own epitaph is without a trace of Christian sentiment—that he had found in the grave a haven *ubi sæva indignatio ulterius cor lacerare nequit*— that he had left in his life an example which all who loved liberty would do well to imitate—this was the only assurance, this the only admonition, which he desired to proclaim from the tomb. It is possible, of course, that his reticence and reserve on religious subjects had its origin in the same cause which led him to conceal so studiously from guests in his house the fact that he daily read prayers to his servants— that it arose from his detestation of pretence and especially of pretentious piety. And this is by no means improbable, for there can be little doubt that, had he been as convinced of the truth of the Christian dogmas as St. Paul himself, he would have avoided ostentatious or enthusiastic profession.[3] But a

---

[1] See his beautiful letter (*Works*, xvii. 197).

[2] Letter to Pope, *Id*. p. 224.

[3] 'There was no vice,' says Delany, 'he so much abhorred as hypocrisy, and of consequence nothing he dreaded so much as to be suspected of it, and this made him often conceal his piety with more care than others take to conceal their vices.'—*Observations*, pp. 43-44.

distinction must be made between the avoidance of
ostentatious or enthusiastic profession and such an
attitude as Swift's. We must take into consideration
the whole tenor of his character and writings, and
the impression conveyed by them is that of a man
who was endeavouring honestly to support a part.
He was convinced of the absolute necessity of maintaining, in the interests of society as well as of particular individuals, the Christian religion with all its
dogmas; he felt that the balance of what he could
accept as sound and true in its teaching was more
and much more than a counterpoise to what might be
unsound and untrue; and he probably felt that what
he could not accept he could not absolutely pronounce
to be false. Applying the test of the politician, the
magistrate, and the philanthropist, he was content to
dispense with the test of the transcendental philosopher.[1] Hence his habit of avoiding all discussion
of such subjects as the immortality of the soul and a
future state, his guarded phrases, his plain unwilling-
ness to commit himself to expressions of his personal
opinions, his appeals to reason rather than to faith, the
ethical as distinguished from the theological character
of his teaching, the absence, in the stress of affliction,
of any indication of faith and hope.

His deficiency on the side of what we commonly
call sentiment is not less remarkable. Sentiment is
never likely to be found in any great degree where the
transcendental instinct is lacking. But the total
atrophy, or rather non-existence, of both in a man

---

[1] Swift's opinions on religion probably differed little from those
expressed so admirably by Polybius, vi. ch. 56, 57; by Strabo, i.
ch. 2, 8; and by Cicero, *De Legibus*, ii. ch. 7.

of strong affections and of acute susceptibility to emotional impression is an anomaly rare indeed in the temper of men. Of sentiment Swift was so wholly devoid that it was unintelligible to him. Its expression in language he regarded as cant, its expression in action as affectation and folly. For him life had no illusions, man no mystery, nature no charm. He looked on woman's beauty with the eye of an anatomist, on earth's beauties with the eye of a chemist. In the passion which not unfrequently transforms even the grossest and most commonplace of human beings into poets he saw only brutal appetite, masquerading in fantastic frippery. And his delight was to strip it bare. All that fancy, all that imagination, all that sentiment had woven round it torn contemptuously away, he gloated with horrid glee over the naked shame of nature. For religious enthusiasm he could discern only physical causes; sometimes he refers it to hysterics or to sexual excitement taking a wrong turn, sometimes to a diseased and disordered brain. More generally he regards it as mere affectation assumed for the purpose of making money or of gratifying vanity by acquiring notoriety. His sole criterion as a critic and judge was unsublimated reason. In his estimate of men he made no allowance for impulse and passion except as indicating depravity or weakness. In his estimate of life and the world generally he saw everything in the clear cold light of the pure intellect. From no mind of which we have expression in record had the Spectres of the Tribe, the Den, the Forum, and the Theatre been so completely exorcised. But, as the eyes of the body may be blinded by excess of light, so the eyes of the mind may by excess of reason be blinded—by the very power which should give them sight. Of the truth by which men live, mere reason indeed obscures almost as much as she reveals. If life took its colour and its pattern from the philosophy of Swift as that philosophy finds embodiment in his ideal king and in his ideal creatures, how insipid would it become, how torpid, how inglorious! Swift's philosophy is indeed in essence precisely the philosophy of Falstaff in his soliloquy on honour :—

What need I be so forward with him that calls not on me? Well, 'tis no matter; honour pricks me on. Yea, but how if honour prick me off when I come on? how then? Can honour set to a leg? no: or an arm? no: or take away the grief of a wound? no. Honour hath no skill in surgery, then? no. What is honour? a word. What is in that word honour? what is that honour? air. A trim reckoning! Who hath it? he that died o' Wednesday. Doth he feel it? no. Doth he hear it? no. 'Tis insensible, then. Yea, to the dead. But will it not live with the living? no. Why? detraction will not suffer it. Therefore I'll none of it. Honour is a mere scutcheon : and so ends my catechism.

Now, apart from transcendental considerations, apart from sentiment, apart, in fine, from all that Swift ignores, how unanswerable is logic like this, how irrefutable the reasoning! But it is reasoning against which all that constitutes the true dignity and beauty of human life rises in revolt. It would paralyse the wings of the soul, dwarf and blight the heroic virtues, and degrade the whole level of action and aspiration. As Shakespeare's generous enthusiast so well says :—

Manhood and honour
Should have hare hearts, would they but fat their thoughts
With this cramm'd reason: reason and respect
Make livers pale, and lustihood deject.

Swift said himself that his favourite author was La Rochefoucauld, 'because I find my whole character in him.'[1] The remark is significant, and the resemblance in some respects between them unquestionable. But his true prototype was Hobbes. Hobbes had none of Swift's acute sensibility, none of his tense and vehement seriousness, nothing of his Titanism, nothing of his humour. But for the rest the analogy between them was complete. The intelligence of both moved only in the sphere of the senses and the pure reason. Pessimists and cynics by both temper and conviction, they were deficient in all those instincts and sympathies on which every true estimate and every true philosophy of humanity must be based. Both resolved mankind into mere animals, and the Yahoos of Swift are the 'natural men' of Hobbes. Both reduced all that ennobles, all that beautifies, all that consecrates life, to a *caput mortuum*. Both denied practically, and even ridiculed as metaphysical thinkers, what they asserted and maintained as ethical political legislators. Both, in effect, eliminated the element of supernaturalism, and defended religion on civil grounds. Hobbes based its sanction and authority on the will of the State, Swift practically on the will of the State Church. When Hobbes wrote 'It is with the mysteries of our religion as with wholesome pills for the sick, which, swallowed whole, have the virtue to cure, but chewed are for the most part cast up again without effect,'[2] he condensed what is in essence the argument of Swift. Both, by nature pure despots, regarded the mass of their fellow-men as fools and

---

[1] Letter to Pope, Nov. 26, 1725.
[2] *Leviathan*, ch. xxxii.

knaves, to be ruled with justice indeed, and, if possible, with clemency, but to be ruled with a rod of iron.

But it must not be forgotten that, if this anti-
ideality and cynicism found its intensest and most
powerful expression in Swift, it was essentially characteristic of the age into which he was born and
in which he died. That age may be compared to a
deep valley between two eminences. On the one side
are the heights to which the enthusiasm of the
Renaissance and the enthusiasm of Puritanism had
elevated the national spirit; on the other side is the
ascent sloping upwards to the equally lofty tablelands
of the idealists of the New World. Between the year
of Swift's birth and the first administration of Pitt, it
may be safely said that in all that ennobles and in all
that beautifies human life and human nature England
had reached her lowest level. The morals and temper
of the London of the Restoration would have disgusted
the Romans of St. Paul, while much of its literature
would hardly have been tolerated by the friends of
Trimalchion. After the accession of Anne, it is
generally supposed that the evil spirit of the preceding
era was exorcised, and that a new and good spirit
entered in. And this is to some extent true. The
example set by the Queen herself, the decency and
decorum observed at her Court, and the writings of
Addison and his circle, undoubtedly exercised a salutary influence on society. But all that was touched
was the surface. The change was more apparent than
real. The filth, the cynicism, the inhumanity, the
unbelief of the former age underlay—a foul sub-
stratum — the specious exterior. The accession of
George I. rendered concealment no longer necessary,

and with some slight modification all became as all had
been before.[1] Wherever we turn we find variously
diluted and variously coloured what we find condensed
in Swift. What is Prior but the poet of disillusion ?
His most elaborate poem was written to show the
nothingness of man and of the world, his *Alma* to
ridicule metaphysics, his most successful tales to
laugh romance to scorn; his best lyrics are but
cynical trifles. What is Gay but an elegant fribble,
who ordered a flippant jest to be inscribed as his epitaph ? [2] Even the fine genius of Pope is without wings,
and many of the passages which exhibit his powers
in their highest perfection are directed to the ignoble
purpose of degrading his species. Mandeville's *Fable
of the Bees* is as shameless a libel on humanity as the
Voyage to the Houyhnhnms, and his *Virgin Unmasked*
would have disgraced Wycherley. In the *Richard-
soniana* we have the very alcohol of cynicism. The
greatest painter of the age devoted his talents to
bringing into prominence all that is most humiliating
and odious in man, and the pens of De Foe and
Smollett vied with the pencil of Hogarth in depicting
and heightening moral and physical ugliness and
depravity. Nor is this spirit less apparent when it
finds urbaner and more refined expression. The

[1] For the temper and tone of the England of Swift see particu-
larly Hartley's *Observations on Man*, ii. 441, not published till 1749,
but written many years before; Butler's *Preface to the Analogy*;
Warburton's *Dedication to the Divine Legation*; Whiston's *Memoirs*,
Part III. pp. 142–213 ; Voltaire, *Lettres sur les Anglais* ; Montesquieu,
Notes on England, where he says, ' Point de religion en Angleterre ;
si quelqu'un parle de religion, tout le monde se met à rire' ; Hervey's
Memoirs ; the *Suffolk Papers*; Atterbury's *Representation*.

[2] Life is a jest : and all things show it.
I thought so once, and now I know it.

correspondence of Pope, of Bolingbroke, of Lady Mary Wortley Montagu, the conversations recorded by Spence, the *Memoirs* of Lord Hervey, and, indeed, the greater part of the polite literature and all the *ana* of the age, are the records of a society which, with *Que sçais-je !* for its motto, and *Nil admirari* for its creed, prided itself on its superiority to enthusiasm, to sentiment, to the ideal. If we turn to theology and philosophy, we find ourselves on the same low level. When Reid wrote, ' Philosophy has no other root but the principles of common sense ; it grows out of them ; it draws its nourishment from them ; severed from this root its honours wither, its sap is dried up, it dies and rots ; [1] and when Pope wrote

> Good sense, which only is the gift of Heaven,
> And, though no science, fairly worth the seven,

they merely expressed what has expression everywhere in the writings of their immediate predecessors and contemporaries. It was the age of the Deistic Controversy, of the sermons of Wake, Gibson, Sherlock, and Hare. The test of religious truth was social utility—its sanction, reason. ' I send my servants to church,' said Anthony Collins, ' that they may neither rob nor murder me ' ; and if he spoke as a freethinker he adduced what was practically the chief argument of the most orthodox theologians of that day in favour of supernaturalism. As the apostle of ideal truth not simply in the technical but in the comprehensive sense of the term, Berkeley stood absolutely alone. To eliminate as far as possible the transcendental element from religion, and to show how life

---

[1] *Inquiry into the Human Mind.* Introduction, p. 4.

may be sustained upon a minimum of moral and spiritual assumption, appears to have been the main object of the divines and moralists of those times.

But to return. Thackeray, in speaking of Swift's last days, has finely said: ' So great a man he seems to me, that thinking of him is like thinking of an empire falling.' The expression is not exaggerated. Swift is the one figure of colossal proportions in the age to which he belonged. Nay, we may go further. Among men whose fame depends mainly on their writings, there is, if we except Aristotle, Shakespeare, and perhaps Bacon, probably no man on record who impresses us with a sense of such enormous intellectual power. He has always the air of a giant sporting among pigmies, crushing or scrutinising, helping or thwarting them, as the mood takes him. Immense strength, immense energy, now frittering themselves away on trifles, now roused for a moment to concentrated action by passion, interest, or bene-volence, but never assuming their true proportions, never developing into full activity—this is what we discern in Swift. We feel how miserably incommen-surate was the part he played with the part which Nature had fitted him to play, how contracted was the stage, how mighty the capacities of the actor. In his pamphlets, in his two great satires, in his poems, in his correspondence, is the impression of a character which there is no mistaking. And it is not among philosophers, poets, and men of letters that we are to look for its prototype or its analogy, but among those who have made and unmade nations—among men like Cæsar and men like Napoleon.

A comparison between Napoleon at St. Helena

and Swift in Ireland has more than once been drawn.
With two great distinctions between them, namely,
that Napoleon was, morally speaking, an essentially
bad man, and Swift an essentially good man, and that
the one was without heart and the other with the heart
of a woman, it would be possible to institute a parallel
not simply between their relative position as exiles
but between their temper and characteristics. Both
scorned the homage which they punctiliously exacted,
and the prizes for which they fought. Devouring ambition, finding in itself not merely the motive but the
centre of action, and originating, if partly from the
lust of dominion, partly also from the restless importunity of superabundant, nay almost preternatural
energy, was the ruling passion of both.[1] Egotists,
despots, and cynics, each owned no equal, each had
no real confidant. The one towered over his kind on
the sublime heights of power, the other in the proud
solitude of his own consciousness. What was potential in the one found full and unimpeded expression;
what was potential in the other perished undeveloped
in embryo. But the genius which could indemnify
itself for the lack of the material and conventional
symbols of supremacy by writing *Gulliver's Travels*

---

[1] To this constitutional restlessness, to this morbid activity of
mind, which was so striking a trait of Napoleon, Swift frequently
refers. Thus in a letter to Kendall, dated February, 16$\frac{91}{92}$, he says,
'A person of great honour in Ireland used to tell me that my mind
was like a conjured spirit that would do mischief if I did not give it
employment. It is this humour which makes me so busy.' Again, in
a letter recently printed by the Historical Manuscripts Commissioners,
'I myself was never very miserable while my thoughts were in a
ferment, for I imagine a dead calm is the troublesomest of our
voyage through the world.'

was in essence of the same superhuman type as the genius which half realised universal empire.

What Swift suffered in failing to attain the prizes which his haughty spirit coveted is only too plain from his diaries and correspondence. His pride amounted to disease. He was always on the watch for fancied slights. If a great man left a letter unanswered for a few days, or a friend let fall an ambiguous word, he was miserable. A man passing him in the streets without touching his hat or a woman failing to drop a curtsey seriously discomposed him.[1] To whatever degree of mere intimacy he admitted a person who could amuse or entertain him, he guarded his dignity with the most jealous care. 'He could not,' says Deane Swift, 'endure to be treated with any sort of familiarity, or that any man living, his three or four old acquaintances with whom he corresponded to the last only excepted, should rank himself in the number of his friends.'[2] His superiority to envy, of which he had not, we are told, the smallest tincture, his indifference to literary fame, and his scrupulous truthfulness in all that related to

[1] To confine illustrations to the diary at Holyhead—' The master of the pacquet boat hath not treated me with the least civility, altho' Watt gave him my name . . . yet my hat is worn to pieces by answering the civilities of the poor inhabitants as they pass by. . . . I am as insignificant here as Parson Brooke is in Dublin. By my conscience, I believe Cæsar would be the same without his army at his back. . . . Not a soul is yet come to Holyhead except a young fellow who smiles when he meets me and would fain be my companion, but it is not come to that yet . . . if I stay here much longer I am afraid all my pride and grandeur will truckle to comply with him.'

[2] *Essay on Swift*, p. 361.

himself, had their origin in the same lofty consciousness of supereminence.

Such were the characteristics and temper of Swift.
And it would seem as if Fortune, perceiving what
opportunities Nature had given her for malicious
sport, had in some spiteful mood resolved to make
his life her cruel plaything. Everything that could
depress, annoy, and irritate was his lot in youth. His
early manhood, initiated by the fatal blunder he made
in taking orders, miserable in itself, involved him in
deeper miseries still. An

> abandon'd wretch, by hope forsook,
> Forsook by hopes, ill fortune's last relief,
> Assign'd for life to unremitting grief;
> For, let Heaven's wrath enlarge these weary days,
> If Hope e'er dawns the smallest of its rays [1]

—it was thus that he could write of himself at a time
when most men are bounding blithely from the start-
ing-post of life. Whenever a ray seemed to pierce
the gloom it was always illusory. Hope after hope
glimmered only to be extinguished. Even the paltry
prizes he despised were beyond his reach, and his
forty-third year found him eating out his heart in
an obscure Irish vicarage. Then came power and
eminence, without the glory and without the guerdon.
A dictator and an underling, a despot and a tool, for
nearly four years of his life, all that could pamper
and flatter, and all that could gall and irritate his
arrogant and sensitive spirit were his mingled portion.
With exile as the reward of services great beyond any
expression of gratitude, in that exile were accumulated

---

[1] *Verses on Sir W. Temple's Illness and Recovery*, written at Moor
Park in 1693.

tenfold all causes of irritation, till irritation became
torture, till torture goaded passion into fury. And
brooding over the life of this unhappy man, wretched
alike in what he owed to Nature and in the spite of
Fortune, hung a phantom horror. As there can be
no doubt that Swift was never insane, and that the
maladies from which he suffered had no connection
with insanity, so there can equally be no doubt that
he was himself convinced of the contrary—was convinced that he carried within him the gradually developing germs of madness, and that his terrible
doom was inevitable.[1]

It has been sometimes supposed that Swift's rage
for obscenity, so inconsistent with the austere purity
of his morals and with his aversion to anything
approaching indecency in conversation, had its origin
in physical disease—that it was, as it so often is, a
phase of insanity. But it is perfectly explicable without resorting to any such hypothesis. An observation
of his own furnishes us with the true key—a nice
man is a man of nasty ideas;[2] and he was one of
the nicest and most fastidious of men. But its expression in its most offensive forms is to be attributed
partly to misanthropy, intensifying this depraved sensibility, and partly to a desire to furnish dissuasives
from vice. Of such poems as the *Lady's Dressing
Room* Delany observes, and probably with perfect
justice, that they were 'the prescriptions of an able

[1] This is placed beyond doubt by the well-known incident recorded by Young in his *Conjectures on Original Composition*. The
incident almost certainly occurred in or about 1717. See Scott,
i. 443-44.
[2] *Thoughts on Various Subjects.*

s 2

physician, who had the health of his patients at heart, but laboured to attain that end not only by strong emetics, but also by all the most offensive drugs and potions that could be administered.' He was, in truth, doing nothing more than the Saints and Fathers of the Church have habitually done, and with the same object. There are passages, for example, in St. Chrysostom and in St. Gregory, which are as nauseous and disgusting as anything that can be found in Swift. But this plea cannot be always, or indeed generally, urged in his defence; and how, in allowing himself such licence, he could see nothing incompatible with his position and behaviour as a clergyman, must remain a mystery.[1] Something is no doubt to be attributed to the age in which he lived, something to his constitution, and more to his rage against his kind. What is certain is that, as his misanthropy intensified, his imagination grew fouler and his filth became more noisome.

II

The writings of Swift are the exact reflection of his character, variously expressing itself on its various sides. Affectation and pretentiousness were his abhorrence; for literary fame he cared nothing, and

---

[1] What is still more surprising is that, although these productions appeared anonymously, it was no secret that they were from the pen of the Dean of St. Patrick's; and how Swift, who in private life and in conversation never forgot and never allowed others to forget the respect due to his cloth, could expose himself to the derogatory retorts which his licence in this respect provoked is inexplicable. Yet so it was. See a ribald poem called *The Dean's Provocation*, which professes to account for the reason of his writing the *Lady's Dressing Room*.

he had therefore no inducement to aspire beyond the
natural level of his powers. He wrote out of the ful-
ness of his mind, as impulse or passion directed,
practically, for the attainment of some immediate
object, or idly, to amuse himself. To books he owed
comparatively little. Butler was his model in verse.
If he had any models in prose, they were the tracts
of Father Parsons, and one of the most powerful
political pieces extant in our language, Silas Titus'
Killing No Murder. As a political pamphleteer,
Swift is without a rival. Fénelon observed of Cicero,
that when the Romans heard him they exclaimed, ' It
is the voice of a God ; ' and of Demosthenes, that when
the Athenians heard him they cried, ' Let us march
against Philip.' The remark indicates the distinction
between Swift's political pieces and the political pieces
of such writers as Bolingbroke, Junius, and Burke.
Compared with him, they appear to be but splendid
sophists, maintaining with all the resources of rhetoric,
and all the experience and skill of practised advocates,
a case for the prosecution or a case for the defence.
If the truth is of little moment to us, we concede to
admiration what we ought to concede only to conviction. But the impression produced by Swift is the
impression produced by a powerful and logical mind,
with no object but the investigation of truth, amply
furnished with the means of ascertaining it, and convinced itself before attempting to convince others.
His profound knowledge of human nature and his
experience of affairs enabled him to bring every
point home, and to assume naturally, and with propriety, an air of authority such as in any mere man
of letters would be affectation.

Swift is a poet only by courtesy. Good sense, humour, and wit are as a rule the distinguishing characteristics of his poetry, though, as Scott well observes, the intensity of his satire sometimes gives to his verses an emphatic violence which borders on grandeur, as in the *Rhapsody* and in the poem on the Last Day. But, if Apollo disowned him, he was not altogether deserted by the Graces, as *Cadenus and Vanessa* shows; and of the attributes of the poet a touch of fancy may certainly be claimed for him. It would, however, be doing him great injustice to deny his claim to a high place among masters of the *sermo pedestris*. As descriptive pieces his *City Shower* and his *Early Morning in London* are pictures worthy of Hogarth; his adaptations from Horace and Ovid are eminently felicitous and pleasing, while the verses on his own death and the *Grand Question Debated* are among the best things of their kind. Some of his other trifles, particularly his Epistles, will always find delighted readers. His verse, though too mechanically monotonous, is unlaboured and flowing, his diction terse and yet easy and natural. In the art of rhyming, an accomplishment on which he especially prided himself, he has few superiors, and his rhymes are as exact and correct as they are ingenious and novel. Even the author of *Don Juan* spoke of himself as contemplating Swift's mastery over rhyme with admiring despair.

It is, of course, as a humorist and satirist that Swift is and will continue to be a power in literature. Models as his political pieces are—in their style nervous, simple, trenchant—in their method lucid, logical —in their tone masculine, vehement—few perhaps but historical students will turn to them, for to none but historical students will their ephemeral matter be intelligible. Two-thirds of his other writings have long ceased to be of interest to the many, but the *Battle of the Books*, the *Tale of a Tub*, the *Arguments against abolishing Christianity*, the *Modest Proposal*, a dozen or two of his poems, and *Gulliver*, will keep his fame fresh in every generation. Here, then, are to be found the qualities upon which his claim to a place among classics must rest. They are easily distinguished. The first attribute of genius is originality, and Swift was essentially original. It is true that he was indebted to others for the hint of his three chief satires, but, as he has himself observed, if a man lights his candle at his neighbour's fire it does not affect his property in the candle which he lights.[1] Probably no other writer with the exception of Dickens has borrowed so little. His images and ideas are almost always his own; his humour is his own; his style is his own. In a well-known passage he claims to have been the first to introduce and teach the use of irony:—

> Arbuthnot is no more my friend,
> Who does to irony pretend,
> Which I was born to introduce,
> Refin'd it first, and taught its use.

This was not strictly true, as he had been anticipated by De Foe, whose *Shortest Way with the Dissenters* appeared nearly two years before the earliest of Swift's writings had been published. But a title to a place among classics depends not merely on originality—it depends also on quality, on the intrinsic value and interest of what is produced. Swift's serious reflections

[1] *Advice to a Young Poet.*

and remarks are the perfection of homely good sense
—shrewd, trenchant, pointed, enriching life with new
and useful truths. But his good sense is without
refinement, without imagination, and without subtlety.
The sphere in which his intelligence worked and
within which his sympathy and insight were bounded
was, comparatively speaking, a narrow one. He had
the eye of a lynx for all that moves on the surface of
life and for all that may be found on the beaten highway of commonplace experience, but the depths he
neither explored nor perhaps even suspected. In his
innumerable aphorisms, generalisations, and precepts
it would be impossible to find one which either indicates delicate discrimination or reveals a glimpse of
ideal truth.

His style has in itself little distinction and no
charm, but for his purposes it is the more effective
from the absence of distinction. A pure medium of
expression, it owes nothing to art, for he disdained
ornament and he disdained elaboration. To eloquence he makes no pretension. Proper words in
proper places was his own ideal of a good style, and
he was satisfied with attaining it.

As a master of irony he has few if any equals. It
was his favourite weapon, tempered as finely as that
with which the Platonic Socrates disarmed Protagoras
and Hippias, and as that with which the author of the
Provincial Letters lacerated the disciples of Le Moine
and Father Annat. But the fineness of its temper
constituted its chief resemblance to the irony of Plato
and Pascal. It is without urbanity, without lightness,
and without grace. Austere and saturnine, bitter
and intense, it would seem strangely out of place as

the ally of pleasantry; and yet seldom has pleasantry been so happily mated. Other humorists may move us to merriment and convulse us with laughter, but the irony of Swift is a source of more delicious enjoyment, of more exquisite pleasure. In its lighter forms it springs from a nice and subtle perception of the unbecoming and the ridiculous in their lighter and more trivial aspects, tempered with scorn and contempt; in its severer, from a similar perception of the same improprieties in their most impressive and most serious aspects, tempered not with scorn merely but with loathing, not with contempt merely but with horror and rage. The extremes are marked by the Dissertations in the *Tale of a Tub* and by the *Directions to Servants* on the one side, by the *Modest Proposal* and the *Voyage to the Houyhnhnms* on the other. And the mean is in the *Voyage to Brobdingnag*. It is in irony that Swift's humour most generally finds expression, and always finds its most characteristic expression. And naturally. Wherever intelligence of clairvoyant insight, however narrow its area, together with a calm or contemptuous consciousness of superiority, is united with acute sensibility and with the keenest perception of the difference between things as they seem and things as they are, irony will always be the note.

The attitude of Swift towards life and man is precisely that of Juvenal's deity—*ridet et odit*—he laughs and loathes. And his humour is the laughter. It is never good-natured. It is always sardonic, presenting a complete contrast to that of Cervantes and to that of Shakespeare. When we turn to the line which Shakespeare put into the mouth of Puck, 'Lord, what

fools these mortals be!' and to the *Tempest*, and then
to the *Voyage to the Houyhnhnms*, and to the poem
in which the Deity dismisses his cowering creatures
from the judgment bar, as too despicable to be
damned—

> I to such blockheads set my wit!
> I damn such fools! Go, go—*you're bit*—

we measure the difference between the humour
'which sees life steadily and sees it whole' and the
humour of the mere Titan.

Swift forms one of an immortal trio. In the
writings of Addison will be mirrored for all time the
image of a beautiful human soul. Humour genial
and kindly as it is exquisite, wit refined and polished
as it is rich and abundant, and a style approaching as
nearly to perfection as it is perhaps possible for style
to do, will unite with the charm of his character in
keeping his memory green. If the poetry of Pope has
not the vogue it once had, the fame of the most
brilliant of poets is secure. He may not have the
homage of the multitude, but he will have in every
generation, as long as our language lasts, the homage
of all who can discern. He stands indeed with Horace,
Juvenal, and Dryden at the head of a great department
of poetry—the poetry of ethics and satire. But the
third of the trio will as a name and as a power over-
shadow the other two. Before his vast proportions
they seem indeed to dwindle into insignificance. And
what figure in that eighteenth century of time is not
dwarfed beside this Momus-Prometheus? Among
men, but not of them, at war with himself, with the

world, and with destiny, he set at naught the warning which Greek wisdom was never weary of repeating—

Born into life we are, and life must be our mould.

He was in temper all that Pindar symbolises in Typhon, and all that revolts Plato in the inharmonious and unmusical soul. And so, while his writings bear the impress of powers such as have rarely been conceded to man, they reflect and return with repulsive fidelity the ugliness and discord of the Titanism which inspired them. Without reverence and without reticence, he gloried in the licence which to the Greeks constituted the last offence against good taste and good sense, and out of the indulgence in which they have coined a synonym for shamelessness—the indiscriminate expression of what ought and what ought not to be said. A cynic and a misanthrope in principle, his philosophy of life is ignoble, base, and false, and his impious mockery extends even to the Deity. A large portion of his works exhibit, and in intense activity, all the worst attributes of our nature—revenge, spite, malignity, uncleanness. His life, indeed, afforded a noble example of duty conscientiously fulfilled, of great services done to his kind, and of an active benevolence which knew no bounds. But it is not by these virtues that he will be remembered. He will live as one of the most commanding and fascinating figures which has ever appeared on the stage of life, and as the protagonist of a drama which can never cease to interest the student of human life and of human nature. In every generation his works will be read, but they will be read not so much for themselves as for their association. The fame of the man will preserve and support the fame of the author. For there is probably no writer of equal power and eminence in whose judgments and conclusions, in whose precepts and teaching, the instincts and experience of progressive humanity will find so little to corroborate.

APPENDICES

I

My opinion, briefly stated, is that Dean Swift's insanity was purely accidental, as much so as if it had been brought on by a coup de soleil or a blow on the head; and I think there are even grounds for believing that he had a blow *in* the head, namely, a slight stroke, which was the real cause of his insanity. I use the word *accidental* insanity in contradistinction to what I call *developmental* insanity, such as the mental disease under which Cowper laboured, or the still better example to be found in the insanity of Tasso. If you will read Black's biography of Tasso—an excellent work—you will see how curiously and gradually he developed into the madman he became, and how clearly the forewarnings of lunacy are to be seen in the still sane periods of his life.

But there was nothing of this kind in Swift. If Swift had developed into a lunatic on the lines of his sane character, he would have been a very different kind of ' person of unsound mind ' to the poor fatuous creature whose vitality survived his intellect in the manner I have read of him. I think I could form a not improbable guess of the kind of madman Swift might have developed into under a strong hereditary tendency, but the history of his case is not of this kind. It is the history of physical disease, and I venture to assert that the details of the disease which have come down to us are sufficient to enable us to form a not improbable diagnosis of the case. It was, no doubt, a case of what you call fatuity, and what doctors call dementia—that is, loss of mental power. There was no delusion, so far as I remember ; but there was this peculiarity—the inability to find words for the expression of the poor remains of thought, although phrases did now and then find utterance under unwonted stimulus. It was, in fact, a case of aphasia with dementia, leading to the expectation that, if one could have seen the brain, a clot, or the effects or remains of a clot, would have been found on or about the third frontal convolution.

I think the psychology and pathology of aphasia have been added to our store of medical knowledge since Sir William Wilde wrote his notes on the closing days of Dean Swift, and I am not sure that he makes any comment upon the often repeated fact that Swift was unable to find words to express his thoughts.

You will gather from the above what my answers must be to your questions, and yet, perhaps, it may be well to answer them categorically, and therefore permit me to say that in my opinion—

A. There is sufficient evidence to render a correct diagnosis of Swift's mental disease possible.

B. There are records of numerous cases in which the phenomena are parallel.

C. It is not physically possible that Swift's fatuity at 75 originated from a surfeit of green fruit when he was 23.

D. The sane part of Swift's life was not likely to have been affected by the latent presence of the insanity.

This question, which I have answered last, seems the most interesting and important, seeing that the ignorant public are but too ready to refer the peculiarities of genius to madness, and that, when a great genius does become insane from some accidental cause, Dryden's lines are only too apt to be quoted.

II

WRIT 'DE LUNATICO INQUIRENDO' AND REPORT OF THE COMMISSION

GEORGE the Second by the Grace of God of Great Britain ffrance and Ireland King Defender of the ffaith and so forth. To our Trusty and welbeloved the R^t honb^{le} Luke Gardner Esqre Eaton Stannard Esqre Recorder of the Citty of Dublin Phillip Tisdall and Bolayn Whitney Esq^{rs} John [?] William Cooper and Dr Thomas Trotter [or Troller] Sr James Somervill Ald^m John Macaroll Ald^m Percival Hunt Ald^m Kirkland Pearson Ald^m'Robert King Thomas Lehunt and Alexander McAuly Esq^{rs} William Harward and John Rochfort Esq^{rs} Charles Grattan and Bellingham Boyle Esq^{rs} Greeting Whereas it is given us to understand by the petition of the Reverend John Grattan and the Reverend James King that the Revd Doctor Jonathan Swift Dean of St Patricks Dublin hath for these nine months past been gradually faileing in his memory and understanding and of such unsound mind and memory that he is incapable of transacting any business or manageing conducting or takeing care either of his Estate or person. We being willing to provide a remedy in this behalf do command you three or more of you that you repair to the said Doctor Jonathan Swift and by all proper ways and meanes you Examine him and moreover by the Oaths of good and lawfull men by whom the truth of the matter may be best known you diligently Inquire whether the said Doctor Jonathan Swift be a person of unsound mind and memory and not capable of takeing care of his person or fortune as aforesaid, and if he be, how long he hath been so, and of what Lands and Tenements Goods and Chattels the said

Doctor Jonathan Swift was possessed off at the time he so
became of unsound mind and memory or at any time since
and what is the yearly value thereof and who is his next
heir and such Inquisition as shall be then found you or
any three or more of you shall openly and distinctly
make return thereof to us in our Chancery in Ireland on
the third day of November next under your seals and the
seals of those by whom the said Inquisition shall be made
together with this Writ Witness our Justices General and
General Governours of our said Kingdom of Ireland at
Dublin the twelfth day of August the Sixteenth year of
our Reign.

DOMVILE.

Ex⁴ Ed Madden dep^{ty} Clk
of the Crown and Hanaper

At the back of the Writ :—

The Execution of the within Commission appears by
ye Inquisition hereunto Annexed

Jo AUFRER
Lu GARDINER
PHIL TISDALL
J ROCHFORT
W^M HARWARD
BELL BOYLE
PERCIVALL HUNT
JOHN MACARELL

An Inquisition Indented taken before us the Right
Honble Luke Gardiner Esqr Philip Tisdall Esqr John
Maccarrell Percival Hunt Aldermⁿ William Harward John
Rochfort and Bellingham Boyle Esq^s Com^{rs} by virtue of
a Commission of our Sovereign Lord George the Second
of Great Brittain France and Ireland King Defender of the
Faith and so forth Bearing Date the Twelfth Day of Aug^t
in the Sixteenth Year of the Reign of his said Majesty at
the Deanery house of St Patricks Dublin the Seventeenth

Day of August in the year of our Lord one thousand seven hund^d and forty two

The Names of the Jury of honest and lawfull men sworn to enquire and Examen of and into the matter Specified in said Comission

Edw^D Hunt Alderm^n
John Adamson Merch^t
Rob^T Donovan Merch^t
Arthur Lamprey Chand^r
Thom^s Hamilton Brewer
John Walsh Carpenter
John Cooke Hosier
John Cummin Carpenter
Erasmus Cope Jeweler
John Sican Merch^t
John Martin Currier
Joshua Barrington Merch^t

Gentlemen

Your Issue is to try and Inquire Whether Doctor Jonathan Swift in the annex^d Comission be a person of unsound mind and Memory and not capable of takeing care of his person or fortune and if he be, how long he hath been so and of what Lands Tenem^ts goods and chattels the said Doctor Jonathan Swift was possessd off at the time he so became of unsound mind and Memory, or at any time since, And what is the yearly value thereof and who is his next Heir.

Wee Find that the Revd Doctor Jonathan Swift in the annexed Comission named is a person of unsound mind and memory and not capable of taking care of his person or Fortune and that he hath been soe since the twentyeth day of May last past And Wee Further find that the said Jonathan Swift was on the said twentyeth day of May, and still is seized and possessed of Lands Thytes [? Tithes] and Tenem^ts of the Clear Yearly value of Eight hundred pounds sterling and also possessed of goods and chattels

T

to the value of ten thousand pounds sterl^g. And It does
not appear to us who is his next Heir

ED: HUNT [Seal to each name] JOHN MARTIN
JOHN ADAMSON   JOSHUA BARRINGTON
ROB: DONOVAN   W^M HARWARD
ARTH^R LAMPREY   J: ROCHFORT
THO^S HAMILTON   BELL BOYLE
JOHN WELSH [sic]   LU GARDINER
JOHN COOKE   PHIL TISDALL
JOHN CUMIN   JOHN MACARELL
ERAS: COPE   PERCIV^{LL} HUNT
J^{NO} SICAN

At the back :—

(1742
Swift - Comission of Lunacy
(and return

rec^d 19th Augt 1742

INDEX

HARDING, printer of the Drapier Letters, arrested, 186; tried, 187; the Bill thrown out, 187

Harley, Earl of Oxford, leader of the Tories, 64; Lord Treasurer, 69; his difficulties, 79; stabbed by Guiscard, 84; his popularity, 85; his correspondence with the agents of the French king, 86; member of the Brothers' Club, 90; quarrel with Nottingham, 104; his activity in the question of Swift's preferment, 114; quarrel with Bolingbroke, 119; his resignation, 122

Herbert, Sir Thomas, possible indebtedness of *Gulliver's Travels* to his *Travels*, 205

Hobbes, compared with Swift, 251

'Hope, Thomas,' pseudonym of Swift, 170

Howard, Mrs., Swift's intimacy with, 216

IRELAND, condition of the country in the earlier years of the eighteenth century, 159; her natural advantages, 159; her treatment by England, 160; famine and pestilence in, 161; torn by feuds and enmities of race, politics, religion, 163; the Middlemen, 164; the provincial gentry, 164; crushing statutes of the English Parliament, 165; the degraded Protestant hierarchy, 166; Grafton succeeded in Lord Lieutenancy by Carteret, 183; deplorable condition of the country in 1729, 221

JOHNSON, Esther, Swift's first meeting with her at Moor Park, 30; her personal appearance and character, 73; her settlement near Swift in Ireland, 76; Swift's relations with her, 76; his *Journal* to her, 78; her alleged marriage with Swift, 146; the evidence against it, 147; the evidence for it, 151; general summary —testimony strongly against it, 156; the verdict of the world, 157; her death, 218

LESSING, his *Miss Sara Sampson*, 157

Lucian, indebtedness of *Gulliver's Travels* to, 205 (*bis*)

Lyon, Dr. John, his testimony against the alleged marriage of Swift and Esther Johnson, 150

MACAULAY, his estimate of Swift, 16, 27

Madden, Dr. Samuel, his testimony as to the alleged marriage of Swift and Esther Johnson, 152

Mason, Monck, his *History and Antiquities of St. Patrick's Cathedral*, its merits and defects, 6

Monck-Berkeley, his *Enquiry into the Life of Dean Swift*, 4; reference to, 154

Montaigne, compared with Swift, 210

NAPOLEON, compared with Swift, 255

Newton, Sir Isaac, his testing of Wood's copper coinage, 178 (*note*), 179

ORRERY, Lord, his *Letters*, their merits and defects, 2; reference to, 151

Oxford, *vide* Harley

PRINTED BY
SPOTTISWOODE AND CO., NEW-STREET SQUARE
LONDON

A List of Books

PUBLISHED BY

CHATTO & WINDUS

214, Piccadilly, London, W.

Sold by all Booksellers, or sent post-free for the published price by the Publishers.

ABOUT.—THE FELLAH: An Egyptian Novel. By EDMOND ABOUT.
Translated by Sir RANDAL ROBERTS. Post 8vo, illustrated boards, **2s.**

ADAMS (W. DAVENPORT), WORKS BY.
 A DICTIONARY OF THE DRAMA. Being a comprehensive Guide to the Plays,
  Playwrights, Players, and Playhouses of the United Kingdom and America.
  Crown 8vo half-bound, **12s. 6d.** [*Preparing.*
 QUIPS AND QUIDDITIES. Selected by W. D. ADAMS. Post 8vo, cloth limp, **2s. 6d.**

AGONY COLUMN (THE) OF "THE TIMES," from 1800 to 1870.
 Edited, with an Introduction, by ALICE CLAY. Post 8vo, cloth limp, **2s. 6d.**

AIDE (HAMILTON), WORKS BY. Post 8vo, illustrated boards, **2s.** each.
 CARR OF CARRLYON. | CONFIDENCES.

ALBERT.—BROOKE FINCHLEY'S DAUGHTER. By MARY ALBERT.
 Post 8vo, picture boards, **2s.**; cloth limp, **2s. 6d.**

ALDEN.—A LOST SOUL. By W. L. ALDEN. Fcap. 8vo, cl. bds., **1s. 6d.**

ALEXANDER (MRS.), NOVELS BY. Post 8vo, illustrated boards, **2s.** each.
 MAID, WIFE, OR WIDOW? | VALERIE'S FATE.

ALLEN (F. M.).—GREEN AS GRASS. By F. M. ALLEN, Author of
 "Through Green Glasses." Frontispiece by J. SMYTH. Cr. 8vo, cloth ex., **3s. 6d.**

ALLEN (GRANT), WORKS BY. Crown 8vo, cloth extra, **6s.** each.
 THE EVOLUTIONIST AT LARGE. | COLIN CLOUT'S CALENDAR.

 Crown 8vo, cloth extra, **3s. 6d.** each; post 8vo, illustrated boards, **2s.** each.
 PHILISTIA. | FOR MAIMIE'S SAKE. | THE TENTS OF SHEM.
 BABYLON. | IN ALL SHADES. | THE GREAT TABOO.
 STRANGE STORIES. | THE DEVIL'S DIE. | DUMARESQ'S DAUGHTER.
 BECKONING HAND. | THIS MORTAL COIL.

 Crown 8vo, cloth extra, **3s. 6d.** each.
 THE DUCHESS OF POWYSLAND. | BLOOD ROYAL.
 IVAN GREET'S MASTERPIECE, &c. With a Frontispiece by S. L. WOOD.
 DR. PALLISER'S PATIENT. Fcap. 8vo, cloth extra, **1s. 6d.**

AMERICAN LITERATURE, A LIBRARY OF, from the Earliest Settlement to the Present Time. Compiled and Edited by EDMUND CLARENCE STEDMAN
 and ELLEN MACKAY HUTCHINSON. Eleven Vols., royal 8vo, cloth extra, **£6 12s.**

ARCHITECTURAL STYLES, A HANDBOOK OF. By A. ROSENGAR-
 TEN. Translated by W. COLLETT-SANDARS. With 639 Illusts. Cr. 8vo, cl. ex., **7s. 6d.**

ART (THE) OF AMUSING: A Collection of Graceful Arts, GAMES,
 Tricks, Puzzles, and Charades. By FRANK BELLEW. 300 Illusts. Cr. 8vo, cl. ex., **4s. 6d.**

ARNOLD (EDWIN LESTER), WORKS BY.
 THE WONDERFUL ADVENTURES OF PHRA THE PHŒNICIAN. With Introduc-
  tion by Sir EDWIN ARNOLD, and 12 Illustrations by H. M. PAGET. Crown 8vo,
  cloth extra, **3s. 6d.**; post 8vo, illustrated boards, **2s.**
 THE CONSTABLE OF ST. NICHOLAS. Crown 8vo, cloth, **3s. 6d.** [*Shortly.*
 BIRD LIFE IN ENGLAND. Crown 8vo, cloth extra, **6s.**

ARTEMUS WARD'S WORKS. With Portrait and Facsimile. Crown
8vo, cloth extra, **7s. 6d.**—Also a POPULAR EDITION, post 8vo, picture boards, **2s.**
THE GENIAL SHOWMAN: Life and Adventures of ARTEMUS WARD. By EDWARD
P. HINGSTON. With a Frontispiece. Crown 8vo, cloth extra, **3s. 6d.**

ASHTON (JOHN), WORKS BY. Crown 8vo, cloth extra, **7s. 6d.** each.
HISTORY OF THE CHAP-BOOKS OF THE 18th CENTURY. With 334 Illusts.
SOCIAL LIFE IN THE REIGN OF QUEEN ANNE. With 85 Illustrations.
HUMOUR, WIT, AND SATIRE OF SEVENTEENTH CENTURY. With 82 Illusts.
ENGLISH CARICATURE AND SATIRE ON NAPOLEON THE FIRST. 115 Illusts.
MODERN STREET BALLADS. With 57 Illustrations.

BACTERIA.—A SYNOPSIS OF THE BACTERIA AND YEAST
FUNGI AND ALLIED SPECIES. By W. B. GROVE, B.A. With 87 Illustrations.
Crown 8vo, cloth extra, **3s. 6d.**

BARDSLEY (REV. C. W.), WORKS BY.
ENGLISH SURNAMES: Their Sources and Significations. Cr. 8vo, cloth, **7s. 6d.**
CURIOSITIES OF PURITAN NOMENCLATURE. Crown 8vo, cloth extra, **6s.**

BARING GOULD (S., Author of "John Herring," &c.), NOVELS BY.
Crown 8vo, cloth extra, **3s. 6d.** each; post 8vo, illustrated boards, **2s.** each.
RED SPIDER. | EVE.

BARRETT (FRANK, Author of "Lady Biddy Fane,") NOVELS BY.
Post 8vo, illustrated boards, **2s.** each; cloth, **2s. 6d.** each.

FETTERED FOR LIFE.	A PRODIGAL'S PROGRESS.
THE SIN OF OLGA ZASSOULICH.	JOHN FORD; and HIS HELPMATE.
BETWEEN LIFE AND DEATH.	A RECOILING VENGEANCE.
FOLLY MORRISON.	HONEST DAVIE.	FOUND GUILTY.
LIEUT. BARNABAS.	FOR LOVE AND HONOUR.
LITTLE LADY LINTON.	

BEACONSFIELD, LORD: A Biography. By T. P. O'CONNOR, M.P.
Sixth Edition. with an Introduction. Crown 8vo, cloth extra, **5s.**

BEAUCHAMP.—GRANTLEY GRANGE: A Novel. By SHELSLEY
BEAUCHAMP. Post 8vo, illustrated boards, **2s.**

BEAUTIFUL PICTURES BY BRITISH ARTISTS: A Gathering of
Favourites from our Picture Galleries, beautifully engraved on Steel. With Notices
of the Artists by SYDNEY ARMYTAGE. M.A. Imperial 4to, cloth extra, gilt edges, **21s.**

BECHSTEIN.—AS PRETTY AS SEVEN, and other German Stories.
Collected by LUDWIG BECHSTEIN. With Additional Tales by the Brothers GRIMM,
and 98 Illustrations by RICHTER. Square 8vo, cloth extra, **6s. 6d.**; gilt edges, **7s. 6d.**

BEERBOHM.—WANDERINGS IN PATAGONIA; or, Life among the
Ostrich Hunters. By JULIUS BEERBOHM. With Illusts. Cr. 8vo, cl. extra, **3s. 6d.**

BENNETT (W. C., LL.D.), WORKS BY. Post 8vo, cloth limp. **2s.** each.
A BALLAD HISTORY OF ENGLAND. | SONGS FOR SAILORS.

BESANT (WALTER), NOVELS BY.
Cr. 8vo. cl. ex., **3s. 6d.** each; post 8vo. illust. bds., **2s.** each; cl. limp, **2s. 6d.** each.
ALL SORTS AND CONDITIONS OF MEN. With Illustrations by FRED. BARNARD.
THE CAPTAINS' ROOM, &c. With Frontispiece by E. J. WHEELER.
ALL IN A GARDEN FAIR. With 6 Illustrations by HARRY FURNISS.
DOROTHY FORSTER. With Frontispiece by CHARLES GREEN.
UNCLE JACK, and other Stories. | CHILDREN OF GIBEON.
THE WORLD WENT VERY WELL THEN. With 12 Illustrations by A. FORESTIER.
HERR PAULUS: His Rise, his Greatness, and his Fall.
FOR FAITH AND FREEDOM. With Illustrations by A. FORESTIER and F. WADDY.
TO CALL HER MINE. &c. With 9 Illustrations by A. FORESTIER.
THE BELL OF ST. PAUL'S.
THE HOLY ROSE, &c. With Frontispiece by F. BARNARD.
ARMOREL OF LYONESSE: A Romance of To-day. With 12 Illusts. by F. BARNARD.
ST. KATHERINE'S BY THE TOWER. With 12 page Illustrations by C. GREEN.
        Crown 8vo, cloth extra, **3s. 6d.** each.
VERBENA CAMELLIA STEPHANOTIS, &c. Frontispiece by GORDON BROWNE.
THE IVORY GATE: A Novel.   [Shortly.
FIFTY YEARS AGO. With 144 Plates and Woodcuts. Crown 8vo, cloth extra, **5s.**
THE EULOGY OF RICHARD JEFFERIES. With Portrait. Cr. 8vo, cl. extra, **6s.**
THE ART OF FICTION. Demy 8vo, **1s.**
LONDON. With 124 Illustrations. Demy 8vo, cloth extra, **18s.**
THE REBEL QUEEN: A Novel. Three Vols.. crown 8vo.   [Shortly,

BESANT (WALTER) AND JAMES RICE, NOVELS BY.

Cr. 8vo, cl. ex., **3s. 6d.** each ; post 8vo, illust. bds,, **2s.** each; cl. limp, **2s. 6d.** each.

READY-MONEY MORTIBOY. | BY CELIA'S ARBOUR.
MY LITTLE GIRL. | THE CHAPLAIN OF THE FLEET.
WITH HARP AND CROWN. | THE SEAMY SIDE.
THIS SON OF VULCAN. | THE CASE OF MR. LUCRAFT, &c.
THE GOLDEN BUTTERFLY. | 'TWAS IN TRAFALGAR'S BAY, &c.
THE MONKS OF THELEMA. | THE TEN YEARS' TENANT, &c.

*** There is also a LIBRARY EDITION of the above Twelve Volumes, handsomely set in new type, on a large crown 8vo page, and bound in cloth extra, **6s.** each.

BEWICK (THOMAS) AND HIS PUPILS. By AUSTIN DOBSON. With 95 Illustrations. Square 8vo, cloth extra, **6s.**

BIERCE.—IN THE MIDST OF LIFE : Tales of Soldiers and Civilians, By AMBROSE BIERCE. Crown 8vo, cloth extra, **6s.**; post 8vo, illustrated boards, **2s.**

BLACKBURN'S (HENRY) ART HANDBOOKS.

ACADEMY NOTES, separate years, from 1875-1887, 1889-1892, each **1s.**
ACADEMY NOTES, 1893. With Illustrations. **1s.**
ACADEMY NOTES, 1875-79. Complete in One Vol., with 600 Illusts. Cloth limp, **6s.**
ACADEMY NOTES, 1880-84. Complete in One Vol. with 700 Illusts. Cloth limp, **6s.**
GROSVENOR NOTES, 1877. **6d.**
GROSVENOR NOTES, separate years, from 1878 to 1890, each **1s.**
GROSVENOR NOTES, Vol. I., 1877-82. With 300 Illusts. Demy 8vo, cloth limp, **6s.**
GROSVENOR NOTES, Vol. II., 1883-87. With 300 Illusts. Demy 8vo, cloth limp, **6s.**
THE NEW GALLERY, 1888-1892. With numerous Illustrations, each **1s.**
THE NEW GALLERY, 1893. With Illustrations. **1s.**
THE NEW GALLERY, Vol. I., 1888-1892. With 250 Illusts. Demy 8vo, cloth, **6s.**
ENGLISH PICTURES AT THE NATIONAL GALLERY. 114 Illustrations. **1s.**
OLD MASTERS AT THE NATIONAL GALLERY. 128 Illustrations. **1s. 6d.**
ILLUSTRATED CATALOGUE TO THE NATIONAL GALLERY. 242 Illusts. cl., **3s.**
THE PARIS SALON, 1893. With Facsimile Sketches. **3s.**
THE PARIS SOCIETY OF FINE ARTS, 1893. With Sketches. **3s. 6d.**

BLAKE (WILLIAM) : India-proof Etchings from his Works by WILLIAM BELL SCOTT. With descriptive Text. Folio, half-bound boards, **21s.**

BLIND (MATHILDE), Poems by. Crown 8vo, cloth extra, **5s.** each.

THE ASCENT OF MAN.
DRAMAS IN MINIATURE. With a Frontispiece by FORD MADOX BROWN.
SONGS AND SONNETS. Fcap. 8vo, vellum and gold.

BOURNE (H. R. FOX), WORKS BY.

ENGLISH MERCHANTS: Memoirs in Illustration of the Progress of British Commerce. With numerous Illustrations. Crown 8vo, cloth extra, **7s. 6d.**
ENGLISH NEWSPAPERS: The History of Journalism. Two Vols., demy 8vo, cl., **25s.**
THE OTHER SIDE OF THE EMIN PASHA RELIEF EXPEDITION. Crown 8vo, cloth extra, **6s.**

BOWERS.—LEAVES FROM A HUNTING JOURNAL. By GEORGE BOWERS. Oblong folio, half-bound. **21s.**

BOYLE (FREDERICK), WORKS BY. Post 8vo, illustrated boards, **2s.** each.

CHRONICLES OF NO-MAN'S LAND. | CAMP NOTES.
SAVAGE LIFE. Crown 8vo, cloth extra, **3s. 6d.**; post 8vo. picture boards, **2s.**

BRAND'S OBSERVATIONS ON POPULAR ANTIQUITIES ; chiefly illustrating the Origin of our Vulgar Customs, Ceremonies, and Superstitions. With the Additions of Sir HENRY ELLIS, and Illustrations. Cr. 8vo. cloth extra, **7s. 6d.**

BREWER (REV. DR.), WORKS BY.

THE READER'S HANDBOOK OF ALLUSIONS, REFERENCES, PLOTS, AND STORIES. Fifteenth Thousand. Crown 8vo, cloth extra, **7s. 6d.**
AUTHORS AND THEIR WORKS, WITH THE DATES: Being the Appendices to "The Reader's Handbook." separately printed. Crown 8vo, cloth limp, **2s.**
A DICTIONARY OF MIRACLES. Crown 8vo, cloth extra, **7s. 6d.**

BREWSTER (SIR DAVID), WORKS BY. Post 8vo cl. ex. **4s. 6d.** each.

MORE WORLDS THAN ONE: Creed of Philosopher and Hope of Christian. Plates.
THE MARTYRS OF SCIENCE: GALILEO, TYCHO BRAHE, and KEPLER. With Portraits.
LETTERS ON NATURAL MAGIC. With numerous Illustrations.

BRILLAT-SAVARIN.—GASTRONOMY AS A FINE ART. By BRILLAT-SAVARIN. Translated by R. E. ANDERSON. M.A. Post 8vo, half-bound, **2s.**

4 BOOKS PUBLISHED BY

BRET HARTE, WORKS BY.
LIBRARY EDITION. In Seven Volumes, crown 8vo, cloth extra, **6s.** each.
BRET HARTE'S COLLECTED WORKS. Arranged and Revised by the Author.
Vol. I. COMPLETE POETICAL AND DRAMATIC WORKS. With Steel Portrait.
Vol. II. LUCK OF ROARING CAMP—BOHEMIAN PAPERS—AMERICAN LEGENDS.
Vol. III. TALES OF THE ARGONAUTS—EASTERN SKETCHES.
Vol. IV. GABRIEL CONROY. | Vol. V. STORIES—CONDENSED NOVELS, &c.
Vol. VI. TALES OF THE PACIFIC SLOPE.
Vol.VII. TALES OF THE PACIFIC SLOPE—II. With Portrait by JOHN PETTIE, R.A.

THE SELECT WORKS OF BRET HARTE, in Prose and Poetry With Introductory
Essay by J. M. BELLEW, Portrait of Author, and 50 Illusts. Cr.8vo, cl. ex., **7s. 6d.**
BRET HARTE'S POETICAL WORKS. Hand-made paper & buckram. Cr.8vo, **4s.6d.**
THE QUEEN OF THE PIRATE ISLE. With 28 original Drawings by KATE
GREENAWAY, reproduced in Colours by EDMUND EVANS. Small 4to, cloth, **5s.**

Crown 8vo, cloth extra, **3s. 6d.** each.
A WAIF OF THE PLAINS. With 60 Illustrations by STANLEY L. WOOD.
A WARD OF THE GOLDEN GATE. With 59 Illustrations by STANLEY L. WOOD
A SAPPHO OF GREEN SPRINGS, &c. With Two Illustrations by HUME NISBET
COLONEL STARBOTTLE'S CLIENT, AND SOME OTHER PEOPLE. With a
Frontispiece by FRED. BARNARD.
SUSY: A Novel. With Frontispiece and Vignette by J. A. CHRISTIE.
SALLY DOWS, &c. With 47 Illustrations by W. D. ALMOND, &c.

Post 8vo, illustrated boards, **2s.** each.
GABRIEL CONROY. | THE LUCK OF ROARING CAMP, &c.
AN HEIRESS OF RED DOG, &c. | CALIFORNIAN STORIES.

Post 8vo, illustrated boards, **2s.** each; cloth limp, **2s. 6d.** each.
FLIP. | MARUJA. | A PHYLLIS OF THE SIERRAS.

Fcap. 8vo. picture cover, **1s.** each.
THE TWINS OF TABLE MOUNTAIN. | JEFF BRIGGS'S LOVE STORY.
SNOW-BOUND AT EAGLE'S.

BRYDGES.—UNCLE SAM AT HOME. By HAROLD BRYDGES. Post
8vo, illustrated boards, **2s.**; cloth limp, **2s. 6d.**

BUCHANAN'S (ROBERT) WORKS. Crown 8vo, cloth extra, **6s.** each.
SELECTED POEMS OF ROBERT BUCHANAN. With Frontispiece by T. DALZIEL.
THE EARTHQUAKE; or, Six Days and a Sabbath.
THE CITY OF DREAM: An Epic Poem. With Two Illustrations by P. MACNAB.
THE WANDERING JEW: A Christmas Carol. Second Edition.
THE OUTCAST: A Rhyme for the Time. With 15 Illustrations by RUDOLF BLIND,
PETER MACNAB, and HUME NISBET. Small demy 8vo, cloth extra, **8s.**
ROBERT BUCHANAN'S COMPLETE POETICAL WORKS. With Steel-plate Por-
trait. Crown 8vo, cloth extra, **7s. 6d.**

Crown 8vo, cloth extra, **3s. 6d.** each; post 8vo, illustrated boards, **2s.** each.
THE SHADOW OF THE SWORD. | LOVE ME FOR EVER. Frontispiece.
A CHILD OF NATURE. Frontispiece. | ANNAN WATER. | FOXGLOVE MANOR
GOD AND THE MAN. With 11 Illus- | THE NEW ABELARD.
trations by FRED. BARNARD. | MATT: A Story of a Caravan. Front.
THE MARTYRDOM OF MADELINE. | THE MASTER OF THE MINE. Front.
With Frontispiece by A. W. COOPER. | THE HEIR OF LINNE.
THE WEDDING-RING. 2 vols., crown 8vo. *[Shortly*

BURTON (CAPTAIN).—THE BOOK OF THE SWORD: Being a
History of the Sword and its Use in all Countries, from the Earliest Times. By
RICHARD F. BURTON. With over 400 Illustrations. Square 8vo, cloth extra, **32s.**

BURTON (ROBERT).
THE ANATOMY OF MELANCHOLY: A New Edition, with translations of the
Classical Extracts. Demy 8vo, cloth extra, **7s. 6d.**
MELANCHOLY ANATOMISED Being an Abridgment, for popular use, of BURTON'S
ANATOMY OF MELANCHOLY. Post 8vo, cloth limp, **2s. 6d.**

CAINE (T. HALL), NOVELS BY. Crown 8vo, cloth extra, **3s. 6d.** each;
post 8vo, illustrated boards, **2s.** each; cloth limp, **2s. 6d.** each.
SHADOW OF A CRIME. | A SON OF HAGAR. | THE DEEMSTER.

CAMERON (COMMANDER).—THE CRUISE OF THE "BLACK
PRINCE" PRIVATEER. By V. LOVETT CAMERON, R.N., C.B. With Two Illustrations by P. MACNAB. Crown 8vo, cloth extra, **5s.**; post 8vo, illustrated boards, **2s.**

CAMERON (MRS. H. LOVETT), NOVELS BY. Post 8vo, illust. bds., **2s.** each.
JULIET'S GUARDIAN | DECEIVERS EVER.

CARLYLE (THOMAS) ON THE CHOICE OF BOOKS. With Life by R. H. SHEPHERD, and Three Illustrations. Post 8vo, cloth extra, **1s. 6d.**
CORRESPONDENCE OF THOMAS CARLYLE AND R. W. EMERSON, 1834 to 1872. Edited by C. E. NORTON. With Portraits. Two Vols., crown 8vo, cloth, **24s.**

CARLYLE (JANE WELSH), LIFE OF. By Mrs. ALEXANDER IRELAND. With Portrait and Facsimile Letter. Small demy 8vo, cloth extra, **7s. 6d.**

CHAPMAN'S (GEORGE) WORKS. Vol. I. contains the Plays complete, including the doubtful ones. Vol. II., the Poems and Minor Translations, with an Introductory Essay by ALGERNON CHARLES SWINBURNE. Vol. III., the Translations of the Iliad and Odyssey. Three Vols., crown 8vo, cloth extra, **6s.** each.

CHATTO AND JACKSON.—A TREATISE ON WOOD ENGRAVING. Historical and Practical. By WILLIAM ANDREW CHATTO and JOHN JACKSON. With an Additional Chapter by HENRY G. BOHN, and 450 fine Illusts. Large 4to, hf.-bd., **28s.**

CHAUCER FOR CHILDREN: A Golden Key. By Mrs. H. R. HAWEIS. With 8 Coloured Plates and 30 Woodcuts. Small 4to, cloth extra, **6s.**
CHAUCER FOR SCHOOLS. By Mrs. H. R. HAWEIS. Demy 8vo, cloth limp, **2s. 6d.**

CLARE.—FOR THE LOVE OF A LASS: A Tale of Tynedale. By AUSTIN CLARE. Post 8vo, picture boards, **2s.**; cloth limp, **2s. 6d.**

CLIVE (MRS. ARCHER), NOVELS BY. Post 8vo, illust. boards, **2s.** each PAUL FERROLL. | WHY PAUL FERROLL KILLED HIS WIFE.

CLODD.—MYTHS AND DREAMS. By EDWARD CLODD, F.R.A.S. Second Edition, Revised. Crown 8vo, cloth extra, **3s. 6d.**

COBBAN (J. MACLAREN), NOVELS BY.
THE CURE OF SOULS. Post 8vo, illustrated boards, **2s.**
THE RED SULTAN. Three Vols., crown 8vo.

COLEMAN (JOHN), WORKS BY.
PLAYERS AND PLAYWRIGHTS I HAVE KNOWN. Two Vols., 8vo, cloth, **24s.**
CURLY: An Actor's Story. With 21 Illusts. by J. C. DOLLMAN. Cr. 8vo, cl., **1s. 6d.**

COLERIDGE.—THE SEVEN SLEEPERS OF EPHESUS. By M. E. COLERIDGE. Fcap. 8vo, cloth, **1s. 6d.**

COLLINS (C. ALLSTON).—THE BAR SINISTER. Post 8vo, **2s.**

COLLINS (MORTIMER AND FRANCES), NOVELS BY.
Crown 8vo, cloth extra, **3s. 6d.** each; post 8vo, illustrated boards, **2s.** each.
FROM MIDNIGHT TO MIDNIGHT. | BLACKSMITH AND SCHOLAR.
TRANSMIGRATION. | YOU PLAY ME FALSE. | A VILLAGE COMEDY.
Post 8vo, illustrated boards, **2s.** each.
SWEET ANNE PAGE. | FIGHT WITH FORTUNE. | SWEET & TWENTY. | FRANCES.

COLLINS (WILKIE), NOVELS BY.
Cr. 8vo, cl. ex., **3s. 6d.** each; post 8vo, illust. bds., **2s.** each; cl. limp, **2s. 6d.** each.
ANTONINA. With a Frontispiece by Sir JOHN GILBERT, R.A.
BASIL. Illustrated by Sir JOHN GILBERT, R.A., and J. MAHONEY.
HIDE AND SEEK. Illustrated by Sir JOHN GILBERT, R.A., and J. MAHONEY.
AFTER DARK. Illustrations by A. B. HOUGHTON. | THE TWO DESTINIES.
THE DEAD SECRET. With a Frontispiece by Sir JOHN GILBERT, R.A.
QUEEN OF HEARTS. With a Frontispiece by Sir JOHN GILBERT, R.A.
THE WOMAN IN WHITE. With Illusts. by Sir J. GILBERT, R.A., and F. A. FRASER.
NO NAME. With Illustrations by Sir J. E. MILLAIS, R.A., and A. W. COOPER.
MY MISCELLANIES. With a Steel-plate Portrait of WILKIE COLLINS.
ARMADALE. With Illustrations by G. H. THOMAS.
THE MOONSTONE. With Illustrations by G. DU MAURIER and F. A. FRASER.
MAN AND WIFE. With Illustrations by WILLIAM SMALL.
POOR MISS FINCH. Illustrated by G. DU MAURIER and EDWARD HUGHES.
MISS OR MRS.? With Illusts. by S. L. FILDES, R.A., and HENRY WOODS, A.R.A.
THE NEW MAGDALEN. Illustrated by G. DU MAURIER and C. S. REINHARDT.
THE FROZEN DEEP. Illustrated by G. DU MAURIER and J. MAHONEY.
THE LAW AND THE LADY. Illusts. by S. L. FILDES, R.A., and SYDNEY HALL.
THE HAUNTED HOTEL. Illustrated by ARTHUR HOPKINS.
THE FALLEN LEAVES. | HEART AND SCIENCE. | THE EVIL GENIUS.
JEZEBEL'S DAUGHTER. | "I SAY NO." | LITTLE NOVELS.
THE BLACK ROBE. | A ROGUE'S LIFE. | THE LEGACY OF CAIN.
BLIND LOVE. With Preface by WALTER BESANT, and Illusts. by A. FORESTIER

COLLINS (JOHN CHURTON, M.A.), BOOKS BY.
ILLUSTRATIONS OF TENNYSON. Crown 8vo, cloth extra, **6s.**
JONATHAN SWIFT: A Biographical and Critical Study. Cr. 8vo, cl. ex., **8s.** [Shortly

COLMAN'S HUMOROUS WORKS: "Broad Grins," "My Nightgown and Slippers," and other Humorous Works of GEORGE COLMAN. With Life by G. B. BUCKSTONE, and Frontispiece by HOGARTH. Crown 8vo, cloth extra, **7s. 6d.**

COLMORE.—A VALLEY OF SHADOWS. By G. COLMORE, Author of "A Conspiracy of Silence." Two Vols., crown 8vo.

COLQUHOUN.—EVERY INCH A SOLDIER: A Novel. By M. J. COLQUHOUN. Post 8vo, illustrated boards, **2s.**

CONVALESCENT COOKERY: A Family Handbook. By CATHERINE RYAN. Crown 8vo, **1s.**; cloth limp, **1s. 6d.**

CONWAY (MONCURE D.), WORKS BY.
DEMONOLOGY AND DEVIL-LORE. 65 Illustrations. Two Vols., 8vo, cloth **28s.**
A NECKLACE OF STORIES. 25 Illusts. by W. J. HENNESSY. Sq. 8vo, cloth, **6s.**
PINE AND PALM: A Novel. Two Vols., crown 8vo, cloth extra, **21s.**
GEORGE WASHINGTON'S RULES OF CIVILITY. Fcap. 8vo, Jap. vellum, **2s. 6d.**

COOK (DUTTON), NOVELS BY.
PAUL FOSTER'S DAUGHTER. Cr. 8vo, cl. ex., **3s. 6d.**; post 8vo, illust. boards, **2s.**
LEO. Post 8vo, illustrated boards, **2s.**

COOPER (EDWARD H.)—GEOFFORY HAMILTON. Two Vols.

CORNWALL.—POPULAR ROMANCES OF THE WEST OF ENG-LAND; or, The Drolls, Traditions, and Superstitions of Old Cornwall. Collected by ROBERT HUNT, F.R.S. Two Steel-plates by GEO. CRUIKSHANK. Cr. 8vo, cl., **7s. 6d.**

COTES.—TWO GIRLS ON A BARGE. By V. CECIL COTES. With 44 Illustrations by F. H. TOWNSEND. Crown 8vo, cloth extra, **3s. 6d.**

CRADDOCK.—THE PROPHET OF THE GREAT SMOKY MOUN-TAINS. By CHARLES EGBERT CRADDOCK. Post 8vo, illust. bds., **2s.**; cl. limp, **2s. 6d.**

CRIM.—ADVENTURES OF A FAIR REBEL. By MATT CRIM. With a Frontispiece. Crown 8vo, cloth extra, **3s. 6d.**; post 8vo, illustrated boards, **2s.**

CROKER (B.M.), NOVELS BY. Crown 8vo, cloth extra, **3s. 6d.** each; post 8vo, illustrated boards, **2s.** each; cloth limp, **2s. 6d.** each.
PRETTY MISS NEVILLE.	DIANA BARRINGTON.
A BIRD OF PASSAGE.	PROPER PRIDE.

A FAMILY LIKENESS. Three Vols., crown 8vo.

CRUIKSHANK'S COMIC ALMANACK. Complete in TWO SERIES: The FIRST from 1835 to 1843; the SECOND from 1844 to 1853. A Gathering of the BEST HUMOUR of THACKERAY, HOOD, MAYHEW, ALBERT SMITH, A'BECKETT, ROBERT BROUGH, &c. With numerous Steel Engravings and Woodcuts by CRUIK-SHANK, HINE, LANDELLS, &c. Two Vols., crown 8vo, cloth gilt, **7s. 6d.** each.
THE LIFE OF GEORGE CRUIKSHANK. By BLANCHARD JERROLD. With 84 Illustrations and a Bibliography. Crown 8vo, cloth extra, **7s. 6d.**

CUMMING (C. F. GORDON), WORKS BY. Demy 8vo, cl. ex., **8s. 6d.** each.
IN THE HEBRIDES. With Autotype Facsimile and 23 Illustrations.
IN THE HIMALAYAS AND ON THE INDIAN PLAINS. With 42 Illustrations.
TWO HAPPY YEARS IN CEYLON. With 28 Illustrations.
VIA CORNWALL TO EGYPT. With Photogravure Frontis. Demy 8vo, cl., **7s. 6d.**

CUSSANS.—A HANDBOOK OF HERALDRY; with Instructions for Tracing Pedigrees and Deciphering Ancient MSS., &c. By JOHN E. CUSSANS. With 408 Woodcuts and 2 Coloured Plates. New edition, revised, crown 8vo, cloth, **6s.**

CYPLES (W.)—HEARTS of GOLD. Cr. 8vo, cl., **3s. 6d.**; post 8vo, bds., **2s.**

DANIEL.—MERRIE ENGLAND IN THE OLDEN TIME. By GEORGE DANIEL. With Illustrations by ROBERT CRUIKSHANK. Crown 8vo, cloth extra, **3s. 6d.**

DAUDET.—THE EVANGELIST; or, Port Salvation. By ALPHONSE DAUDET. Crown 8vo, cloth extra, **3s. 6d.**; post 8vo, illustrated boards, **2s.**

DAVENANT.—HINTS FOR PARENTS ON THE CHOICE OF A PRO-FESSION FOR THEIR SONS. By F. DAVENANT, M.A. Post 8vo, **1s.**; cl., **1s. 6d.**

DAVIES (DR. N. E. YORKE-), WORKS BY.
Crown 8vo, **1s.** each: cloth limp, **1s. 6d.** each.
ONE THOUSAND MEDICAL MAXIMS AND SURGICAL HINTS.
NURSERY HINTS: A Mother's Guide in Health and Disease.
FOODS FOR THE FAT: A Treatise on Corpulency, and a Dietary for its Cure.
AIDS TO LONG LIFE. Crown 8vo, **2s.**; cloth limp, **2s. 6d.**

DAVIES' (SIR JOHN) COMPLETE POETICAL WORKS, for the first time Collected and Edited, with Memorial-Introduction and Notes, by the Rev. A. B. GROSART, D.D. Two Vols., crown 8vo, cloth boards, **12s.**

DAWSON.—THE FOUNTAIN OF YOUTH: A Novel of Adventure. By ERASMUS DAWSON, M.B. Edited by PAUL DEVON. With Two Illustrations by HUME NISBET. Crown 8vo, cloth extra, **3s. 6d.**; post 8vo, illustrated boards, **2s.**

DE GUERIN.—THE JOURNAL OF MAURICE DE GUERIN. Edited by G. S. TREBUTIEN. With a Memoir by SAINTE-BEUVE. Translated from the 20th French Edition by JESSIE P. FROTHINGHAM. Fcap, 8vo, half-bound, **2s. 6d.**

DE MAISTRE.—A JOURNEY ROUND MY ROOM. By XAVIER DE MAISTRE. Translated by HENRY ATTWELL. Post 8vo, cloth limp, **2s. 6d.**

DE MILLE.—A CASTLE IN SPAIN. By JAMES DE MILLE. With a Frontispiece. Crown 8vo, cloth extra, **3s. 6d.**; post 8vo, illustrated boards, **2s.**

DERBY (THE).—THE BLUE RIBBON OF THE TURF: A Chronicle of the RACE FOR THE DERBY, from Diomed to Donovan. With Brief Accounts of THE OAKS. By LOUIS HENRY CURZON Crown 8vo, cloth limp, **2s. 6d.**

DERWENT (LEITH), NOVELS BY. Cr.8vo,cl., **3s.6d.** ea.; post 8vo,bds.,**2s.**ea.
OUR LADY OF TEARS. | CIRCE'S LOVERS.

DICKENS (CHARLES), NOVELS BY. Post 8vo, illustrated boards, **2s.** each.
SKETCHES BY BOZ. | NICHOLAS NICKLEBY.
THE PICKWICK PAPERS. | OLIVER TWIST.
THE SPEECHES OF CHARLES DICKENS, 1841-1870. With a New Bibliography. Edited by RICHARD HERNE SHEPHERD. Crown 8vo, cloth extra, **6s.**—Also a SMALLER EDITION, in the *Mayfair Library*, post 8vo, cloth limp, **2s. 6d.**
ABOUT ENGLAND WITH DICKENS. By ALFRED RIMMER. With 57 Illustrations by C. A. VANDERHOOF, ALFRED RIMMER, and others. Sq. 8vo, cloth extra, **7s. 6d.**

DICTIONARIES.
A DICTIONARY OF MIRACLES: Imitative, Realistic, and Dogmatic. By the Rev E. C. BREWER, LL.D. Crown 8vo, cloth extra, **7s. 6d.**
THE READER'S HANDBOOK OF ALLUSIONS, REFERENCES, PLOTS, AND STORIES. By the Rev. E. C. BREWER, LL.D. With an ENGLISH BIBLIOGRAPHY Fifteenth Thousand. Crown 8vo, cloth extra, **7s. 6d.**
AUTHORS AND THEIR WORKS, WITH THE DATES. Cr. 8vo, cloth limp, **2s.**
FAMILIAR SHORT SAYINGS OF GREAT MEN. With Historical and Explanatory Notes. By SAMUEL A. BENT, A.M. Crown 8vo, cloth extra, **7s. 6d.**
SLANG DICTIONARY: Etymological, Historical, and Anecdotal. Cr. 8vo, cl., **6s. 6d.**
WOMEN OF THE DAY: A Biographical Dictionary. By F. HAYS. Cr. 8vo, cl., **5s.**
WORDS, FACTS, AND PHRASES: A Dictionary of Curious, Quaint, and Out-of-the-Way Matters. By ELIEZER EDWARDS. Crown 8vo, cloth extra, **7s. 6d.**

DIDEROT.—THE PARADOX OF ACTING. Translated, with Annotations, from Diderot's "Le Paradoxe sur le Comédien," by WALTER HERRIES POLLOCK. With a Preface by HENRY IRVING. Crown 8vo, parchment, **4s. 6d.**

DOBSON (AUSTIN), WORKS BY.
THOMAS BEWICK & HIS PUPILS. With 95 Illustrations. Square 8vo, cloth, **6s.**
FOUR FRENCHWOMEN. Fcap. 8vo, hf.-roxburghe, with a Portrait, **2s. 6d.**—Also, a Library Edition, with 4 Portraits, crown 8vo, buckram, gilt top, **6s.**
EIGHTEENTH CENTURY VIGNETTES. Crown 8vo, buckram, gilt top, **6s.**

DOBSON (W. T.)—POETICAL INGENUITIES AND ECCENTRICITIES. Post 8vo, cloth limp, **2s. 6d.**

DONOVAN (DICK), DETECTIVE STORIES BY.
Post 8vo. illustrated boards, **2s.** each; cloth limp, **2s. 6d.** each.
THE MAN-HUNTER. | WANTED! | A DETECTIVE'S TRIUMPHS.
CAUGHT AT LAST! | IN THE GRIP OF THE LAW.
TRACKED AND TAKEN. | FROM INFORMATION RECEIVED.
WHO POISONED HETTY DUNCAN? | LINK BY LINK. [*Shortly*.
Crown 8vo, cloth extra, **3s. 6d.** each; post 8vo, illustrated boards, **2s.** each;
cloth limp, **2s. 6d.** each.
THE MAN FROM MANCHESTER. With 23 Illustrations.
TRACKED TO DOOM. With 6 full-page Illustrations by GORDON BROWNE.

DOYLE (CONAN).—THE FIRM OF GIRDLESTONE. By A. CONAN DOYLE, Author of "Micah Clarke." Crown 8vo, cloth extra, **3s. 6d.**

DRAMATISTS, THE OLD. With Vignette Portraits. Cr. 8vo, cl. ex., **6s.** per Vol.
  BEN JONSON'S WORKS. With Notes Critical and Explanatory, and a Bio-
    graphical Memoir by WM. GIFFORD. Edited by Col. CUNNINGHAM. Three Vols.
  CHAPMAN'S WORKS. Complete in Three Vols. Vol. I. contains the Plays
    complete; Vol. II., Poems and Minor Translations, with an Introductory Essay
    by A. C. SWINBURNE ; Vol. III., Translations of the Iliad and Odyssey.
  MARLOWE'S WORKS. Edited, with Notes, by Col. CUNNINGHAM. One Vol.
  MASSINGER'S PLAYS. From GIFFORD'S Text. Edit by Col. CUNNINGHAM. OneVol.

DUNCAN (SARA JEANNETTE), WORKS BY.
            Crown 8vo, cloth extra, **7s. 6d.** each.
  A SOCIAL DEPARTURE: How Orthodocia and ; Went round the World by Our-
    selves. With 111 Illustrations by F. H. TOWNSEND.
  AN AMERICAN GIRL IN LONDON. With 80 Illustrations by F. H. TOWNSEND.
  THE SIMPLE ADVENTURES OF A MEMSAHIB. With 37 Illusts.   [*Shortly.*

DYER.—THE FOLK-LORE OF PLANTS. By Rev. T. F. THISELTON
  DYER, M.A. Crown 8vo, cloth extra, **6s.**

EARLY ENGLISH POETS. Edited, with Introductions and Annota-
  tions, by Rev. A. B. GROSART, D.D. Crown 8vo, cloth boards, **6s.** per Volume.
  FLETCHER'S (GILES) COMPLETE POEMS. One Vol.
  DAVIES' (SIR JOHN) COMPLETE POETICAL WORKS. Two Vols.
  HERRICK'S (ROBERT) COMPLETE COLLECTED POEMS. Three Vols.
  SIDNEY'S (SIR PHILIP) COMPLETE POETICAL WORKS. Three Vols.

EDGCUMBE.—ZEPHYRUS : A Holiday in Brazil and on the River Plate.
  By E. R. PEARCE EDGCUMBE. With 41 Illustrations. Crown 8vo, cloth extra, **5s.**

EDWARDES (MRS. ANNIE), NOVELS BY.
  A POINT OF HONOUR. Post 8vo, illustrated boards, **2s.**
  ARCHIE LOVELL. Crown 8vo, cloth extra, **3s. 6d.** ; post 8vo, illust. boards, **2s.**

EDWARDS (ELIEZER).—WORDS, FACTS, AND PHRASES : A
  Dictionary of Curious, Quaint, and Out-of-the-Way Matters. By ELIEZER EDWARDS.
  Crown 8vo, cloth extra, **7s. 6d.**

EDWARDS (M. BETHAM-), NOVELS BY.
  KITTY. Post 8vo, illustrated boards, **2s.** ; cloth limp, **2s. 6d.**
  FELICIA. Post 8vo, illustrated boards, **2s.**

EGERTON.—SUSSEX FOLK & SUSSEX WAYS. By Rev. J. C. EGERTON.
  With Introduction by Rev. Dr. H. WACE, and 4 Illustrations. Cr. 8vo, cloth ex., **5s.**

EGGLESTON (EDWARD).—ROXY : A Novel. Post 8vo, illust. bds., **2s.**

ENGLISHMAN'S HOUSE, THE : A Practical Guide to all interested in
  Selecting or Building a House ; with Estimates of Cost, Quantities, &c. By C. J.
  RICHARDSON. With Coloured Frontispiece and 600 Illusts. Crown 8vo, cloth, **7s. 6d.**

EWALD (ALEX. CHARLES, F.S.A.), WORKS BY.
  THE LIFE AND TIMES OF PRINCE CHARLES STUART, Count of Albany
    (THE YOUNG PRETENDER). With a Portrait. Crown 8vo, cloth extra, **7s. 6d.**
  STORIES FROM THE STATE PAPERS. With an Autotype. Crown 8vo, cloth, **6s.**

EYES, OUR : How to Preserve Them from Infancy to Old Age. By
  JOHN BROWNING, F.R.A.S. With 70 Illusts. Eighteenth Thousand. Crown 8vo, **1s.**

FAMILIAR SHORT SAYINGS OF GREAT MEN. By SAMUEL ARTHUR
  BENT, A.M. Fifth Edition, Revised and Enlarged. Crown 8vo, cloth extra, **7s. 6d.**

FARADAY (MICHAEL), WORKS BY. Post 8vo, cloth extra, **4s. 6d.** each.
  THE CHEMICAL HISTORY OF A CANDLE: Lectures delivered before a Juvenile
    Audience. Edited by WILLIAM CROOKES. F.C.S. With numerous Illustrations.
  ON THE VARIOUS FORCES OF NATURE, AND THEIR RELATIONS TO
    EACH OTHER. Edited by WILLIAM CROOKES, F.C.S. With Illustrations.

FARRER (J. ANSON), WORKS BY.
  MILITARY MANNERS AND CUSTOMS. Crown 8vo, cloth extra, **6s.**
  WAR : Three Essays, reprinted from "Military Manners." Cr. 8vo, **1s.** ; cl., **1s. 6d.**

FENN (G. MANVILLE), NOVELS BY.
  THE NEW MISTRESS. Cr. 8vo, cloth extra, **3s. 6d.** ; post 8vo, illust. boards, **2s.**
  WITNESS TO THE DEED. Three Vo's, crown 8vo.

FIN-BEC.—THE CUPBOARD PAPERS: Observations on the Art of Living and Dining. By FIN-BEC. Post 8vo, cloth limp, **2s. 6d.**

FIREWORKS, THE COMPLETE ART OF MAKING; or, The Pyrotechnist's Treasury. By THOMAS KENTISH. With 267 Illustrations. Cr. 8vo, cl., **5s.**

FITZGERALD (PERCY, M.A., F.S.A.), WORKS BY.
THE WORLD BEHIND THE SCENES. Crown 8vo, cloth extra, **3s. 6d.**
LITTLE ESSAYS: Passages from Letters of CHARLES LAMB. Post 8vo, cl., **2s. 6d.**
A DAY'S TOUR: Journey through France and Belgium. With Sketches. Cr. 4to, **1s.**
FATAL ZERO. Crown 8vo, cloth extra, **3s. 6d.** : post 8vo, illustrated boards, **2s.**
Post 8vo, illustrated boards, **2s.** each.
BELLA DONNA. | LADY OF BRANTOME. | THE SECOND MRS. TILLOTSON.
POLLY. | NEVER FORGOTTEN. | SEVENTY-FIVE BROOKE STREET.
LIFE OF JAMES BOSWELL (of Auchinleck). With an Account of his Sayings, Doings, and Writings; and Four Portraits. Two Vols., demy 8vo, cloth, **24s.**

FLAMMARION.—URANIA: A Romance. By CAMILLE FLAMMARION. Translated by AUGUSTA RICE STETSON. With 87 Illustrations by DE BIELER, MYRBACH, and GAMBARD. Crown 8vo, cloth extra, **5s.**

FLETCHER'S (GILES, B.D.) COMPLETE POEMS: Christ's Victorie in Heaven, Christ's Victorie on Earth, Christ's Triumph over Death, and Minor Poems. With Notes by Rev. A. B. GROSART, D.D. Crown 8vo, cloth boards, **6s.**

FLUDYER (HARRY) AT CAMBRIDGE: A Series of Family Letters. Post 8vo, picture cover, **1s.**; cloth limp, **1s. 6d.**

FONBLANQUE (ALBANY).—FILTHY LUCRE. Post 8vo, illust. bds., **2s.**

FRANCILLON (R. E.), NOVELS BY.
Crown 8vo, cloth extra, **3s. 6d.** each; post 8vo, illustrated boards, **2s.** each.
ONE BY ONE. | QUEEN COPHETUA. | A REAL QUEEN. | KING OR KNAVE?
OLYMPIA. Post 8vo, illust. bds., **2s.** | ESTHER'S GLOVE. Fcap. 8vo, pict. cover, **1s.**
ROMANCES OF THE LAW. Crown 8vo, cloth, **6s.**; post 8vo, illust. boards, **2s.**
ROPES OF SAND. 3 vols., crown 8vo.

FREDERIC (HAROLD), NOVELS BY.
SETH'S BROTHER'S WIFE. Post 8vo, illustrated boards, **2s.**
THE LAWTON GIRL. Cr. 8vo, cloth ex., **6s.**; post 8vo, illustrated boards, **2s.**

FRENCH LITERATURE, A HISTORY OF. By HENRY VAN LAUN. Three Vols., demy 8vo, cloth boards, **7s. 6d.** each.

FRERE.—PANDURANG HARI; or, Memoirs of a Hindoo. With Preface by Sir BARTLE FRERE. Crown 8vo, cloth, **3s. 6d.**; post 8vo, illust. bds., **2s.**

FRISWELL (HAIN).—ONE OF TWO: A Novel. Post 8vo, illust. bds., **2s.**

FROST (THOMAS), WORKS BY. Crown 8vo, cloth extra, **3s. 6d.** each.
CIRCUS LIFE AND CIRCUS CELEBRITIES. | LIVES OF THE CONJURERS.
THE OLD SHOWMEN AND THE OLD LONDON FAIRS.

FRY'S (HERBERT) ROYAL GUIDE TO THE LONDON CHARITIES.
Showing their Name, Date of Foundation, Objects, Income, Officials, &c. Edited by JOHN LANE. Published Annually. Crown 8vo, cloth, **1s. 6d.**

GARDENING BOOKS. Post 8vo, **1s.** each; cloth limp, **1s. 6d.** each.
A YEAR'S WORK IN GARDEN AND GREENHOUSE: Practical Advice as to the Management of the Flower, Fruit, and Frame Garden. By GEORGE GLENNY.
HOUSEHOLD HORTICULTURE. By TOM and JANE JERROLD. Illustrated.
THE GARDEN THAT PAID THE RENT. By TOM JERROLD.
OUR KITCHEN GARDEN: The Plants we Grow, and How we Cook Them. By TOM JERROLD. Crown 8vo, cloth, 1s. 6d.
MY GARDEN WILD, AND WHAT I GREW THERE. By FRANCIS G. HEATH Crown 8vo, cloth extra, gilt edges, **6s.**

GARRETT.—THE CAPEL GIRLS: A Novel. By EDWARD GARRETT. Crown 8vo, cloth extra, **3s. 6d.**; post 8vo, illustrated boards, **2s.**

GENTLEMAN'S MAGAZINE, THE. 1s. Monthly. In addition to Articles upon subjects in Literature, Science, and Art, **"TABLE TALK"** by SYLVANUS URBAN, and **"PAGES ON PLAYS"** by JUSTIN H. McCARTHY, appear monthly. *** *Bound Volumes for recent years kept in stock, **8s. 6d.** each; Cases for binding, **2s.**

GENTLEMAN'S ANNUAL, THE. Published Annually in November. 1s.
The 1892 Annual, written by T. W. SPEIGHT. is entitled "**THE LOUDWATER TRAGEDY.**"

GERMAN POPULAR STORIES. Collected by the Brothers GRIMM and Translated by EDGAR TAYLOR. With Introduction by JOHN RUSKIN, and 22 Steel Plates after GEORGE CRUIKSHANK. Square 8vo, cloth, **6s. 6d.**; gilt edges, **7s. 6d.**

GIBBON (CHARLES), NOVELS BY.
Crown 8vo, cloth extra, **3s. 6d.** each; post 8vo, illustrated boards, **2s. each.**
ROBIN GRAY. | LOVING A DREAM. | THE GOLDEN SHAFT.
THE FLOWER OF THE FOREST. | OF HIGH DEGREE.

Post 8vo, illustrated boards, **2s.** each.
THE DEAD HEART. | IN LOVE AND WAR.
FOR LACK OF GOLD. | A HEART'S PROBLEM.
WHAT WILL THE WORLD SAY? | BY MEAD AND STREAM.
FOR THE KING. | A HARD KNOT. | THE BRAES OF YARROW.
QUEEN OF THE MEADOW. | FANCY FREE. | IN HONOUR BOUND.
IN PASTURES GREEN. | HEART'S DELIGHT. | BLOOD-MONEY.

GIBNEY (SOMERVILLE).—SENTENCED! Cr. 8vo, 1s. ; cl., 1s. 6d.

GILBERT (WILLIAM), NOVELS BY. Post 8vo, illustrated boards, **2s.** each.
DR. AUSTIN'S GUESTS. | JAMES DUKE, COSTERMONGER.
THE WIZARD OF THE MOUNTAIN.

GILBERT (W. S.), ORIGINAL PLAYS BY. Two Series, 2s. 6d. each.
The FIRST SERIES contains: The Wicked World—Pygmalion and Galatea—Charity—The Princess—The Palace of Truth—Trial by Jury.
The SECOND SERIES: Broken Hearts—Engaged—Sweethearts—Gretchen—Dan'l Druce—Tom Cobb—H.M.S. "Pinafore"—The Sorcerer—Pirates of Penzance.

EIGHT ORIGINAL COMIC OPERAS written by W. S. GILBERT. Containing: The Sorcerer—H.M.S. "Pinafore"—Pirates of Penzance—Iolanthe—Patience—Princess Ida—The Mikado—Trial by Jury. Demy 8vo, cloth limp, **2s. 6d.**
THE "GILBERT AND SULLIVAN" BIRTHDAY BOOK: Quotations for Every Day in the Year, Selected from Plays by W. S. GILBERT set to Music by Sir A. SULLIVAN. Compiled by ALEX. WATSON. Royal 16mo, Jap. leather, **2s. 6d.**

GLANVILLE (ERNEST), NOVELS BY.
Crown 8vo, cloth extra, **3s. 6d.** each; post 8vo, illustrated boards, **2s.** each.
THE LOST HEIRESS: A Tale of Love, Battle, and Adventure. With 2 Illusts.
THE FOSSICKER: A Romance of Mashonaland. With 2 Illusts. by HUME NISBET.

GLENNY.—A YEAR'S WORK IN GARDEN AND GREENHOUSE: Practical Advice to Amateur Gardeners as to the Management of the Flower, Fruit, and Frame Garden. By GEORGE GLENNY. Post 8vo, **1s.**; cloth limp, **1s. 6d.**

GODWIN.—LIVES OF THE NECROMANCERS. By WILLIAM GODWIN. Post 8vo, cloth limp, **2s.**

GOLDEN TREASURY OF THOUGHT, THE: An Encyclopædia of QUOTATIONS. Edited by THEODORE TAYLOR. Crown 8vo, cloth gilt, **7s. 6d.**

GOODMAN.—THE FATE OF HERBERT WAYNE. By E. J. GOODMAN, Author of "Too Curious." Crown 8vo, cloth, **3s. 6d.**

GOWING.—FIVE THOUSAND MILES IN A SLEDGE: A Midwinter Journey Across Siberia. By LIONEL F. GOWING. With 30 Illustrations by C. J. UREN, and a Map by E. WELLER. Large crown 8vo, cloth extra, **8s.**

GRAHAM.—THE PROFESSOR'S WIFE: A Story By LEONARD GRAHAM. Fcap. 8vo, picture cover. **1s.**

GREEKS AND ROMANS, THE LIFE OF THE, described from Antique Monuments. By ERNST GUHL and W. KONER. Edited by Dr. F. HUEFFER. With 545 Illustrations. Large crown 8vo, cloth extra, **7s. 6d.**

GREENWOOD (JAMES), WORKS BY. Cr. 8vo, cloth extra, **3s. 6d.** each.
THE WILDS OF LONDON. | LOW-LIFE DEEPS.

GREVILLE (HENRY), NOVELS BY:
NIKANOR. Translated by ELIZA E. CHASE. With 8 Illustrations. Crown 8vo, cloth extra, **6s.**; post 8vo, illustrated boards, **2s.**
A NOBLE WOMAN. Crown 8vo, cloth extra, **5s.**; post 8vo, illustrated boards, **2s.**

GRIFFITH.—CORINTHIA MARAZION: A Novel. By CECIL GRIFFITH, Author of "Victory Deane," &c. Crown 8vo, cloth extra, **3s. 6d.**

HABBERTON (JOHN, Author of "Helen's Babies"), **NOVELS BY.**
Post 8vo, illustrated boards **2s.** each; cloth limp, **2s. 6d.** each.
BRUETON'S BAYOU. | COUNTRY LUCK.

HAIR, THE: Its Treatment in Health, Weakness, and Disease. Translated from the German of Dr. J. PINCUS. Crown 8vo, **1s.**; cloth, **1s. 6d.**

HAKE (DR. THOMAS GORDON), POEMS BY. Cr. 8vo, cl. ex., **6s.** each.
NEW SYMBOLS. | LEGENDS OF THE MORROW. | THE SERPENT PLAY.
MAIDEN ECSTASY. Small 4to, cloth extra, **8s.**

HALL.—SKETCHES OF IRISH CHARACTER. By Mrs. S. C. HALL.
With numerous Illustrations on Steel and Wood by MACLISE, GILBERT, HARVEY, and GEORGE CRUIKSHANK. Medium 8vo, cloth extra, **7s. 6d.**

HALLIDAY (ANDR.).—EVERY-DAY PAPERS. Post 8vo, bds., 2s.

HANDWRITING, THE PHILOSOPHY OF. With over 100 Facsimiles and Explanatory Text. By DON FELIX DE SALAMANCA. Post 8vo, cloth limp, **2s. 6d.**

HANKY-PANKY: Easy Tricks, White Magic, Sleight of Hand, &c.
Edited by W. H. CREMER. With 200 Illustrations. Crown 8vo, cloth extra, **4s. 6d.**

HARDY (LADY DUFFUS). — PAUL WYNTER'S SACRIFICE. 2s.

HARDY (THOMAS). — UNDER THE GREENWOOD TREE. By
THOMAS HARDY, Author of "Far from the Madding Crowd." With Portrait and 15 Illustrations. Crown 8vo, cloth extra, **3s. 6d.**; post 8vo, illustrated boards, **2s.**

HARPER.—THE BRIGHTON ROAD: Old Times and New on a Classic Highway. By CHARLES G. HARPER. With a Photogravure Frontispiece and 90 Illustrations. Demy 8vo, cloth extra, **16s.**

HARWOOD.—THE TENTH EARL. By J. BERWICK HARWOOD. Post 8vo, illustrated boards, **2s.**

HAWEIS (MRS. H. R.), WORKS BY. Square 8vo, cloth extra, **6s.** each.
THE ART OF BEAUTY. With Coloured Frontispiece and 91 Illustrations.
THE ART OF DECORATION. With Coloured Frontispiece and 74 Illustrations.
CHAUCER FOR CHILDREN. With 8 Coloured Plates and 30 Woodcuts.
THE ART OF DRESS. With 32 Illustrations. Post 8vo, **1s.**; cloth, **1s. 6d.**
CHAUCER FOR SCHOOLS. Demy 8vo. cloth limp, **2s. 6d.**

HAWEIS (Rev. H. R., M.A.).—AMERICAN HUMORISTS: WASHINGTON IRVING, OLIVER WENDELL HOLMES, JAMES RUSSELL LOWELL, ARTEMUS WARD, MARK TWAIN, and BRET HARTE. Third Edition. Crown 8vo, cloth extra, **6s.**

HAWLEY SMART.—WITHOUT LOVE OR LICENCE: A Novel. By
HAWLEY SMART. Crown 8vo, cloth extra, **3s. 6d.**; post 8vo, illustrated boards, **2s.**

HAWTHORNE. —OUR OLD HOME. By NATHANIEL HAWTHORNE.
Annotated with Passages from the Author's Note-book, and Illustrated with 31 Photogravures. Two Vols., crown 8vo, buckram, gilt top, **15s.**

HAWTHORNE (JULIAN), NOVELS BY.
Crown 8vo, cloth extra, **3s. 6d.** each; post 8vo, illustrated boards, **2s.** each.
GARTH. | ELLICE QUENTIN. | BEATRIX RANDOLPH. | DUST.
SEBASTIAN STROME. | DAVID POINDEXTER.
FORTUNE'S FOOL. | THE SPECTRE OF THE CAMERA.
Post 8vo, illustrated boards, **2s.** each.
MISS CADOGNA. | LOVE—OR A NAME.
MRS. GAINSBOROUGH'S DIAMONDS. Fcap. 8vo. illustrated cover, **1s.**

HEATH.—MY GARDEN WILD, AND WHAT I GREW THERE.
By FRANCIS GEORGE HEATH. Crown 8vo, cloth extra, gilt edges, **6s.**

HELPS (SIR ARTHUR), WORKS BY. Post 8vo. cloth limp, **2s. 6d.** each.
ANIMALS AND THEIR MASTERS. | SOCIAL PRESSURE.
IVAN DE BIRON: A Novel. Cr. 8vo, cl. extra, **3s. 6d.**; post 8vo, illust. bds., **2s.**

HENDERSON.—AGATHA PAGE: A Novel. By ISAAC HENDERSON.
Crown 8vo. cloth extra. **3s. 6d.**

HENTY.—RUJUB, THE JUGGLER. By G. A. HENTY. Three Vols.

HERMAN.—A LEADING LADY. By HENRY HERMAN, joint-Author of "The Bishops' Bible." Post 8vo. illustrated boards, **2s.**; cloth extra, **2s. 6d.**

HERRICK'S (ROBERT) HESPERIDES, NOBLE NUMBERS, AND COMPLETE COLLECTED POEMS. With Memorial-Introduction and Notes by the Rev. A. B. GROSART, D.D.; Steel Portrait, &c. Three Vols., crown 8vo, cl. bds., **18s.**

HERTZKA.—FREELAND: A Social Anticipation. By Dr. THEODOR HERTZKA. Translated by ARTHUR RANSOM. Crown 8vo, cloth extra, **6s.**

HESSE-WARTEGG.—TUNIS: The Land and the People. By Chevalier ERNST VON HESSE-WARTEGG. With 22 Illustrations. Cr. 8vo, cloth extra, **3s. 6d.**

HILL.—TREASON-FELONY: A Novel. By JOHN HILL. Two Vols.

HINDLEY (CHARLES), WORKS BY.
TAVERN ANECDOTES AND SAYINGS: Including Reminiscences connected with Coffee Houses, Clubs, &c. With Illustrations. Crown 8vo, cloth, **3s. 6d.**
THE LIFE AND ADVENTURES OF A CHEAP JACK. Cr. 8vo, cloth ex., **3s. 6d.**

HOEY.—THE LOVER'S CREED. By Mrs. CASHEL HOEY. Post 8vo, **2s.**

HOLLINGSHEAD (JOHN).—NIAGARA SPRAY. Crown 8vo, **1s.**

HOLMES.—THE SCIENCE OF VOICE PRODUCTION AND VOICE PRESERVATION. By GORDON HOLMES, M.D. Crown 8vo, **1s.**; cloth, **1s. 6d.**

HOLMES (OLIVER WENDELL), WORKS BY.
THE AUTOCRAT OF THE BREAKFAST-TABLE. Illustrated by J. GORDON THOMSON. Post 8vo, cloth limp, **2s. 6d.**—Another Edition, in smaller type, with an Introduction by G. A. SALA. Post 8vo, cloth limp, **2s.**
THE AUTOCRAT OF THE BREAKFAST-TABLE and THE PROFESSOR AT THE BREAKFAST-TABLE. In One Vol. Post 8vo, half-bound, **2s.**

HOOD'S (THOMAS) CHOICE WORKS, in Prose and Verse. With Life of the Author, Portrait, and 200 Illustrations. Crown 8vo, cloth extra, **7s. 6d.**
HOOD'S WHIMS AND ODDITIES. With 85 Illustrations. Post 8vo, printed on laid paper and half-bound, **2s.**

HOOD (TOM).—FROM NOWHERE TO THE NORTH POLE: A Noah's Arkæological Narrative. By TOM HOOD. With 25 Illustrations by W. BRUNTON and E. C. BARNES. Square 8vo, cloth extra, gilt edges, **6s.**

HOOK'S (THEODORE) CHOICE HUMOROUS WORKS; including his Ludicrous Adventures, Bons Mots, Puns, and Hoaxes. With Life of the Author, Portraits, Facsimiles, and Illustrations. Crown 8vo, cloth extra, **7s. 6d.**

HOOPER.—THE HOUSE OF RABY: A Novel. By Mrs. GEORGE HOOPER. Post 8vo, illustrated boards, **2s.**

HOPKINS.—"'TWIXT LOVE AND DUTY:" A Novel. By TIGHE HOPKINS. Post 8vo, illustrated boards, **2s.**

HORNE. — ORION: An Epic Poem. By RICHARD HENGIST HORNE. With Photographic Portrait by SUMMERS. Tenth Edition. Cr. 8vo, cloth extra, **7s.**

HORSE (THE) AND HIS RIDER: An Anecdotic Medley. By "THORMANBY." Crown 8vo, cloth extra, **6s.**

HUNGERFORD (MRS.), Author of "Molly Bawn," **NOVELS BY.**
Post 8vo, illustrated boards, **2s.** each; cloth limp, **2s. 6d.** each.
A MAIDEN ALL FORLORN. | IN DURANCE VILE. | A MENTAL STRUGGLE.
MARVEL. | A MODERN CIRCE.
LADY VERNER'S FLIGHT. Two Vols., crown 8vo.

HUNT.—ESSAYS BY LEIGH HUNT: A TALE FOR A CHIMNEY CORNER, &c. Edited by EDMUND OLLIER. Post 8vo, printed on laid paper and half-bd., **2s.**

HUNT (MRS. ALFRED), NOVELS BY.
Crown 8vo, cloth extra, **3s. 6d.** each; post 8vo, illustrated boards, **2s.** each.
THE LEADEN CASKET. | SELF-CONDEMNED. | THAT OTHER PERSON.
THORNICROFT'S MODEL. Post 8vo, illustrated boards, **2s.**
MRS. JULIET. Three Vols., crown 8vo.

HUTCHISON.—HINTS ON COLT-BREAKING. By W. M. HUTCHISON. With 25 Illustrations. Crown 8vo, cloth extra, **3s. 6d.**

HYDROPHOBIA: An Account of M. PASTEUR'S System; Technique of his Method, and Statistics. By RENAUD SUZOR, M.B. Crown 8vo, cloth extra, **6s.**

IDLER (THE): A Monthly Magazine. Edited by JEROME K. JEROME and ROBERT E. BARR. Profusely Illustrated. Sixpence Monthly.—Vols. I. and II. now ready, cloth extra, **5s.** each; Cases for Binding, **1s. 6d.**

INGELOW (JEAN).—FATED TO BE FREE. Post 8vo, illustrated bds., **2s.**

INDOOR PAUPERS. By ONE OF THEM. Crown 8vo, **1s.**; cloth, **1s. 6d.**

INNKEEPER'S HANDBOOK (THE) AND LICENSED VICTUALLER'S MANUAL. By J. TREVOR-DAVIES. Crown 8vo, **1s.**; cloth, **1s. 6d.**

IRISH WIT AND HUMOUR, SONGS OF. Collected and Edited by A. PERCEVAL GRAVES. Post 8vo, cloth limp, **2s. 6d.**

JAMES.—A ROMANCE OF THE QUEEN'S HOUNDS. By CHARLES JAMES. Post 8vo, picture cover, **1s.**; cloth limp, **1s. 6d.**

JANVIER.—PRACTICAL KERAMICS FOR STUDENTS. By CATHERINE A. JANVIER. Crown 8vo, cloth extra, **6s.**

JAY (HARRIETT), NOVELS BY. Post 8vo, illustrated boards, **2s.** each.
THE DARK COLLEEN. | THE QUEEN OF CONNAUGHT.

JEFFERIES (RICHARD), WORKS BY. Post 8vo, cloth limp, **2s. 6d.** each.
NATURE NEAR LONDON. | THE LIFE OF THE FIELDS. | THE OPEN AIR.
*** Also the HAND-MADE PAPER EDITION, crown 8vo, buckram, gilt top, **6s.** each.
THE EULOGY OF RICHARD JEFFERIES. By WALTER BESANT. Second Edition. With a Photograph Portrait. Crown 8vo, cloth extra, **6s.**

JENNINGS (H. J.), WORKS BY.
CURIOSITIES OF CRITICISM. Post 8vo, cloth limp, **2s. 6d.**
LORD TENNYSON: A Biographical Sketch. With a Photograph. Cr. 8vo, cl., **6s.**

JEROME.—STAGELAND. By JEROME K. JEROME. With 64 Illustrations by J. BERNARD PARTRIDGE. Square 8vo, picture cover, **1s.**; cloth limp, **2s.**

JERROLD.—THE BARBER'S CHAIR; & THE HEDGEHOG LETTERS. By DOUGLAS JERROLD. Post 8vo, printed on laid paper and half-bound, **2s.**

JERROLD (TOM), WORKS BY. Post 8vo, **1s.** each; cloth limp, **1s. 6d.** each.
THE GARDEN THAT PAID THE RENT.
HOUSEHOLD HORTICULTURE: A Gossip about Flowers. Illustrated.
OUR KITCHEN GARDEN: The Plants, and How we Cook Them. Cr. 8vo,cl.,**1s.6d.**

JESSE.—SCENES AND OCCUPATIONS OF A COUNTRY LIFE. By EDWARD JESSE. Post 8vo, cloth limp, **2s.**

JONES (WILLIAM, F.S.A.), WORKS BY. Cr.8vo, cl. extra, **7s. 6d.** each.
FINGER-RING LORE: Historical, Legendary, and Anecdotal. With nearly 300 Illustrations. Second Edition, Revised and Enlarged.
CREDULITIES, PAST AND PRESENT. Including the Sea and Seamen, Miners, Talismans, Word and Letter Divination, Exorcising and Blessing of Animals, Birds, Eggs, Luck, &c. With an Etched Frontispiece.
CROWNS AND CORONATIONS: A History of Regalia. With 100 Illustrations.

JONSON'S (BEN) WORKS. With Notes Critical and Explanatory, and a Biographical Memoir by WILLIAM GIFFORD. Edited by Colonel CUNNINGHAM. Three Vols., crown 8vo, cloth extra, **6s.** each.

JOSEPHUS, THE COMPLETE WORKS OF. Translated by WHISTON. Containing "The Antiquities of the Jews" and "The Wars of the Jews." With 52 Illustrations and Maps. Two Vols., demy 8vo, half-bound, **12s. 6d.**

KEMPT.—PENCIL AND PALETTE: Chapters on Art and Artists. By ROBERT KEMPT. Post 8vo, cloth limp, **2s. 6d.**

KERSHAW. — COLONIAL FACTS AND FICTIONS: Humorous Sketches. By MARK KERSHAW. Post 8vo, illustrated boards, **2s.**; cloth, **2s. 6d.**

KEYSER. — CUT BY THE MESS: A Novel. By ARTHUR KEYSER. Crown 8vo, picture cover, **1s.**; cloth limp, **1s. 6d.**

KING (R. ASHE), NOVELS BY. Cr. 8vo, cl., **3s. 6d.** ea.; post 8vo, bds., **2s.** ea.
A DRAWN GAME. | "THE WEARING OF THE GREEN."
Post 8vo, illustrated boards, **2s.** each.
PASSION'S SLAVE. | BELL BARRY.

KNIGHTS (THE) OF THE LION: A Romance of the Thirteenth Century. Edited, with an Introduction, by the MARQUESS of LORNE, K.T. Cr. 8vo, cl. ex., **6s.**

KNIGHT.—THE PATIENT'S VADE MECUM : How to Get Most Benefit from Medical Advice. By WILLIAM KNIGHT, M.R.C.S., and EDWARD KNIGHT, L.R.C.P. Crown 8vo, **1s.**; cloth limp, **1s. 6d.**

LAMB'S (CHARLES) COMPLETE WORKS, in Prose and Verse, including "Poetry for Children" and "Prince Dorus." Edited, with Notes and Introduction, by R. H. SHEPHERD. With Two Portraits and Facsimile of a page of the "Essay on Roast Pig." Crown 8vo, half-bound, **7s. 6d.**
THE ESSAYS OF ELIA. Post 8vo, printed on laid paper and half-bound, **2s.**
LITTLE ESSAYS: Sketches and Characters by CHARLES LAMB, selected from his Letters by PERCY FITZGERALD. Post 8vo, cloth limp, **2s. 6d.**
THE DRAMATIC ESSAYS OF CHARLES LAMB. With Introduction and Notes by BRANDER MATTHEWS, and Steel-plate Portrait. Fcap. 8vo, hf.-bd., **2s. 6d.**

LANDOR.—CITATION AND EXAMINATION OF WILLIAM SHAKS-PEARE, &c., before Sir THOMAS LUCY, touching Deer-stealing, 19th September, 1582. To which is added, **A CONFERENCE OF MASTER EDMUND SPENSER** with the Earl of Essex, touching the State of Ireland, 1595. By WALTER SAVAGE LANDOR. Fcap. 8vo, half-Roxburghe, **2s. 6d.**

LANE.—THE THOUSAND AND ONE NIGHTS, commonly called in England **THE ARABIAN NIGHTS' ENTERTAINMENTS.** Translated from the Arabic, with Notes, by EDWARD WILLIAM LANE. Illustrated by many hundred Engravings from Designs by HARVEY. Edited by EDWARD STANLEY POOLE. With a Preface by STANLEY LANE-POOLE. Three Vols., demy 8vo, cloth extra, **7s. 6d.** each.

LARWOOD (JACOB), WORKS BY.
THE STORY OF THE LONDON PARKS. With Illusts. Cr. 8vo, cl. extra, **3s. 6d.**
ANECDOTES OF THE CLERGY: The Antiquities, Humours, and Eccentricities of the Cloth. Post 8vo, printed on laid paper and half-bound, **2s.**
Post 8vo, cloth limp, **2s. 6d.** each.
FORENSIC ANECDOTES. | **THEATRICAL ANECDOTES.**

LEIGH (HENRY S.), WORKS BY.
CAROLS OF COCKAYNE. Printed on hand-made paper, bound in buckram, **5s.**
JEUX D'ESPRIT. Edited by HENRY S. LEIGH. Post 8vo, cloth limp, **2s. 6d.**

LEYS (JOHN).—THE LINDSAYS : A Romance. Post 8vo, illust. bds., **2s.**

LIFE IN LONDON; or, The History of JERRY HAWTHORN and COR-INTHIAN TOM. With CRUIKSHANK's Coloured Illustrations. Crown 8vo, cloth extra, **7s. 6d.**   [*New Edition preparing.*

LINTON (E. LYNN), WORKS BY.   Post 8vo, cloth limp, **2s. 6d.** each.
WITCH STORIES. | **OURSELVES:** ESSAYS ON WOMEN.
Crown 8vo, cloth extra, **3s. 6d.** each; post 8vo, illustrated boards, **2s.** each.
SOWING THE WIND. | **UNDER WHICH LORD?**
PATRICIA KEMBALL. | **"MY LOVE!"** | **IONE.**
ATONEMENT OF LEAM DUNDAS. | **PASTON CAREW, Millionaire & Miser.**
THE WORLD WELL LOST.
Post 8vo, illustrated boards, **2s.** each.
THE REBEL OF THE FAMILY. | **WITH A SILKEN THREAD.**
FREESHOOTING : Extracts from the Works of Mrs. LYNN LINTON. Post 8vo, cloth, **2s. 6d.**

LONGFELLOW'S POETICAL WORKS. With numerous Illustrations on Steel and Wood. Crown 8vo, cloth extra, **7s. 6d.**

LUCY.—GIDEON FLEYCE : A Novel. By HENRY W. LUCY. Crown 8vo, cloth extra, **3s. 6d.**; post 8vo, illustrated boards, **2s.**

LUSIAD (THE) OF CAMOENS. Translated into English Spenserian Verse by ROBERT FFRENCH DUFF. With 14 Plates. Demy 8vo, cloth boards, **18s.**

MACALPINE (AVERY), NOVELS BY.
TERESA ITASCA. Crown 8vo, cloth extra, **1s.**
BROKEN WINGS. With 6 Illusts. by W. J. HENNESSY. Crown 8vo, cloth extra, **6s.**

MACCOLL (HUGH), NOVELS BY.
MR. STRANGER'S SEALED PACKET. Crown 8vo, cloth extra, **5s.** ; post 8vo, illustrated boards, **2s.**
EDNOR WHITLOCK. Crown 8vo, cloth extra, **6s.**

MACDONELL.—QUAKER COUSINS : A Novel. By AGNES MACDONELL. Crown 8vo, cloth extra, **3s. 6d.** ; post 8vo, illustrated boards, **2s.**

McCARTHY (JUSTIN, M.P.), WORKS BY.

A HISTORY OF OUR OWN TIMES, from the Accession of Queen Victoria to the General Election of 1880. Four Vols. demy 8vo, cloth extra, **12s.** each.—Also a POPULAR EDITION, in Four Vols., crown 8vo, cloth extra, **6s.** each.—And a JUBILEE EDITION, with an Appendix of Events to the end of 1886, in Two Vols., large crown 8vo, cloth extra, **7s. 6d.** each.

A SHORT HISTORY OF OUR OWN TIMES. One Vol., crown 8vo, cloth extra, **6s.** —Also a CHEAP POPULAR EDITION, post 8vo, cloth limp, **2s. 6d.**

A HISTORY OF THE FOUR GEORGES. Four Vols. demy 8vo, cloth extra, **12s.** each.   [Vols. I. & II. *ready.*

Cr. 8vo, cl. extra, **3s. 6d.** each : post 8vo, illust. bds., **2s.** each ; cl. limp, **2s. 6d.** each.

THE WATERDALE NEIGHBOURS.	**MISS MISANTHROPE.**
MY ENEMY'S DAUGHTER.	**DONNA QUIXOTE.**
A FAIR SAXON.	**THE COMET OF A SEASON.**
LINLEY ROCHFORD.	**MAID OF ATHENS.**
DEAR LADY DISDAIN.	**CAMIOLA:** A Girl with a Fortune.

THE DICTATOR. Three Vols., crown 8vo.   [*Shortly.*

"THE RIGHT HONOURABLE." By JUSTIN MCCARTHY, M.P., and Mrs. CAMPBELL-PRAED. Fourth Edition. Crown 8vo, cloth extra, **6s.**

McCARTHY (JUSTIN H.), WORKS BY.

THE FRENCH REVOLUTION. Four Vols., 8vo, **12s.** each. [Vols. I. & II. *ready.*

AN OUTLINE OF THE HISTORY OF IRELAND. Crown 8vo, **1s.** ; cloth, **1s. 6d**

IRELAND SINCE THE UNION : Irish History, 1798-1886. Crown 8vo, cloth, **6s.**

HAFIZ IN LONDON : Poems. Small 8vo, gold cloth, **3s. 6d.**

HARLEQUINADE : Poems. Small 4to, Japanese vellum, **8s.**

OUR SENSATION NOVEL. Crown 8vo, picture cover, **1s.** ; cloth limp, **1s. 6d.**

DOOM! An Atlantic Episode. Crown 8vo, picture cover, **1s.**

DOLLY : A Sketch. Crown 8vo, picture cover, **1s.** ; cloth limp, **1s. 6d.**

LILY LASS : A Romance. Crown 8vo, picture cover, **1s.** ; cloth limp, **1s. 6d.**

THE THOUSAND AND ONE DAYS : Persian Tales. Edited by JUSTIN H. MCCARTHY. With 2 Photogravures by STANLEY L. WOOD. Two Vols., crown 8vo, half-bound, **12s.**

MACDONALD (GEORGE, LL.D.), WORKS BY.

WORKS OF FANCY AND IMAGINATION. Ten Vols., cl. extra, gilt edges, in cloth case, **21s.** Or the Vols. may be had separately, in grolier cl., at **2s. 6d.** each.

Vol. I. WITHIN AND WITHOUT.—THE HIDDEN LIFE.

„ II. THE DISCIPLE.—THE GOSPEL WOMEN.—BOOK OF SONNETS.—ORGAN SONGS.

„ III. VIOLIN SONGS.—SONGS OF THE DAYS AND NIGHTS.—A BOOK OF DREAMS.—ROADSIDE POEMS.—POEMS FOR CHILDREN.

„ IV. PARABLES.—BALLADS.—SCOTCH SONGS.

„ V. & VI. PHANTASTES: A Faerie Romance. | Vol. VII. THE PORTENT.

„ VIII. THE LIGHT PRINCESS.—THE GIANT'S HEART.—SHADOWS.

„ IX. CROSS PURPOSES.—THE GOLDEN KEY.—THE CARASOYN.—LITTLE DAYLIGHT

„ X. THE CRUEL PAINTER.—THE WOW o' RIVVEN.—THE CASTLE.—THE BROKEN SWORDS.—THE GRAY WOLF.—UNCLE CORNELIUS.

POETICAL WORKS OF GEORGE MACDONALD. Collected and arranged by the Author. 2 vols., crown 8vo, buckram, **12s.**

A THREEFOLD CORD. Edited by GEORGE MACDONALD. Post 8vo, cloth, **5s.**

HEATHER AND SNOW : A Novel. 2 vols., crown 8vo.

MACGREGOR. — PASTIMES AND PLAYERS : Notes on Popular
Games. By ROBERT MACGREGOR. Post 8vo. cloth limp, **2s. 6d.**

MACKAY.—INTERLUDES AND UNDERTONES ; or, Music at Twilight.
By CHARLES MACKAY, LL.D. Crown 8vo, cloth extra, **6s.**

MACLISE PORTRAIT GALLERY (THE) OF ILLUSTRIOUS LITER-
ARY CHARACTERS : **85 PORTRAITS ;** with Memoirs — Biographical, Critical, Bibliographical, and Anecdotal—illustrative of the Literature of the former half of the Present Century, by WILLIAM BATES, B.A. Crown 8vo, cloth extra, **7s. 6d.**

MACQUOID (MRS.), WORKS BY. Square 8vo, cloth extra, **7s. 6d.** each.

IN THE ARDENNES. With 50 Illustrations by THOMAS R. MACQUOID.

PICTURES AND LEGENDS FROM NORMANDY AND BRITTANY. With 34 Illustrations by THOMAS R. MACQUOID.

THROUGH NORMANDY. With 92 Illustrations by T. R. MACQUOID, and a Map.

THROUGH BRITTANY. With 35 Illustrations by T. R. MACQUOID, and a Map.

ABOUT YORKSHIRE. With 67 Illustrations by T. R. MACQUOID.

Post 8vo, illustrated boards, **2s.** each,

THE EVIL EYE, and other Stories. | **LOST ROSE.**

MAGIC LANTERN, THE, and its Management: including full Practical Directions. By T. C. HEPWORTH. 10 Illustrations. Cr. 8vo, **1s.**; cloth, **1s. 6d.**

MAGICIAN'S OWN BOOK, THE: Performances with Cups and Balls, Eggs, Hats, Handkerchiefs, &c. All from actual Experience. Edited by W. H. CREMER. With 200 Illustrations. Crown 8vo, cloth extra, **4s. 6d.**

MAGNA CHARTA: An Exact Facsimile of the Original in the British Museum, 3 feet by 2 feet, with Arms and Seals emblazoned in Gold and Colours, **5s.**

MALLOCK (W. H.), WORKS BY.
> THE NEW REPUBLIC. Post 8vo, picture cover, **2s.**; cloth limp, **2s. 6d.**
> THE NEW PAUL & VIRGINIA: Positivism on an Island. Post 8vo, cloth, **2s. 6d.**
> POEMS. Small 4to, parchment, **8s.**
> IS LIFE WORTH LIVING? Crown 8vo, cloth extra, **6s.**
> A ROMANCE OF THE NINETEENTH CENTURY. Crown 8vo, cloth, **6s.**

MALLORY'S (SIR THOMAS) MORT D'ARTHUR: The Stories of King Arthur and of the Knights of the Round Table. (A Selection.) Edited by B. MONTGOMERIE RANKING. Post 8vo, cloth limp, **2s.**

MARK TWAIN, WORKS BY. Crown 8vo, cloth extra, **7s. 6d.** each.
> THE CHOICE WORKS OF MARK TWAIN. Revised and Corrected throughout by the Author. With Life, Portrait, and numerous Illustrations.
> ROUGHING IT, and INNOCENTS AT HOME. With 200 Illusts. by F. A. FRASER.
> MARK TWAIN'S LIBRARY OF HUMOUR. With 197 Illustrations.

Crown 8vo, cloth extra (illustrated), **7s. 6d.** each; post 8vo, illust. boards, **2s.** each.
> THE INNOCENTS ABROAD; or, New Pilgrim's Progress. With 234 Illustrations. (The Two-Shilling Edition is entitled MARK TWAIN'S PLEASURE TRIP.)
> THE GILDED AGE. By MARK TWAIN and C. D. WARNER. With 212 Illustrations.
> THE ADVENTURES OF TOM SAWYER. With 111 Illustrations.
> A TRAMP ABROAD. With 314 Illustrations.
> THE PRINCE AND THE PAUPER. With 190 Illustrations.
> LIFE ON THE MISSISSIPPI. With 300 Illustrations.
> ADVENTURES OF HUCKLEBERRY FINN. With 174 Illusts. by E. W. KEMBLE.
> A YANKEE AT THE COURT OF KING ARTHUR. With 220 Illusts. by BEARD.
> MARK TWAIN'S SKETCHES. Post 8vo, illustrated boards, **2s.**
> THE STOLEN WHITE ELEPHANT, &c. Cr. 8vo, cl., **6s.**; post 8vo, illust. bds., **2s.**

Crown 8vo, cloth extra, **3s. 6d.** each.
> THE AMERICAN CLAIMANT. With 81 Illustrations by HAL HURST, &c.
> THE £1,000,000 BANK-NOTE, and other New Stories.

MARLOWE'S WORKS. Including his Translations. Edited, with Notes and Introductions, by Col. CUNNINGHAM. Crown 8vo, cloth extra, **6s.**

MARRYAT (FLORENCE), NOVELS BY. Post 8vo, illust. boards, **2s.** each.
> A HARVEST OF WILD OATS. | FIGHTING THE AIR.
> OPEN! SESAME! | WRITTEN IN FIRE.

MASSINGER'S PLAYS. From the Text of WILLIAM GIFFORD. Edited by Col. CUNNINGHAM. Crown 8vo, cloth extra. **6s.**

MASTERMAN.—HALF-A-DOZEN DAUGHTERS: A Novel. By J. MASTERMAN. Post 8vo, illustrated boards, **2s.**

MATTHEWS.—A SECRET OF THE SEA, &c. By BRANDER MATTHEWS. Post 8vo, illustrated boards, **2s.**; cloth limp, **2s. 6d.**

MAYHEW.—LONDON CHARACTERS AND THE HUMOROUS SIDE OF LONDON LIFE. By HENRY MAYHEW. With Illusts. Crown 8vo, cloth, **3s. 6d.**

MENKEN.—INFELICIA: Poems by ADAH ISAACS MENKEN. With Illustrations by F. E. LUMMIS and F. O. C. DARLEY. Small 4to, cloth extra, **7s. 6d.**

MERRICK.—THE MAN WHO WAS GOOD. By LEONARD MERRICK, Author of "Violet Moses," &c. Post 8vo, illustrated boards, **2s.**

MEXICAN MUSTANG (ON A), through Texas to the Rio Grande. By A. E. SWEET and J. ARMOY KNOX. With 265 Illusts. Cr. 8vo, cloth extra, **7s. 6d.**

MIDDLEMASS (JEAN), NOVELS BY. Post 8vo, illust. boards, **2s.** each.
> TOUCH AND GO. | MR. DORILLION.

MILLER.—PHYSIOLOGY FOR THE YOUNG; or, The House of Life: Human Physiology, with its application to the Preservation of Health. By Mrs. F. FENWICK MILLER. With numerous Illustrations. Post 8vo, cloth limp, **2s. 6d.**

MILTON (J. L.), WORKS BY. Post 8vo, 1s. each; cloth, 1s. 6d. each.
THE HYGIENE OF THE SKIN. With Directions for Diet, Soaps, Baths, &c.
THE BATH IN DISEASES OF THE SKIN.
THE LAWS OF LIFE, AND THEIR RELATION TO DISEASES OF THE SKIN.
THE SUCCESSFUL TREATMENT OF LEPROSY. Demy 8vo, 1s.

MINTO (WM.)—WAS SHE GOOD OR BAD? Cr. 8vo, 1s. ; cloth, 1s. 6d.

MITFORD.—THE GUN-RUNNER: A Romance of Zululand. By
BERTRAM MITFORD. With Frontispiece by S. L. WOOD. Cr. 8vo, 3s. 6d. [Shortly.

MOLESWORTH (MRS.), NOVELS BY.
HATHERCOURT RECTORY. Post 8vo, illustrated boards, 2s.
THAT GIRL IN BLACK. Crown 8vo, cloth, 1s. 6d.

MOORE (THOMAS), WORKS BY.
THE EPICUREAN; and ALCIPHRON. Post 8vo, half-bound, 2s.
PROSE AND VERSE, Humorous, Satirical, and Sentimental, by THOMAS MOORE;
with Suppressed Passages from the MEMOIRS OF LORD BYRON. Edited by R.
HERNE SHEPHERD. With Portrait. Crown 8vo, cloth extra, 7s. 6d.

MUDDOCK (J. E.), STORIES BY.
STORIES WEIRD AND WONDERFUL. Post 8vo, illust. boards, 2s.; cloth, 2s. 6d.
THE DEAD MAN'S SECRET; or, The Valley of Gold. With Frontispiece by
F. BARNARD. Crown 8vo, cloth extra, 5s.; post 8vo, illustrated boards, 2s.
FROM THE BOSOM OF THE DEEP. Post 8vo, illustrated boards, 2s.
MAID MARIAN AND ROBIN HOOD: A Romance of Old Sherwood Forest. With
12 Illustrations by STANLEY L. WOOD. Crown 8vo, cloth extra, 5s.

MURRAY (D. CHRISTIE), NOVELS BY.
Crown 8vo, cloth extra, 3s. 6d. each; post 8vo, illustrated boards. 2s. each.

A LIFE'S ATONEMENT.	HEARTS.	BY THE GATE OF THE SEA.
JOSEPH'S COAT.	WAY OF THE WORLD	A BIT OF HUMAN NATURE.
COALS OF FIRE.	A MODEL FATHER.	FIRST PERSON SINGULAR
VAL STRANGE.	OLD BLAZER'S HERO.	CYNIC FORTUNE.

BOB MARTIN'S LITTLE GIRL. Crown 8vo, cloth extra, 3s. 6d.
TIME'S REVENGES. Three Vols., crown 8vo.

MURRAY (D. CHRISTIE) & HENRY HERMAN, WORKS BY.
ONE TRAVELLER RETURNS. Cr. 8vo, cl. extra, 6s.; post 8vo, illust. bds., 2s.
Crown 8vo, cloth extra, 3s. 6d. each; post 8vo, illustrated boards, 2s. each.
PAUL JONES'S ALIAS. With 13 Illustrations. | THE BISHOPS' BIBLE.

MURRAY (HENRY), NOVELS BY.
A GAME OF BLUFF. Post 8vo, illustrated boards, 2s.; cloth, 2s. 6d.
A SONG OF SIXPENCE. Post 8vo, cloth extra, 2s. 6d.

NEWBOLT.—TAKEN FROM THE ENEMY. By HENRY NEWBOLT.
Fcap. 8vo, cloth boards, 1s. 6d.

NISBET (HUME), BOOKS BY.
"BAIL UP!" Crown 8vo, cloth extra, 3s. 6d.; post 8vo, illustrated boards, 2s.
DR. BERNARD ST. VINCENT. Post 8vo, illustrated boards, 2s.
LESSONS IN ART. With 21 Illustrations. Crown 8vo, cloth extra, 2s. 6d.
WHERE ART BEGINS. With 27 Illusts. Square 8vo, cloth extra, 7s. 6d.

NOVELISTS.—HALF-HOURS WITH THE BEST NOVELISTS OF
THE CENTURY. Edit. by H. T. MACKENZIE BELL. Cr. 8vo, cl., 3s. 6d. [Preparing.

O'HANLON (ALICE), NOVELS BY. Post 8vo, illustrated boards, 2s. each.
THE UNFORESEEN. | CHANCE? OR FATE?

OHNET (GEORGES), NOVELS BY.
DOCTOR RAMEAU. 9 Illusts. by E. BAYARD. Cr. 8vo, cl., 6s.; post 8vo, bds., 2s.
A LAST LOVE. Crown 8vo, cloth, 5s.; post 8vo, boards, 2s.
A WEIRD GIFT. Crown 8vo, cloth, 3s. 6d.; post 8vo, boards, 2s.

OLIPHANT (MRS.), NOVELS BY. Post 8vo, illustrated boards, 2s. each.
THE PRIMROSE PATH. | THE GREATEST HEIRESS IN ENGLAND
WHITELADIES. With Illustrations by ARTHUR HOPKINS and HENRY WOODS,
A.R.A. Crown 8vo, cloth extra, 3s. 6d.; post 8vo, illustrated boards, 2s.

O'REILLY (HARRINGTON).—FIFTY YEARS ON THE TRAIL: Adventures of JOHN Y. NELSON. 100 Illusts. by P. FRENZENY. Crown 8vo, 3s. 6d.

O'REILLY (MRS.).—PHŒBE'S FORTUNES, Post 8vo, illust. bds., 2s.

OUIDA, NOVELS BY. Cr. 8vo, cl., **3s. 6d.** each; post 8vo, llust. bds., **2s. each.**

HELD IN BONDAGE.	FOLLE-FARINE.	MOTHS.
TRICOTRIN.	A DOG OF FLANDERS.	PIPISTRELLO.
STRATHMORE.	PASCAREL.	A VILLAGE COMMUNE.
CHANDOS.	TWO LITTLE WOODEN	IN MAREMMA.
CECIL CASTLEMAINE'S	SHOES.	BIMBI. | SYRLIN.
GAGE.	SIGNA.	WANDA.
IDALIA.	IN A WINTER CITY.	FRESCOES. | OTHMAR.
UNDER TWO FLAGS.	ARIADNE.	PRINCESS NAPRAXINE.
PUCK.	FRIENDSHIP.	GUILDEROY. | RUFFINO.

BIMBI. Presentation Edition, with Nine Illustrations by EDMUND H. GARRETT. Square 8vo, cloth, **5s.**

SANTA BARBARA, &c. Square 8vo, cloth, **6s.**; crown 8vo, cloth, **3s. 6d.**

WISDOM, WIT, AND PATHOS, selected from the Works of OUIDA by F. SYDNEY MORRIS. Post 8vo, cloth extra, **5s.** CHEAP EDITION, illustrated boards, **2s.**

PAGE (H. A.), WORKS BY.
THOREAU: His Life and Aims. With Portrait. Post 8vo, cloth limp, **2s. 6d.**
ANIMAL ANECDOTES. Arranged on a New Principle. Crown 8vo, cloth extra, **5s.**

PARLIAMENTARY ELECTIONS AND ELECTIONEERING, A HISTORY OF, from the Stuarts to Queen Victoria. By JOSEPH GREGO. A New Edition, with 93 Illustrations. Demy 8vo, cloth extra, **7s. 6d.**

PASCAL'S PROVINCIAL LETTERS. A New Translation, with Historical Introduction and Notes by T. M'CRIE, D.D. Post 8vo, cloth limp. **2s.**

PAUL.—GENTLE AND SIMPLE. By MARGARET A. PAUL. With Frontispiece by HELEN PATERSON. Crown 8vo, cloth, **3s. 6d.**; post 8vo, illust. boards, **2s.**

PAYN (JAMES), NOVELS BY.
Crown 8vo, cloth extra, **3s. 6d.** each; post 8vo, illustrated boards, **2s.** each.

LOST SIR MASSINGBERD.	A GRAPE FROM A THORN.
WALTER'S WORD.	FROM EXILE.
LESS BLACK THAN WE'RE	THE CANON'S WARD.
PAINTED.	THE TALK OF THE TOWN.
BY PROXY.	HOLIDAY TASKS.
HIGH SPIRITS.	GLOW-WORM TALES.
UNDER ONE ROOF.	THE MYSTERY OF MIRBRIDGE.
A CONFIDENTIAL AGENT.	THE WORD AND THE WILL.

Post 8vo, illustrated boards, **2s.** each.

HUMOROUS STORIES.	FOUND DEAD.
THE FOSTER BROTHERS.	GWENDOLINE'S HARVEST.
THE FAMILY SCAPEGRACE.	A MARINE RESIDENCE.
MARRIED BENEATH HIM.	MIRK ABBEY.|SOME PRIVATE VIEWS.
BENTINCK'S TUTOR.	NOT WOOED, BUT WON.
A PERFECT TREASURE.	TWO HUNDRED POUNDS REWARD.
A COUNTY FAMILY.	THE BEST OF HUSBANDS.
LIKE FATHER, LIKE SON.	HALVES. | THE BURNT MILLION.
A WOMAN'S VENGEANCE.	FALLEN FORTUNES.
CARLYON'S YEAR. CECIL'S TRYST.	WHAT HE COST HER.
MURPHY'S MASTER.	KIT: A MEMORY. | FOR CASH ONLY.
AT HER MERCY.	A PRINCE OF THE BLOOD.
THE CLYFFARDS OF CLYFFE.	SUNNY STORIES.

IN PERIL AND PRIVATION: Stories of MARINE ADVENTURE. With 17 Illustrations. Crown 8vo, cloth extra, **3s. 6d.**

NOTES FROM THE "NEWS." Crown 8vo, portrait cover, **1s.**; cloth, **1s. 6d.**

PENNELL (H. CHOLMONDELEY), WORKS BY. Post 8vo, cl., **2s. 6d.** each.
PUCK ON PEGASUS. With Illustrations.
PEGASUS RE-SADDLED. With Ten full-page Illustrations by G. DU MAURIER.
THE MUSES OF MAYFAIR. Vers de Société, Selected by H. C. PENNELL.

PHELPS (E. STUART), WORKS BY. Post 8vo, **1s.** each; cloth, **1s. 6d.** each.

BEYOND THE GATES. By the Author	AN OLD MAID'S PARADISE.
of " The Gates Ajar."	BURGLARS IN PARADISE.

JACK THE FISHERMAN. Illustrated by C. W. REED. Cr. 8vo, **1s.**; cloth, **1s. 6d,**

PIRKIS (C. L.), NOVELS BY.
TROOPING WITH CROWS. Fcap. 8vo, picture cover, **1s.**
LADY LOVELACE. Post 8vo, illustrated boards, **2s.**

PLANCHE (J. R.), WORKS BY.
THE PURSUIVANT OF ARMS. With Six Plates, and 209 Illusts. Cr. 8vo, cl. **7s. 6d.**
SONGS AND POEMS, 1819–1879. Introduction by Mrs. MACKARNESS. Cr. 8vo, cl., **6s.**

PLUTARCH'S LIVES OF ILLUSTRIOUS MEN. Translated from the
Greek, with Notes Critical and Historical, and a Life of Plutarch, by JOHN and
WILLIAM LANGHORNE. With Portraits. Two Vols., demy 8vo, half-bound, **10s. 6d.**

POE'S (EDGAR ALLAN) CHOICE WORKS, in Prose and Poetry. Introduction by CHAS. BAUDELAIRE, Portrait, and Facsimiles. Cr. 8vo, cloth, **7s. 6d.**
THE MYSTERY OF MARIE ROGET, &c. Post 8vo. illustrated boards, **2s.**

POPE'S POETICAL WORKS. Post 8vo, cloth limp, 2s.

PRAED (MRS. CAMPBELL), NOVELS BY. Post 8vo, illust. bds., **2s.** ea.
THE ROMANCE OF A STATION. | THE SOUL OF COUNTESS ADRIAN.
"THE RIGHT HONOURABLE." By Mrs. CAMPBELL PRAED and JUSTIN McCARTHY,
M.P. Crown 8vo, cloth extra, **6s.**

PRICE (E. C.), NOVELS BY.
Crown 8vo, cloth extra, **3s. 6d.** each; post 8vo, illustrated boards, **2s.** each.
VALENTINA. | THE FOREIGNERS. | MRS. LANCASTER'S RIVAL.
GERALD. Post 8vo, illustrated boards, **2s.**

PRINCESS OLGA.—RADNA; or, The Great Conspiracy of 1881. By
the Princess OLGA. Crown 8vo, cloth extra, **6s.**

PROCTOR (RICHARD A., B.A.), WORKS BY.
FLOWERS OF THE SKY. With 55 Illusts. Small crown 8vo, cloth extra, **3s. 6d.**
EASY STAR LESSONS. With Star Maps for Every Night in the Year. Cr. 8vo, **6s.**
FAMILIAR SCIENCE STUDIES. Crown 8vo, cloth extra, **6s.**
SATURN AND ITS SYSTEM. With 13 Steel Plates. Demy 8vo, cloth ex., **10s. 6d.**
MYSTERIES OF TIME AND SPACE. With Illustrations. Cr. 8vo, cloth extra, **6s.**
THE UNIVERSE OF SUNS. With numerous Illustrations. Cr. 8vo, cloth ex., **6s.**
WAGES AND WANTS OF SCIENCE WORKERS. Crown 8vo, **1s. 6d.**

PRYCE.—MISS MAXWELL'S AFFECTIONS. By RICHARD PRYCE.
Frontispiece by HAL LUDLOW. Cr. 8vo, cl., **3s. 6d.**; post 8vo, illust. boards., **2s.**

RAMBOSSON.—POPULAR ASTRONOMY. By J. RAMBOSSON, Laureate
of the Institute of France. With numerous Illusts. Crown 8vo, cloth extra, **7s. 6d.**

RANDOLPH.—AUNT ABIGAIL DYKES: A Novel. By Lt.-Colonel
GEORGE RANDOLPH, U.S.A. Crown 8vo, cloth extra, **7s. 6d.**

READE (CHARLES), NOVELS BY.
Crown 8vo, cloth extra, illustrated, **3s. 6d.** each; post 8vo, illust. bds., **2s.** each.
PEG WOFFINGTON. Illustrated by S. L. FILDES, R.A.—Also a POCKET EDITION,
set in New Type, in Elzevir style, fcap. 8vo, half-leather, **2s. 6d.**
CHRISTIE JOHNSTONE. Illustrated by WILLIAM SMALL.—Also a POCKET EDITION,
set in New Type, in Elzevir style, fcap. 8vo, half-leather, **2s. 6d.**
IT IS NEVER TOO LATE TO MEND. Illustrated by G. J. PINWELL.
COURSE OF TRUE LOVE NEVER DID RUN SMOOTH. Illust. HELEN PATERSON.
THE AUTOBIOGRAPHY OF A THIEF, &c. Illustrated by MATT STRETCH.
LOVE ME LITTLE, LOVE ME LONG. Illustrated by M. ELLEN EDWARDS.
THE DOUBLE MARRIAGE. Illusts. by Sir JOHN GILBERT, R.A., and C. KEENE.
THE CLOISTER AND THE HEARTH. Illustrated by CHARLES KEENE.
HARD CASH. Illustrated by F. W. LAWSON.
GRIFFITH GAUNT. Illustrated by S. L. FILDES, R.A., and WILLIAM SMALL.
FOUL PLAY. Illustrated by GEORGE DU MAURIER.
PUT YOURSELF IN HIS PLACE. Illustrated by ROBERT BARNES.
A TERRIBLE TEMPTATION. Illustrated by EDWARD HUGHES and A. W. COOPER.
A SIMPLETON. Illustrated by KATE CRAUFURD.
THE WANDERING HEIR. Illust. by H. PATERSON, S. L. FILDES, C. GREEN, &c.
A WOMAN-HATER. Illustrated by THOMAS COULDERY.
SINGLEHEART AND DOUBLEFACE. Illustrated by P. MACNAB.
GOOD STORIES OF MEN AND OTHER ANIMALS. Illust. by E. A. ABBEY, &c.
THE JILT, and other Stories. Illustrated by JOSEPH NASH.
A PERILOUS SECRET. Illustrated by FRED. BARNARD.
READIANA. With a Steel-plate Portrait of CHARLES READE.
BIBLE CHARACTERS: Studies of David, Paul, &c. Fcap. 8vo, leatherette, **1s.**
THE CLOISTER AND THE HEARTH. With an Introduction by WALTER BESANT.
Elzevir Edition. 4 vols., post 8vo, each with Front., cl. ex., gilt top, **14s.** the set.

SELECTIONS FROM THE WORKS OF CHARLES READE. Cr. 8vo, buckram, **6s.**

RIDDELL (MRS. J. H.), NOVELS BY.
Crown 8vo, cloth extra, **3s. 6d.** each; post 8vo, illustrated boards, **2s.** each.
THE PRINCE OF WALES'S GARDEN PARTY. | **WEIRD STORIES.**
Post 8vo, illustrated boards, **2s.** each.
THE UNINHABITED HOUSE. | **HER MOTHER'S DARLING.**
MYSTERY IN PALACE GARDENS. | **THE NUN'S CURSE.**
FAIRY WATER. | **IDLE TALES.**

RIMMER (ALFRED), WORKS BY. Square 8vo, cloth gilt, **7s. 6d.** each.
OUR OLD COUNTRY TOWNS. With 55 Illustrations.
RAMBLES ROUND ETON AND HARROW. With 50 Illustrations.
ABOUT ENGLAND WITH DICKENS. With 58 Illusts. by C. A. VANDERHOOF, &c.

RIVES (Amélie).—BARBARA DERING. By AMÉLIE RIVES, Author
of "The Quick or the Dead?" Crown 8vo, cloth extra, **3s. 6d.**

ROBINSON CRUSOE. By DANIEL DEFOE. (MAJOR'S EDITION.) With
57 Illustrations by GEORGE CRUIKSHANK. Post 8vo, half-bound, **2s.**

ROBINSON (F. W.), NOVELS BY.
WOMEN ARE STRANGE. Post 8vo, illustrated boards, **2s.**
THE HANDS OF JUSTICE. Cr. 8vo, cloth ex., **3s. 6d.**; post 8vo, illust. bds., **2s.**

ROBINSON (PHIL), WORKS BY. Crown 8vo, cloth extra, **6s.** each.
THE POETS' BIRDS. | **THE POETS' BEASTS.**
THE POETS AND NATURE: REPTILES, FISHES, AND INSECTS.

ROCHEFOUCAULD'S MAXIMS AND MORAL REFLECTIONS. With
Notes, and an Introductory Essay by SAINTE-BEUVE. Post 8vo, cloth limp, **2s.**

ROLL OF BATTLE ABBEY, THE : A List of the Principal Warriors
who came from Normandy with William the Conqueror, and Settled in this Country,
A.D. 1066–7. With Arms emblazoned in Gold and Colours. Handsomely printed, **5s.**

ROWLEY (HON. HUGH), WORKS BY. Post 8vo, cloth, **2s. 6d.** each.
PUNIANA: RIDDLES AND JOKES. With numerous Illustrations.
MORE PUNIANA. Profusely Illustrated.

RUNCIMAN (JAMES), STORIES BY. Post 8vo, bds., **2s.** ea.; cl., **2s. 6d.** ea.
SKIPPERS AND SHELLBACKS. | **GRACE BALMAIGN'S SWEETHEART.**
SCHOOLS AND SCHOLARS.

RUSSELL (W. CLARK), BOOKS AND NOVELS BY:
Cr. 8vo, cloth extra, **6s.** each; post 8vo, illust. boards, **2s.** each; cloth limp, **2s. 6d.** ea.
ROUND THE GALLEY-FIRE. | **A BOOK FOR THE HAMMOCK.**
IN THE MIDDLE WATCH. | **MYSTERY OF THE "OCEAN STAR."**
A VOYAGE TO THE CAPE. | **THE ROMANCE OF JENNY HARLOWE.**
Cr. 8vo, cl. extra, **3s. 6d.** ea.; post 8vo, illust. boards, **2s.** ea.; cloth limp, **2s. 6d.** ea.
AN OCEAN TRAGEDY. | **MY SHIPMATE LOUISE.**
ALONE ON A WIDE WIDE SEA.
ON THE FO'K'SLE HEAD. Post 8vo, illust. boards, **2s.**; cloth limp, **2s. 6d.**

SAINT AUBYN (ALAN), NOVELS BY.
Crown 8vo, cloth extra, **3s. 6d.** each; post 8vo, illust. boards, **2s.** each.
A FELLOW OF TRINITY. Note by OLIVER WENDELL HOLMES and Frontispiece.
THE JUNIOR DEAN.
Fcap. 8vo, cloth boards, **1s. 6d.** each.
THE OLD MAID'S SWEETHEART. | **MODEST LITTLE SARA.**
THE MASTER OF ST. BENEDICT'S. Two Vols., crown 8vo.

SALA (G. A.).—GASLIGHT AND DAYLIGHT. Post 8vo, boards, 2s.

SANSON.—SEVEN GENERATIONS OF EXECUTIONERS : Memoirs
of the Sanson Family (1688 to 1847). Crown 8vo, cloth extra, **3s. 6d.**

SAUNDERS (JOHN), NOVELS BY.
Crown 8vo, cloth extra, **3s. 6d.** each; post 8vo, illustrated boards, **2s.** each.
GUY WATERMAN. | **THE LION IN THE PATH.** | **THE TWO DREAMERS.**
BOUND TO THE WHEEL. Crown 8vo, cloth extra, **3s. 6d.**

SAUNDERS (KATHARINE), NOVELS BY.
Crown 8vo, cloth extra, **3s. 6d.** each; post 8vo, illustrated boards, **2s.** each.
MARGARET AND ELIZABETH. | **HEART SALVAGE.**
THE HIGH MILLS. | **SEBASTIAN.**
JOAN MERRYWEATHER. Post 8vo, illustrated boards, **2s.**
GIDEON'S ROCK. Crown 8vo, cloth extra, **3s. 6d.**

SCIENCE-GOSSIP. Edited by Dr. J. E. TAYLOR, F.L.S., &c. Devoted to Geology, Botany, Physiology, Chemistry, Zoology, Microscopy, Telescopy, Physiography, &c. **4d.** Monthly. Pts. 1 to 300, **8d.** each; Pts. 301 to date, **4d.** each. Vols. I. to XIX., **7s. 6d.** each; Vols. XX. to date, **5s.** each. Cases for Binding, **1s. 6d.**

SCOTLAND YARD, Past and Present: Experiences of 37 Years. By Ex-Chief-Inspector CAVANAGH. Post 8vo, illustrated boards, **2s.**; cloth, **2s. 6d.**

SECRET OUT, THE : One Thousand Tricks with Cards; with Entertaining Experiments in Drawing-room or "White Magic." By W. H. CREMER. With 300 Illustrations. Crown 8vo, cloth extra, **4s. 6d.**

SEGUIN (L. G.), WORKS BY.
THE COUNTRY OF THE PASSION PLAY (OBERAMMERGAU) and the Highlands of Bavaria. With Map and 37 Illustrations. Crown 8vo, cloth extra, **3s. 6d.**
WALKS IN ALGIERS. With 2 Maps and 16 Illusts. Crown 8vo, cloth extra. **6s.**

SENIOR (WM.).—BY STREAM AND SEA. Post 8vo, cloth, 2s. 6d.

SHAKESPEARE FOR CHILDREN: LAMB'S TALES FROM SHAKE-SPEARE. With Illustrations, coloured and plain, by J. MOYR SMITH. Cr. 4to, **6s.**

SHARP.—CHILDREN OF TO-MORROW : A Novel. By WILLIAM SHARP. Crown 8vo, cloth extra, **6s.**

SHARP, LUKE (ROBERT BARR), STORIES BY.
IN A STEAMER CHAIR. With 2 Illustrations. Crown 8vo, cloth extra, **3s. 6d.**
FROM WHOSE BOURNE, &c. With 47 Illustrations. *[Shortly.*

SHELLEY.—THE COMPLETE WORKS IN VERSE AND PROSE OF PERCY BYSSHE SHELLEY. Edited, Prefaced, and Annotated by R. HERNE SHEPHERD. Five Vols., crown 8vo, cloth boards, **3s. 6d.** each.
POETICAL WORKS, in Three Vols.:
  Vol. I. Introduction by the Editor; Posthumous Fragments of Margaret Nicholson; Shelley's Correspondence with Stockdale; The Wandering Jew; Queen Mab, with the Notes; Alastor, and other Poems; Rosalind and Helen; Prometheus Unbound; Adonais, &c.
  Vol. II. Laon and Cythna; The Cenci; Julian and Maddalo; Swellfoot the Tyrant; The Witch of Atlas; Epipsychidion; Hellas.
  Vol. III. Posthumous Poems; The Masque of Anarchy; and other Pieces.
PROSE WORKS, in Two Vols.:
  Vol. I. The Two Romances of Zastrozzi and St. Irvyne; the Dublin and Marlow Pamphlets; A Refutation of Deism; Letters to Leigh Hunt, and some Minor Writings and Fragments.
  Vol. II. The Essays; Letters from Abroad; Translations and Fragments, Edited by Mrs. SHELLEY. With a Bibliography of Shelley, and an Index of the Prose Works.

SHERARD (R. H.).—ROGUES : A Novel. Crown 8vo, **1s.**; cloth, **1s. 6d.**

SHERIDAN (GENERAL). — PERSONAL MEMOIRS OF GENERAL P. H. SHERIDAN. With Portraits and Facsimiles. Two Vols., demy 8vo, cloth, **24s.**

SHERIDAN'S (RICHARD BRINSLEY) COMPLETE WORKS. With Life and Anecdotes. Including his Dramatic Writings, his Works in Prose and Poetry, Translations, Speeches and Jokes. 10 Illusts. Cr. 8vo, hf.-bound, **7s. 6d.**
THE RIVALS, THE SCHOOL FOR SCANDAL, and other Plays. Post 8vo, printed on laid paper and half-bound. **2s.**
SHERIDAN'S COMEDIES: THE RIVALS and THE SCHOOL FOR SCANDAL. Edited, with an Introduction and Notes to each Play, and a Biographical Sketch, by BRANDER MATTHEWS. With Illustrations. Demy 8vo, half-parchment, **12s. 6d.**

SIDNEY'S (SIR PHILIP) COMPLETE POETICAL WORKS, including all those in "Arcadia." With Portrait, Memorial-Introduction, Notes, &c. by the Rev. A. B. GROSART, D.D. Three Vols., crown 8vo. cloth boards, **18s.**

SIGNBOARDS : Their History. With Anecdotes of Famous Taverns and Remarkable Characters. By JACOB LARWOOD and JOHN CAMDEN HOTTEN. With Coloured Frontispiece and 94 Illustrations. Crown 8vo, cloth extra, **7s. 6d.**

SIMS (GEORGE R.), WORKS BY.
Post 8vo, illustrated boards, **2s.** each; cloth limp, **2s. 6d.** each.
ROGUES AND VAGABONDS. | MARY JANE MARRIED.
THE RING O' BELLS. | TALES OF TO-DAY.
MARY JANE'S MEMOIRS. | DRAMAS OF LIFE. With 60 Illustrations.
TINKLETOP'S CRIME. With a Frontispiece by MAURICE GREIFFENHAGEN.
ZEPH: A Circus Story, &c.
    Crown 8vo, picture cover, **1s.** each; cloth, **1s. 6d.** each.
HOW THE POOR LIVE; and HORRIBLE LONDON.
THE DAGONET RECITER AND READER: being Readings and Recitations in Prose and Verse, selected from his own Works by GEORGE R. SIMS.
THE CASE OF GEORGE CANDLEMAS. | DAGONET DITTIES.

SISTER DORA: A Biography. By MARGARET LONSDALE. With Four Illustrations. Demy 8vo, picture cover, **4d.**; cloth, **6d.**

SKETCHLEY.—A MATCH IN THE DARK. By ARTHUR SKETCHLEY. Post 8vo, illustrated boards, **2s.**

SLANG DICTIONARY (THE): Etymological, Historical, and Anecdotal. Crown 8vo, cloth extra, **6s. 6d.**

SMITH (J. MOYR), WORKS BY.
THE PRINCE OF ARGOLIS. With 130 Illusts. Post 8vo, cloth extra, **3s. 6d.**
TALES OF OLD THULE. With numerous Illustrations. Crown 8vo, cloth gilt, **6s.**
THE WOOING OF THE WATER WITCH. Illustrated. Post 8vo, cloth, **6s.**

SOCIETY IN LONDON. By A FOREIGN RESIDENT. Crown 8vo, **1s.**; cloth, **1s. 6d.**

SOCIETY IN PARIS: The Upper Ten Thousand. A Series of Letters from Count PAUL VASILI to a Young French Diplomat. Crown 8vo, cloth, **6s.**

SOMERSET. — SONGS OF ADIEU. By Lord HENRY SOMERSET. Small 4to, Japanese vellum, **6s.**

SPALDING.—ELIZABETHAN DEMONOLOGY: An Essay on the Belief in the Existence of Devils. By T. A. SPALDING. LL.B. Crown 8vo, cloth extra, **5s.**

SPEIGHT (T. W.), NOVELS BY.
Post 8vo, illustrated boards, **2s.** each.
THE MYSTERIES OF HERON DYKE. | HOODWINKED; and THE SANDY-
BY DEVIOUS WAYS, &c. | CROFT MYSTERY. [TRAGEDY.
THE GOLDEN HOOP. | BACK TO LIFE. | THE LOUDWATER
Post 8vo, cloth limp, **1s. 6d.** each.
A BARREN TITLE. | WIFE OR NO WIFE?
THE SANDYCROFT MYSTERY. Crown 8vo, picture cover, **1s.**

SPENSER FOR CHILDREN. By M. H. TOWRY. With Illustrations by WALTER J. MORGAN. Crown 4to, cloth gilt, **6s.**

STARRY HEAVENS (THE): A POETICAL BIRTHDAY BOOK. Royal 16mo, cloth extra, **2s. 6d.**

STAUNTON.—THE LAWS AND PRACTICE OF CHESS. With an Analysis of the Openings. By HOWARD STAUNTON. Edited by ROBERT B. WORMALD. Crown 8vo, cloth extra, **5s.**

STEDMAN (E. C.), WORKS BY.
VICTORIAN POETS. Thirteenth Edition. Crown 8vo, cloth extra, **9s.**
THE POETS OF AMERICA. Crown 8vo, cloth extra, **9s.**

STERNDALE. — THE AFGHAN KNIFE: A Novel. By ROBERT ARMITAGE STERNDALE. Cr. 8vo, cloth extra, **3s. 6d.**; post 8vo, illust. boards, **2s.**

STEVENSON (R. LOUIS), WORKS BY. Post 8vo, cl. limp, **2s. 6d.** each.
TRAVELS WITH A DONKEY. Seventh Edit. With a Frontis. by WALTER CRANE.
AN INLAND VOYAGE. Fourth Edition. With a Frontispiece by WALTER CRANE.
Crown 8vo, buckram, gilt top, **6s.** each.
FAMILIAR STUDIES OF MEN AND BOOKS. Sixth Edition.
THE SILVERADO SQUATTERS. With a Frontispiece. Third Edition.
THE MERRY MEN. Third Edition. | UNDERWOODS: Poems. Fifth Edition.
MEMORIES AND PORTRAITS. Third Edition.
VIRGINIBUS PUERISQUE, and other Papers. Seventh Edition. | BALLADS.
ACROSS THE PLAINS, with other Memories and Essays.
NEW ARABIAN NIGHTS. Eleventh Edition. Crown 8vo, buckram, gilt top, **6s.**; post 8vo, illustrated boards, **2s.**
THE SUICIDE CLUB; and THE RAJAH'S DIAMOND. (From NEW ARABIAN NIGHTS.) With Six Illustrations by J. BERNARD PARTRIDGE. Crown 8vo, cloth extra, **5s.**
PRINCE OTTO. Sixth Edition. Post 8vo, illustrated boards, **2s.**
FATHER DAMIEN: An Open Letter to the Rev. Dr. Hyde. Second Edition. Crown 8vo, hand-made and brown paper, **1s.**

STODDARD. — SUMMER CRUISING IN THE SOUTH SEAS. By C. WARREN STODDARD. Illustrated by WALLIS MACKAY. Cr. 8vo, cl. extra, **3s. 6d.**

STORIES FROM FOREIGN NOVELISTS. With Notices by HELEN and ALICE ZIMMERN. Crown 8vo, cloth extra, **3s. 6d.**; post 8vo, illustrated boards, **2s.**

STRANGE MANUSCRIPT (A) FOUND IN A COPPER CYLINDER. With 19 Illustrations by GILBERT GAUL. Third Edition. Crown 8vo, cloth extra, 5s.

STRANGE SECRETS. Told by CONAN DOYLE, PERCY FITZGERALD, FLORENCE MARRYAT, &c. Cr. 8vo, cl. ex., Eight Illusts., 6s.; post 8vo, illust. bds., 2s.

STRUTT'S SPORTS AND PASTIMES OF THE PEOPLE OF ENGLAND; including the Rural and Domestic Recreations, May Games, Mummeries, Shows, &c., from the Earliest Period to the Present Time. Edited by WILLIAM HONE. With 140 Illustrations. Crown 8vo, cloth extra, 7s. 6d.

SUBURBAN HOMES (THE) OF LONDON : A Residential Guide. With a Map, and Notes on Rental, Rates, and Accommodation. Crown 8vo, cloth, 7s. 6d.

SWIFT'S (DEAN) CHOICE WORKS, in Prose and Verse. With Memoir, Portrait, and Facsimiles of the Maps in "Gulliver's Travels." Cr. 8vo, cl., 7s. 6d.
GULLIVER'S TRAVELS, and A TALE OF A TUB. Post 8vo, half-bound, 2s.
JONATHAN SWIFT: A Study. By J. CHURTON COLLINS. Cr. 8vo. cloth, 8s. [Shortly.

SWINBURNE (ALGERNON C.), WORKS BY.

SELECTIONS FROM POETICAL WORKS OF A. C. SWINBURNE. Fcap. 8vo, 6s.	ESSAYS AND STUDIES. Crown 8vo, 12s.
ATALANTA IN CALYDON. Crown 8vo, 6s.	ERECHTHEUS : A Tragedy. Crown 8vo, 6s.
CHASTELARD : A Tragedy. Crown 8vo, 7s.	SONGS OF THE SPRINGTIDES. Crown 8vo, 6s.
POEMS AND BALLADS. FIRST SERIES. Crown 8vo or fcap. 8vo, 9s.	STUDIES IN SONG. Crown 8vo, 7s.
	MARY STUART: A Tragedy. Crown 8vo, 8s.
POEMS AND BALLADS. SECOND SERIES. Crown 8vo or fcap. 8vo, 9s.	TRISTRAM OF LYONESSE. Crown 8vo, 9s.
	A CENTURY OF ROUNDELS. Small 4to, 8s.
POEMS AND BALLADS. THIRD SERIES. Crown 8vo, 7s.	A MIDSUMMER HOLIDAY. Crown 8vo, 7s.
	MARINO FALIERO: A Tragedy. Crown 8vo, 6s.
SONGS BEFORE SUNRISE. Crown 8vo, 10s. 6d.	A STUDY OF VICTOR HUGO. Crown 8vo, 6s.
BOTHWELL : A Tragedy. Crown 8vo, 12s. 6d.	M'SCELLANIES. Crown 8vo, 12s.
SONGS OF TWO NATIONS. Crown 8vo, 6s.	LOCRINE : A Tragedy. Crown 8vo, 6s.
GEORGE CHAPMAN. (See Vol. II. of G. CHAPMAN'S Works.) Crown 8vo, 6s.	A STUDY OF BEN JONSON. Crown 8vo, 7s.
	THE SISTERS : A Tragedy. Crown 8vo, 6s.

SYMONDS.—WINE, WOMEN, AND SONG : Mediæval Latin Students' Songs. With Essay and Trans. by J. ADDINGTON SYMONDS. Fcap. 8vo, parchment, 6s.

SYNTAX'S (DR.) THREE TOURS : In Search of the Picturesque, in Search of Consolation, and in Search of a Wife. With ROWLANDSON's Coloured Illustrations, and Life of the Author by J. C. HOTTEN. Crown 8vo. cloth extra, 7s. 6d.

TAINE'S HISTORY OF ENGLISH LITERATURE. Translated by HENRY VAN LAUN. Four Vols., small demy 8vo, cl. bds., 30s.—POPULAR EDITION, Two Vols., large crown 8vo, cloth extra. 15s.

TAYLOR'S (BAYARD) DIVERSIONS OF THE ECHO CLUB : Burlesques of Modern Writers. Post 8vo, cloth limp, 2s.

TAYLOR (DR. J. E., F.L.S.), WORKS BY. Cr. 8vo, cl. ex., 7s. 6d. each.
THE SAGACITY AND MORALITY OF PLANTS: A Sketch of the Life and Conduct of the Vegetable Kingdom. With a Coloured Frontispiece and 100 Illustrations.
OUR COMMON BRITISH FOSSILS, and Where to Find Them. 331 Illustrations.
THE PLAYTIME NATURALIST. With 366 Illustrations. Crown 8vo, cloth, 5s.

TAYLOR'S (TOM) HISTORICAL DRAMAS. Containing "Clancarty," "Jeanne Darc," "'Twixt Axe and Crown," "The Fool's Revenge," "Arkwright's Wife," "Anne Boleyn," "Plot and Passion." Crown 8vo, cloth extra, 7s. 6d.
⁎ The Plays may also be had separately, at 1s. each.

TENNYSON (LORD): A Biographical Sketch. By H. J. JENNINGS. With a Photograph-Portrait. Crown 8vo, cloth extra, 6s.—Cheap Edition, post 8vo, portrait cover, 1s.; cloth, 1s. 6d.

THACKERAYANA : Notes and Anecdotes. Illustrated by Hundreds of Sketches by WILLIAM MAKEPEACE THACKERAY. Crown 8vo, cloth extra, 7s. 6d.

THAMES.—A NEW PICTORIAL HISTORY OF THE THAMES. By A. S. KRAUSSE. With 340 Illustrations. Post 8vo, 1s.; cloth, 1s. 6d.

THIERS.—HISTORY OF THE CONSULATE & EMPIRE OF FRANCE UNDER NAPOLEON. By A. THIERS. Translated by D. FORBES CAMPBELL and JOHN STEBBING. New Edition, reset in a specially-cast type, with 36 Steel Plates. 12 vols, demy 8vo, cloth extra, 12s. each. (First Volume ready September next.)

THOMAS (BERTHA), NOVELS BY. Cr. 8vo, cl., 3s. 6d. ea.; post 8vo, 2s. ea.
THE VIOLIN-PLAYER. | PROUD MAISIE,
CRESSIDA. Post 8vo, illustrated boards, 2s.

THOMSON'S SEASONS, and CASTLE OF INDOLENCE. With Introduction by ALLAN CUNNINGHAM, and 48 Illustrations. Post 8vo, half-bound, **2s.**

THORNBURY (WALTER), WORKS BY. Cr. 8vo, cl. extra, **7s. 6d.** each.
THE LIFE AND CORRESPONDENCE OF J. M. W. TURNER. Founded upon Letters and Papers furnished by his Friends. With Illustrations in Colours.
HAUNTED LONDON. Edit. by E. WALFORD, M.A. Illusts. by F. W. FAIRHOLT, F.S.A.
Post 8vo, illustrated boards, **2s.** each.
OLD STORIES RE-TOLD. | TALES FOR THE MARINES.

TIMBS (JOHN), WORKS BY. Crown 8vo, cloth extra, **7s. 6d.** each.
THE HISTORY OF CLUBS AND CLUB LIFE IN LONDON: Anecdotes of its Famous Coffee-houses, Hostelries, and Taverns. With 42 Illustrations.
ENGLISH ECCENTRICS AND ECCENTRICITIES: Stories of Delusions, Impostures, Sporting Scenes, Eccentric Artists, Theatrical Folk, &c. 48 Illustrations.

TROLLOPE (ANTHONY), NOVELS BY.
Crown 8vo, cloth extra, **3s. 6d.** each; post 8vo, illustrated boards, **2s.** each.
THE WAY WE LIVE NOW. | MR. SCARBOROUGH'S FAMILY.
FRAU FROHMANN. | MARION FAY. | THE LAND-LEAGUERS.
Post 8vo, illustrated boards, **2s.** each.
KEPT IN THE DARK. | AMERICAN SENATOR.
GOLDEN LION OF GRANPERE. | JOHN CALDIGATE.

TROLLOPE (FRANCES E.), NOVELS BY.
Crown 8vo, cloth extra, **3s. 6d.** each; post 8vo, illustrated boards, **2s.** each.
LIKE SHIPS UPON THE SEA. | MABEL'S PROGRESS. | ANNE FURNESS.

TROLLOPE (T. A.).—DIAMOND CUT DIAMOND. Post 8vo, illust. bds., **2s.**

TROWBRIDGE.—FARNELL'S FOLLY: A Novel. By J. T. TROWBRIDGE. Post 8vo, illustrated boards, **2s.**

TYTLER (C. C. FRASER-).—MISTRESS JUDITH: A Novel. By C. C. FRASER-TYTLER. Crown 8vo, cloth extra, **3s. 6d.**; post 8vo, illust. boards, **2s.**

TYTLER (SARAH), NOVELS BY.
Crown 8vo, cloth extra, **3s. 6d.** each; post 8vo, illustrated boards, **2s.** each.
THE BRIDE'S PASS. | BURIED DIAMONDS.
LADY BELL. | THE BLACKHALL GHOSTS.
Post 8vo, illustrated boards, **2s.** each.
WHAT SHE CAME THROUGH. | BEAUTY AND THE BEAST.
CITOYENNE JACQUELINE. | DISAPPEARED.
SAINT MUNGO'S CITY. | THE HUGUENOT FAMILY.
NOBLESSE OBLIGE.

VILLARI.—A DOUBLE BOND. By LINDA VILLARI. Fcap. 8vo, picture cover. **1s.**

WALT WHITMAN, POEMS BY. Edited, with Introduction, by WILLIAM M. ROSSETTI. With Portrait. Cr. 8vo, hand-made paper and buckram, **6s.**

WALTON AND COTTON'S COMPLETE ANGLER; or, The Contemplative Man's Recreation, by IZAAK WALTON; and Instructions how to Angle for a Trout or Grayling in a clear Stream, by CHARLES COTTON. With Memoirs and Notes by Sir HARRIS NICOLAS, and 61 Illustrations. Crown 8vo, cloth antique, **7s. 6d.**

WARD (HERBERT), WORKS BY.
FIVE YEARS WITH THE CONGO CANNIBALS. With 92 Illustrations by the Author, VICTOR PERARD, and W. B. DAVIS. Third ed. Roy. 8vo, cloth ex., **14s.**
MY LIFE WITH STANLEY'S REAR GUARD. With a Map by F. S. WELLER, F.R.G.S. Post 8vo, **1s.**; cloth, **1s. 6d.**

WARNER.—A ROUNDABOUT JOURNEY. By CHARLES DUDLEY WARNER. Crown 8vo, cloth extra, **6s.**

WARRANT TO EXECUTE CHARLES I. A Facsimile, with the 59 Signatures and Seals. Printed on paper 22 in. by 14 in. **2s.**
WARRANT TO EXECUTE MARY QUEEN OF SCOTS. A Facsimile, including Queen Elizabeth's Signature and the Great Seal. **2s.**

WASSERMANN (LILLIAS), NOVELS BY.
THE DAFFODILS. Crown 8vo, **1s.**; cloth, **1s. 6d.**
THE MARQUIS OF CARABAS. By AARON WATSON and LILLIAS WASSERMANN, 3 vols., crown 8vo.

WALFORD (EDWARD, M.A.), WORKS BY.
WALFORD'S COUNTY FAMILIES OF THE UNITED KINGDOM (1893). Containing the Descent, Birth, Marriage, Education, &c., of 12,000 Heads of Families their Heirs, Offices, Addresses, Clubs, &c. Royal 8vo, cloth gilt, **50s.**
WALFORD'S WINDSOR PEERAGE, BARONETAGE, AND KNIGHTAGE (1893). Crown 8vo, cloth extra, **12s. 6d.**
WALFORD'S SHILLING PEERAGE (1893). Containing a List of the House of Lords, Scotch and Irish Peers, &c. 32mo, cloth, **1s.**
WALFORD'S SHILLING BARONETAGE (1893). Containing a List of the Baronets of the United Kingdom, Biographical Notices, Addresses, &c. 32mo, cloth, **1s.**
WALFORD'S SHILLING KNIGHTAGE (1893). Containing a List of the Knights of the United Kingdom, Biographical Notices, Addresses, &c. 32mo, cloth, **1s.**
WALFORD'S SHILLING HOUSE OF COMMONS (1893). Containing a List of all Members of the New Parliament, their Addresses, Clubs, &c. 32mo, cloth, **1s.**
WALFORD'S COMPLETE PEERAGE, BARONETAGE, KNIGHTAGE, AND HOUSE OF COMMONS (1893). Royal 32mo, cloth extra, gilt edges, **5s.**
TALES OF OUR GREAT FAMILIES. Crown 8vo, cloth extra, **3s. 6d.**

WEATHER, HOW TO FORETELL THE, WITH POCKET SPECTROSCOPE. By F. W. CORY. With 10 Illustrations. Cr. 8vo, **1s.**; cloth, **1s. 6d.**

WESTALL (William).—TRUST-MONEY. Three Vols., crown 8vo.

WHIST.—HOW TO PLAY SOLO WHIST. By ABRAHAM S. WILKS and CHARLES F. PARDON. New Edition. Post 8vo, cloth limp, **2s.**

WHITE.—THE NATURAL HISTORY OF SELBORNE. By GILBERT WHITE, M.A. Post 8vo, printed on laid paper and half-bound, **2s.**

WILLIAMS (W. MATTIEU, F.R.A.S.), WORKS BY.
SCIENCE IN SHORT CHAPTERS. Crown 8vo, cloth extra, **7s. 6d.**
A SIMPLE TREATISE ON HEAT. With Illusts. Cr. 8vo, cloth limp, **2s. 6d.**
THE CHEMISTRY OF COOKERY. Crown 8vo, cloth extra, **6s.**
THE CHEMISTRY OF IRON AND STEEL MAKING. Crown 8vo, cloth extra, **9s.**

WILLIAMSON (MRS. F. H.).—A CHILD WIDOW. Post 8vo, bds., **2s.**

WILSON (DR. ANDREW, F.R.S.E.), WORKS BY.
CHAPTERS ON EVOLUTION. With 259 Illustrations. Cr. 8vo, cloth extra, **7s. 6d.**
LEAVES FROM A NATURALIST'S NOTE-BOOK. Post 8vo, cloth limp, **2s. 6d.**
LEISURE-TIME STUDIES. With Illustrations. Crown 8vo, cloth extra, **6s.**
STUDIES IN LIFE AND SENSE. With numerous Illusts. Cr. 8vo, cl. ex., **6s.**
COMMON ACCIDENTS: HOW TO TREAT THEM. Illusts. Cr. 8vo, **1s.**; cl., **1s. 6d.**
GLIMPSES OF NATURE. With 35 Illustrations. Crown 8vo, cloth extra, **3s. 6d.**

WINTER (J. S.), STORIES BY. Post 8vo, illustrated boards, **2s.** each; cloth limp, **2s. 6d.** each.
CAVALRY LIFE. | **REGIMENTAL LEGENDS.**
A SOLDIER'S CHILDREN. With 34 Illustrations by E. G. THOMSON and E. STUART HARDY. Crown 8vo, cloth extra, **3s. 6d.**

WISSMANN.—MY SECOND JOURNEY THROUGH EQUATORIAL AFRICA. By HERMANN VON WISSMANN. With 92 Illusts. Demy 8vo, **16s.**

WOOD.—SABINA : A Novel. By Lady WOOD. Post 8vo, boards, **2s.**

WOOD (H. F.), DETECTIVE STORIES BY. Cr. 8vo, **6s.** ea.; post 8vo, bds. **2s.**
PASSENGER FROM SCOTLAND YARD. | **ENGLISHMAN OF THE RUE CAIN.**

WOOLLEY.—RACHEL ARMSTRONG; or, Love and Theology. By CELIA PARKER WOOLLEY. Post 8vo, illustrated boards, **2s.**; cloth, **2s. 6d.**

WRIGHT (THOMAS), WORKS BY. Crown 8vo, cloth extra, **7s. 6d.** each.
CARICATURE HISTORY OF THE GEORGES. With 400 Caricatures, Squibs, &c.
HISTORY OF CARICATURE AND OF THE GROTESQUE IN ART, LITERATURE, SCULPTURE, AND PAINTING. Illustrated by F. W. FAIRHOLT, F.S.A.

WYNMAN.—MY FLIRTATIONS. By MARGARET WYNMAN. With 13 Illustrations by J. BERNARD PARTRIDGE. Crown 8vo, cloth extra, **3s. 6d.**

YATES (EDMUND), NOVELS BY. Post 8vo, illustrated boards, **2s.** each.
LAND AT LAST. | **THE FORLORN HOPE.** | **CASTAWAY.**

ZOLA (EMILE), NOVELS BY. Crown 8vo, cloth extra, **3s. 6d.** each.
THE DOWNFALL. Translated by E. A. VIZETELLY. Third Edition.
THE DREAM. Translated by ELIZA CHASE. With 8 Illustrations by JEANNIOT.

LISTS OF BOOKS CLASSIFIED IN SERIES.

, *For fuller cataloguing, see alphabetical arrangement, pp. 1-25.*

THE MAYFAIR LIBRARY. Post 8vo, cloth limp, **2s. 6d.** per Volume.

A Journey Round My Room. By XAVIER DE MAISTRE.
Quips and Quiddities. By W. D. ADAMS.
The Agony Column of "The Times."
Melancholy Anatomised: Abridgment of "Burton's Anatomy of Melancholy."
The Speeches of Charles Dickens.
Poetical Ingenuities. By W. T. DOBSON.
The Cupboard Papers. By FIN-BEC.
W. S. Gilbert's Plays. FIRST SERIES.
W. S. Gilbert's Plays. SECOND SERIES.
Songs of Irish Wit and Humour.
Animals and Masters. By Sir A. HELPS.
Social Pressure. By Sir A. HELPS.
Curiosities of Criticism. H. J. JENNINGS.
Holmes's Autocrat of Breakfast-Table.
Pencil and Palette. By R. KEMPT.
Little Essays: from LAMB's Letters.

Forensic Anecdotes. By JACOB LARWOOD.
Theatrical Anecdotes. JACOB LARWOOD.
Jeux d'Esprit. Edited by HENRY S. LEIGH.
Witch Stories. By E. LYNN LINTON.
Ourselves. By E. LYNN LINTON.
Pastimes & Players. By R. MACGREGOR.
New Paul and Virginia. W. H. MALLOCK.
New Republic. By W. H. MALLOCK.
Puck on Pegasus. By H. C. PENNELL.
Pegasus Re-Saddled. By H. C. PENNELL.
Muses of Mayfair. Ed. H. C. PENNELL.
Thoreau: His Life & Aims. By H. A. PAGE.
Puniana. By Hon. HUGH ROWLEY.
More Puniana. By Hon. HUGH ROWLEY.
The Philosophy of Handwriting.
By Stream and Sea. By WM. SENIOR.
Leaves from a Naturalist's Note-Book. By Dr. ANDREW WILSON.

THE GOLDEN LIBRARY. Post 8vo, cloth limp, **2s.** per Volume.

Bayard Taylor's Diversions of the Echo Club.
Bennett's Ballad History of England.
Bennett's Songs for Sailors.
Godwin's Lives of the Necromancers.
Pope's Poetical Works.
Holmes's Autocrat of Breakfast Table.

Jesse's Scenes of Country Life.
Leigh Hunt's Tale for a Chimney Corner.
Mallory's Mort d'Arthur: Selections.
Pascal's Provincial Letters.
Rochefoucauld's Maxims & Reflections.

THE WANDERER'S LIBRARY. Crown 8vo, cloth extra, **3s. 6d.** each.

Wanderings in Patagonia. By JULIUS BEERBOHM. Illustrated.
Camp Notes. By FREDERICK BOYLE.
Savage Life. By FREDERICK BOYLE.
Merrie England in the Olden Time. By G. DANIEL. Illustrated by CRUIKSHANK.
Circus Life. By THOMAS FROST.
Lives of the Conjurers. THOMAS FROST.
The Old Showmen and the Old London Fairs. By THOMAS FROST.
Low-Life Deeps. By JAMES GREENWOOD.

Wilds of London. JAMES GREENWOOD.
Tunis. Chev. HESSE-WARTEGG. 22 Illusts.
Life and Adventures of a Cheap Jack.
World Behind the Scenes. P. FITZGERALD.
Tavern Anecdotes and Sayings.
The Genial Showman. By E. P. HINGSTON
Story of London Parks. JACOB LARWOOD.
London Characters. By HENRY MAYHEW.
Seven Generations of Executioners.
Summer Cruising in the South Seas. By C. WARREN STODDARD. Illustrated.

POPULAR SHILLING BOOKS.

Harry Fludyer at Cambridge.
Jeff Briggs's Love Story. BRET HARTE.
Twins of Table Mountain. BRET HARTE.
Snow-bound at Eagle's. By BRET HARTE.
A Day's Tour. By PERCY FITZGERALD.
Esther's Glove. By R. E. FRANCILLON.
Sentenced! By SOMERVILLE GIBNEY.
The Professor's Wife. By L. GRAHAM.
Mrs. Gainsborough's Diamonds. By JULIAN HAWTHORNE.
Niagara Spray. By J. HOLLINGSHEAD.
A Romance of the Queen's Hounds. By CHARLES JAMES.
Garden that Paid Rent. TOM JERROLD.
Cut by the Mess. By ARTHUR KEYSER.
Teresa Itasca. By A. MACALPINE.
Our Sensation Novel. J. H. MCCARTHY.
Doom! By JUSTIN H. MCCARTHY.
Dolly. By JUSTIN H. MCCARTHY.

Lily Lass. JUSTIN H. MCCARTHY.
Was She Good or Bad? By W. MINTO.
Notes from the "News." By JAS. PAYN.
Beyond the Gates. By E. S. PHELPS.
Old Maid's Paradise. By E. S. PHELPS.
Burglars in Paradise. By E. S. PHELPS.
Jack the Fisherman. By E. S. PHELPS.
Trooping with Crows. By C. L. PIRKIS.
Bible Characters. By CHARLES READE.
Rogues. By R. H. SHERARD.
The Dagonet Reciter. By G. R. SIMS.
How the Poor Live. By G. R. SIMS.
Case of George Candlemas. G. R. SIMS.
Sandycroft Mystery. T. W. SPEIGHT.
Hoodwinked. By T. W. SPEIGHT.
Father Damien. By R. L. STEVENSON.
A Double Bond. By LINDA VILLARI.
My Life with Stanley's Rear Guard. By HERBERT WARD.

HANDY NOVELS. Fcap. 8vo, cloth boards, **1s. 6d.** each.

The Old Maid's Sweetheart. A. ST. AUBYN
Modest Little Sara. ALAN ST. AUBYN.
Seven Sleepers of Ephesus. M. E. COLERIDGE.

Taken from the Enemy. H. NEWBOLT.
A Lost Soul. By W. L. ALDEN.
Dr. Palliser's Patient. G. ALLEN.

MY LIBRARY.

Choice Works, printed on laid paper, bound half-Roxburghe, **2s. 6d.** each.

Four Frenchwomen. By AUSTIN DOBSON.
Citation and Examination of William Shakspeare. By W. S. LANDOR.
The Journal of Maurice de Guerin.

Christie Johnstone. By CHARLES READE. With a Photogravure Frontispiece.
Peg Woffington. By CHARLES READE.
The Dramatic Essays of Charles Lamb.

THE POCKET LIBRARY. Post 8vo, printed on laid paper and hf.-bd., **2s.** each.

The Essays of Elia. By CHARLES LAMB.
Robinson Crusoe. Edited by JOHN MAJOR. With 37 Illusts. by GEORGE CRUIKSHANK.
Whims and Oddities. By THOMAS HOOD. With 85 Illustrations.
The Barber's Chair, and The Hedgehog Letters. By DOUGLAS JERROLD.
Gastronomy. By BRILLAT-SAVARIN.
The Epicurean, &c. By THOMAS MOORE.
Leigh Hunt's Essays. Ed. E. OLLIER.

White's Natural History of Selborne.
Gulliver's Travels, and The Tale of a Tub. By Dean SWIFT.
The Rivals, School for Scandal, and other Plays by RICHARD BRINSLEY SHERIDAN.
Anecdotes of the Clergy. J. LARWOOD.
Thomson's Seasons. Illustrated.
The Autocrat of the Breakfast-Table and The Professor at the Breakfast-Table. By OLIVER WENDELL HOLMES.

THE PICCADILLY NOVELS.

LIBRARY EDITIONS OF NOVELS, many Illustrated, crown 8vo, cloth extra, **3s. 6d.** each.

By F. M. ALLEN.
Green as Grass.

By GRANT ALLEN.
Philistia. | The Tents of Shem.
Babylon | For Maimie's Sake.
Strange Stories. | The Devil's Die.
Beckoning Hand. | This Mortal Coil.
In all Shades. | The Great Taboo.
Dumaresq's Daughter. | Blood Royal.
The Duchess of Powysland.
Ivan Greet's Masterpiece.

By EDWIN L. ARNOLD.
Phra the Phœnician.

By ALAN ST. AUBYN.
A Fellow of Trinity.

By Rev. S. BARING GOULD.
Red Spider. | Eve.

By W. BESANT & J. RICE.
My Little Girl. | By Celia's Arbour.
Case of Mr. Lucraft. | Monks of Thelema.
This Son of Vulcan. | The Seamy Side.
Golden Butterfly. | Ten Years' Tenant.
Ready-Money Mortiboy.
With Harp and Crown.
'Twas in Trafalgar's Bay.
The Chaplain of the Fleet.

By WALTER BESANT.
All Sorts and Conditions of Men.
The Captains' Room. | Herr Paulus.
All in a Garden Fair
The World Went Very Well Then.
For Faith and Freedom.
Dorothy Forster. | The Holy Rose.
Uncle Jack. | Armorel of Lyon-
Children of Gibeon. | esse.
Bell of St. Paul's. | St. Katherine's by
To Call Her Mine. | the Tower.

By ROBERT BUCHANAN.
The Shadow of the Sword. | Matt.
A Child of Nature. | Heir of Linne.
The Martyrdom of Madeline.
God and the Man. | The New Abelard.
Love Me for Ever. | Foxglove Manor.
Annan Water. | Master of the Mine.

By HALL CAINE.
The Shadow of a Crime.
A Son of Hagar. | The Deemster.

MORT. & FRANCES COLLINS.
Transmigration.
From Midnight to Midnight.
Blacksmith and Scholar.
Village Comedy. | You Play Me False.

By WILKIE COLLINS.
Armadale. | The Frozen Deep.
After Dark. | The Two Destinies.
No Name. | Law and the Lady.
Antonina. | Basil. | Haunted Hotel.
Hide and Seek. | The Fallen Leaves.
The Dead Secret. | Jezebel's Daughter.
Queen of Hearts. | The Black Robe.
My Miscellanies. | Heart and Science.
Woman in White. | "I Say No."
The Moonstone. | Little Novels.
Man and Wife. | The Evil Genius.
Poor Miss Finch. | The Legacy of Cain
Miss or Mrs? | A Rogue's Life.
New Magdalen. | Blind Love.

By DUTTON COOK.
Paul Foster's Daughter.

By MATT CRIM.
Adventures of a Fair Rebel.

By B. M. CROKER.
Diana Barrington. | Pretty Miss Neville.
Proper Pride. | A Bird of Passage.

By WILLIAM CYPLES.
Hearts of Gold.

By ALPHONSE DAUDET.
The Evangelist; or, Port Salvation.

By ERASMUS DAWSON.
The Fountain of Youth.

By JAMES DE MILLE.
A Castle in Spain.

By J. LEITH DERWENT.
Our Lady of Tears. | Circe's Lovers.

By DICK DONOVAN.
Tracked to Doom.

By Mrs. ANNIE EDWARDES.
Archie Lovell.

By G. MANVILLE FENN.
The New Mistress.

By PERCY FITZGERALD.
Fatal Zero.

By R. E. FRANCILLON.
Queen Cophetua. | A Real Queen.
One by One. | King or Knave.
Pref. by Sir BARTLE FRERE.
Pandurang Hari.

THE PICCADILLY (3/6) NOVELS—*continued.*

By EDWARD GARRETT.
The Capel Girls.

By CHARLES GIBBON.
Robin Gray. | The Golden Shaft.
Loving a Dream. | Of High Degree.
The Flower of the Forest.

By E. GLANVILLE.
The Lost Heiress. | The Fossicker.

By CECIL GRIFFITH.
Corinthia Marazion.

By THOMAS HARDY.
Under the Greenwood Tree.

By BRET HARTE.
A Waif of the Plains.
A Ward of the Golden Gate.
A Sappho of Green Springs.
Colonel Starbottle's Client.
Susy. | Sally Dows.

By JULIAN HAWTHORNE.
Garth. | Dust.
Ellice Quentin. | Fortune's Fool.
Sebastian Strome. | Beatrix Randolph.
David Poindexter's Disappearance.
The Spectre of the Camera.

By Sir A. HELPS.
Ivan de Biron.

By ISAAC HENDERSON.
Agatha Page.

By Mrs. ALFRED HUNT.
The Leaden Casket. | Self-Condemned.
That other Person.

By R. ASHE KING.
A Drawn Game.
"The Wearing of the Green."

By E. LYNN LINTON.
Patricia Kemball. | Ione.
Under which Lord? | Paston Carew.
"My Love!" | Sowing the Wind.
The Atonement of Leam Dundas.
The World Well Lost.

By HENRY W. LUCY.
Gideon Fleyce.

By JUSTIN McCARTHY.
A Fair Saxon. | Donna Quixote.
Linley Rochford. | Maid of Athens.
Miss Misanthrope. | Camiola.
The Waterdale Neighbours.
My Enemy's Daughter.
Dear Lady Disdain.
The Comet of a Season.

By AGNES MACDONELL.
Quaker Cousins.

By BERTRAM MITFORD.
The Gun-Runner.

By D. CHRISTIE MURRAY.
Life's Atonement. | Val Strange.
Joseph's Coat. | Hearts.
Coals of Fire. | A Model Father.
Old Blazer's Hero.
By the Gate of the Sea.
A Bit of Human Nature.
First Person Singular. | Cynic Fortune.
The Way of the World.

By MURRAY & HERMAN.
The Bishops' Bible.
Paul Jones's Alias.

By HUME NISBET.
"Bail Up!"

By GEORGES OHNET.
A Weird Gift.

By Mrs. OLIPHANT.
Whiteladies.

THE PICCADILLY (3/6) NOVELS—*continued.*

By OUIDA.
Held in Bondage. | Two Little Wooden
Strathmore. | Shoes.
Chandos. | In a Winter City.
Under Two Flags. | Ariadne.
Idalia. | Friendship.
CecilCastlemaine's | Moths. | Ruffino.
Gage. | Pipistrello.
Tricotrin. | Puck. | AVillageCommune
Folle Farine. | Bimbi. | Wanda.
A Dog of Flanders. | Frescoes. | Othmar.
Pascarel. | Signa. | In Maremma.
Princess Naprax- | Syrlin. | Guilderoy.
ine. | Santa Barbara.

By MARGARET A. PAUL.
Gentle and Simple.

By JAMES PAYN.
Lost Sir Massingberd.
Less Black than We're Painted.
A Confidential Agent.
A Grape from a Thorn.
In Peril and Privation.
The Mystery of Mirbridge.
The Canon's Ward.
Walter's Word. | Talk of the Town
By Proxy. | Holiday Tasks.
High Spirits. | The Burnt Million.
Under One Roof. | The Word and the
From Exile. | Will.
Glow-worm Tales. | Sunny Stories.

By E. C. PRICE.
Valentina. | The Foreigners.
Mrs. Lancaster's Rival.

By RICHARD PRYCE.
Miss Maxwell's Affections.

By CHARLES READE.
It Is Never Too Late to Mend.
The Double Marriage.
Love Me Little, Love Me Long.
The Cloister and the Hearth.
The Course of True Love.
The Autobiography of a Thief.
Put Yourself in his Place.
A Terrible Temptation.
Singleheart and Doubleface.
Good Stories of Men and other Animals.
Hard Cash. | Wandering Heir.
Peg Woffington. | A Woman-Hater.
ChristieJohnstone. | A Simpleton.
Griffith Gaunt. | Readiana.
Foul Play. | The Jilt.
A Perilous Secret.

By Mrs. J. H. RIDDELL.
The Prince of Wales's Garden Party.
Weird Stories.

By F. W. ROBINSON.
Women are Strange.
The Hands of Justice.

By W. CLARK RUSSELL.
An Ocean Tragedy.
My Shipmate Louise.
Alone on a Wide Wide Sea.

By JOHN SAUNDERS.
Guy Waterman. | Two Dreamers.
Bound to the Wheel.
The Lion in the Path.

By KATHARINE SAUNDERS.
Margaret and Elizabeth.
Gideon's Rock. | Heart Salvage.
The High Mills. | Sebastian.

THE PICCADILLY (3/6) NOVELS—*continued.*
By LUKE SHARP.
In a Steamer Chair.
From Whose Bourne.
By HAWLEY SMART.
Without Love or Licence.
By R. A. STERNDALE.
The Afghan Knife.
By BERTHA THOMAS.
Proud Maisie. | The Violin-player.
By FRANCES E. TROLLOPE.
Like Ships upon the Sea.
Anne Furness. | Mabel's Progress.
By IVAN TURGENIEFF, &c.
Stories from Foreign Novelists.

THE PICCADILLY (3/6) NOVELS—*continued.*
By ANTHONY TROLLOPE.
Frau Frohmann. | Kept in the Dark.
Marion Fay. | Land-Leaguers.
The Way We Live Now.
Mr. Scarborough's Family.
By C. C. FRASER-TYTLER.
Mistress Judith.
By SARAH TYTLER.
The Bride's Pass. | Lady Bell.
Buried Diamonds.
The Blackhall Ghosts.
By MARK TWAIN.
The American Claimant.
The £1,000,000 Bank-note.
By J. S. WINTER.
A Soldier's Children.

CHEAP EDITIONS OF POPULAR NOVELS.
Post 8vo, illustrated boards, **2s.** each.

By ARTEMUS WARD.
Artemus Ward Complete.
By EDMOND ABOUT.
The Fellah.
By HAMILTON AIDE.
Carr of Carrlyon. | Confidences.
By MARY ALBERT.
Brooke Finchley's Daughter.
By Mrs. ALEXANDER.
Maid, Wife, or Widow? | Valerie' Fate.
By GRANT ALLEN.
Strange Stories. | The Devil's Die.
Philistia. | This Mortal Coil.
Babylon. | In all Shades.
The Beckoning Hand.
For Maimie's Sake. | Tents of Shem.
Great Taboo. | Dumaresq's Daughter.
By E. LESTER ARNOLD.
Phra the Phœnician.
By ALAN ST. AUBYN.
A Fellow of Trinity. | The Junior Dean.
By Rev. S. BARING GOULD.
Red Spider. | Eve.
By FRANK BARRETT.
Fettered for Life.
Between Life and Death.
The Sin of Olga Zassoulich.
Folly Morrison. | Honest Davie.
Lieut. Barnabas. | A Prodigal's Progress.
Found Guilty. | A Recoiling Vengeance.
For Love and Honour.
John Ford; and His Helpmate.
Little Lady Linton.
By W. BESANT & J. RICE.
This Son of Vulcan. | By Celia's Arbour.
My Little Girl. | Monks of Thelema.
Case of Mr. Lucraft. | The Seamy Side.
Golden Butterfly. | Ten Years' Tenant.
Ready-Money Mortiboy.
With Harp and Crown.
'Twas in Trafalgar's Bay.
The Chaplain of the Fleet.
By SHELSLEY BEAUCHAMP.
Grantley Grange.
By AMBROSE BIERCE.
In the Midst of Life.
By FREDERICK BOYLE.
Camp Notes. | Savage Life.
Chronicles of No-man's Land.

By WALTER BESANT.
Dorothy Forster. | Uncle Jack.
Children of Gibeon. | Herr Paulus.
All Sorts and Conditions of Men.
The Captains' Room.
All in a Garden Fair.
The World Went Very Well Then.
For Faith and Freedom.
To Call Her Mine.
The Bell of St. Paul's. | The Holy Rose.
Armorel of Lyonesse.
St. Katherine's by the Tower.
By BRET HARTE.
Californian Stories. | Gabriel Conroy
An Heiress of Red Dog. | Flip.
The Luck of Roaring Camp. | Maruja.
A Phyllis of the Sierras.
By HAROLD BRYDGES.
Uncle Sam at Home.
By ROBERT BUCHANAN.
The Shadow of the | The Martyrdom of
Sword. | Madeline.
A Child of Nature. | Annan Water.
God and the Man. | The New Abelard.
Love Me for Ever. | Matt.
Foxglove Manor. | The Heir of Linne.
The Master of the Mine.
By HALL CAINE.
The Shadow of a Crime.
A Son of Hagar. | The Deemster.
By Commander CAMERON.
The Cruise of the "Black Prince."
By Mrs. LOVETT CAMERON.
Deceivers Ever. | Juliet's Guardian.
By AUSTIN CLARE.
For the Love of a Lass.
By Mrs. ARCHER CLIVE.
Paul Ferroll.
Why Paul Ferroll Killed his Wife.
By MACLAREN COBBAN.
The Cure of Souls.
By C. ALLSTON COLLINS.
The Bar Sinister.
MORT. & FRANCES COLLINS.
Sweet Anne Page. | Transmigration.
From Midnight to Midnight.
Fight with Fortune. | Village Comedy.
Sweet and Twenty. | You Play me False.
Blacksmith and Scholar. | Frances.

Two-Shilling Novels—*continued*.

By WILKIE COLLINS.

Armadale.	My Miscellanies.
After Dark.	Woman in White.
No Name.	The Moonstone.
Antonina. | Basil.	Man and Wife.
Hide and Seek.	Poor Miss Finch.
The Dead Secret.	The Fallen Leaves.
Queen of Hearts.	Jezebel's Daughter
Miss or Mrs?	The Black Robe.
New Magdalen.	Heart and Science.
The Frozen Deep.	"I Say No."
Law and the Lady.	The Evil Genius.
The Two Destinies.	Little Novels.
Haunted Hotel.	Legacy of Cain.
A Rogue's Life.	Blind Love.

By M. J. COLQUHOUN.
Every Inch a Soldier.

By DUTTON COOK.
Leo. | Paul Foster's Daughter.

By C. EGBERT CRADDOCK.
Prophet of the Great Smoky Mountains.

By MATT CRIM.
Adventures of a Fair Rebel.

By B. M. CROKER.
Pretty Miss Neville. | Bird of Passage.
Diana Barrington. | Proper Pride.

By WILLIAM CYPLES.
Hearts of Gold.

By ALPHONSE DAUDET.
The Evangelist; or, Port Salvation.

By ERASMUS DAWSON.
The Fountain of Youth.

By JAMES DE MILLE.
A Castle in Spain.

By J. LEITH DERWENT.
Our Lady of Tears. | Circe's Lovers.

By CHARLES DICKENS.
Sketches by Boz. | Oliver Twist.
Pickwick Papers. | Nicholas Nickleby.

By DICK DONOVAN.
The Man-Hunter. | Caught at Last!
Tracked and Taken. | Wanted!
Who Poisoned Hetty Duncan?
The Man from Manchester.
A Detective's Triumphs.
In the Grip of the Law.
From Information Received.
Tracked to Doom. | Link by Link.

By Mrs. ANNIE EDWARDES.
A Point of Honour. | Archie Lovell.

By M. BETHAM-EDWARDS.
Felicia. | Kitty.

By EDWARD EGGLESTON.
Roxy.

By G. MANVILLE FENN.
The New Mistress.

By PERCY FITZGERALD.
Bella Donna. | Polly.
Never Forgotten. | Fatal Zero.
The Second Mrs. Tillotson.
Seventy-five Brooke Street.
The Lady of Brantome.

By PERCY FITZGERALD and others.
Strange Secrets.

ALBANY DE FONBLANQUE.
Filthy Lucre.

By R. E. FRANCILLON.
Olympia.	Queen Cophetua.
One by One.	King or Knave?
A Real Queen.	Romances of Law.

Two-Shilling Novels—*continued*.

By HAROLD FREDERICK.
Seth's Brother's Wife.
The Lawton Girl.

Pref. by Sir BARTLE FRERE.
Pandurang Hari.

By HAIN FRISWELL.
One of Two.

By EDWARD GARRETT.
The Capel Girls.

By CHARLES GIBBON.

Robin Gray.	In Honour Bound.
Fancy Free.	Flower of Forest.
For Lack of Gold.	Braes of Yarrow.
What will the World Say?	The Golden Shaft.
	Of High Degree.
In Love and War.	Mead and Stream.
For the King.	Loving a Dream.
In Pastures Green.	A Hard Knot.
Queen of Meadow.	Heart's Delight.
A Heart's Problem.	Blood-Money.
The Dead Heart.	

By WILLIAM GILBERT.
Dr. Austin's Guests. | James Duke.
The Wizard of the Mountain.

By ERNEST GLANVILLE.
The Lost Heiress. | The Fossicker.

By HENRY GREVILLE.
A Noble Woman. | Nikanor.

By JOHN HABBERTON.
Brueton's Bayou. | Country Luck.

By ANDREW HALLIDAY.
Every-Day Papers.

By Lady DUFFUS HARDY.
Paul Wynter's Sacrifice.

By THOMAS HARDY.
Under the Greenwood Tree.

By J. BERWICK HARWOOD.
The Tenth Earl.

By JULIAN HAWTHORNE.
Garth.	Sebastian Strome.
Ellice Quentin.	Dust.
Fortune's Fool.	Beatrix Randolph.
Miss Cadogna.	Love—or a Name.

David Poindexter's Disappearance.
The Spectre of the Camera.

By Sir ARTHUR HELPS.
Ivan de Biron.

By HENRY HERMAN.
A Leading Lady.

By Mrs. CASHEL HOEY.
The Lover's Creed.

By Mrs. GEORGE HOOPER.
The House of Raby.

By TIGHE HOPKINS.
'Twixt Love and Duty.

By Mrs. HUNGERFORD.
A Maiden all Forlorn.
In Durance Vile. | A Mental Struggle.
Marvel. | A Modern Circe.

By Mrs. ALFRED HUNT.
Thornicroft's Model. | Self-Condemned.
That Other Person. | Leaden Casket.

By JEAN INGELOW.
Fated to be Free.

By HARRIETT JAY.
The Dark Colleen.
The Queen of Connaught.

By MARK KERSHAW.
Colonial Facts and Fictions.

TWO-SHILLING NOVELS—*continued.*

By R. ASHE KING.
A Drawn Game. | Passion's Slave.
"The Wearing of the Green."
Bell Barry.

By JOHN LEYS.
The Lindsays.

By E. LYNN LINTON.
Patricia Kemball. | Paston Carew.
World Well Lost. | "My Love!"
Under which Lord? | Ione.
The Atonement of Leam Dundas.
With a Silken Thread.
The Rebel of the Family.
Sowing the Wind.

By HENRY W. LUCY.
Gideon Fleyce.

By JUSTIN McCARTHY.
A Fair Saxon. | Donna Quixote.
Linley Rochford. | Maid of Athens.
Miss Misanthrope. | Camiola.
Dear Lady Disdain.
The Waterdale Neighbours.
My Enemy's Daughter.
The Comet of a Season.

By HUGH MACCOLL.
Mr. Stranger's Sealed Packet.

By AGNES MACDONELL.
Quaker Cousins.

KATHARINE S. MACQUOID.
The Evil Eye. | Lost Rose.

By W. H. MALLOCK.
The New Republic.

By FLORENCE MARRYAT.
Open! Sesame! | Fighting the Air.
A Harvest of Wild Oats.
Written in Fire.

By J. MASTERMAN.
Half-a-dozen Daughters.

By BRANDER MATTHEWS.
A Secret of the Sea.

By LEONARD MERRICK.
The Man who was Good.

By JEAN MIDDLEMASS.
Touch and Go. | Mr. Dorillion.

By Mrs. MOLESWORTH.
Hathercourt Rectory.

By J. E. MUDDOCK.
Stories Weird and Wonderful.
The Dead Man's Secret.
From the Bosom of the Deep.

By D. CHRISTIE MURRAY.
A Model Father. | Old Blazer's Hero.
Joseph's Coat. | Hearts.
Coals of Fire. | Way of the World.
Val Strange. | Cynic Fortune.
A Life's Atonement.
By the Gate of the Sea.
A Bit of Human Nature.
First Person Singular.

By MURRAY and HERMAN.
One Traveller Returns.
Paul Jones's Alias.
The Bishops' Bible.

By HENRY MURRAY.
A Game of Bluff.

By HUME NISBET.
"Bail Up!"
Dr. Bernard St. Vincent.

By ALICE O'HANLON.
The Unforeseen. | Chance? or Fate?

TWO-SHILLING NOVELS—*continued.*

By GEORGES OHNET.
Doctor Rameau. | A Last Love.
A Weird Gift.

By Mrs. OLIPHANT.
Whiteladies. | The Primrose Path.
The Greatest Heiress in England.

By Mrs. ROBERT O'REILLY.
Phœbe's Fortunes.

By OUIDA.
Held in Bondage. | Two Little Wooden
Strathmore. | Shoes.
Chandos. | Friendship.
Under Two Flags. | Moths.
Idalia. | Pipistrello.
CecilCastlemaine's | A Village Com-
  Gage. | mune.
Tricotrin. | Bimbi.
Puck. | Wanda.
Folle Farine. | Frescoes.
A Dog of Flanders. | In Maremma.
Pascarel. | Othmar.
Signa. | Guilderoy.
Princess Naprax- | Ruffino.
  ine. | Syrlin.
In a Winter City. | Ouida's Wisdom,
Ariadne. | Wit, and Pathos.

MARGARET AGNES PAUL.
Gentle and Simple.

By JAMES PAYN.
Bentinck's Tutor. | £200 Reward.
Murphy's Master. | Marine Residence.
A County Family. | Mirk Abbey.
At Her Mercy. | By Proxy.
Cecil's Tryst. | Under One Roof.
Clyffards of Clyffe. | High Spirits.
Foster Brothers. | Carlyon's Year.
Found Dead. | From Exile.
Best of Husbands. | For Cash Only.
Walter's Word. | Kit.
Halves. | The Canon's Ward.
Fallen Fortunes. | Talk of the Town.
Humorous Stories. | Holiday Tasks.
Lost Sir Massingberd.
A Perfect Treasure.
A Woman's Vengeance.
The Family Scapegrace.
What He Cost Her.
Gwendoline's Harvest.
Like Father, Like Son.
Married Beneath Him.
Not Wooed, but Won.
Less Black than We're Painted.
A Confidential Agent.
Some Private Views.
A Grape from a Thorn.
Glow-worm Tales.
The Mystery of Mirbridge.
The Burnt Million.
The Word and the Will.
A Prince of the Blood.
Sunny Stories.

By C. L. PIRKIS.
Lady Lovelace.

By EDGAR A. POE.
The Mystery of Marie Roget.

By Mrs. CAMPBELL PRAED.
The Romance of a Station.
The Soul of Countess Adrian.

By E. C. PRICE.
Valentina. | The Foreigners.
Mrs. Lancaster's Rival. | Gerald.

Two-Shilling Novels—*continued.*
By RICHARD PRYCE.
Miss Maxwell's Affections.
By CHARLES READE.
It is Never Too Late to Mend.
Christie Johnstone.
Put Yourself in His Place.
The Double Marriage.
Love Me Little, Love Me Long.
The Cloister and the Hearth.
The Course of True Love.
Autobiography of a Thief.
A Terrible Temptation.
The Wandering Heir. | Hard Cash.
Singleheart and Doubleface.
Good Stories of Men and other Animals.
Peg Woffington. | A Simpleton.
Griffith Gaunt. | Readiana.
Foul Play. | A Woman-Hater.
A Perilous Secret. | The Jilt.
By Mrs. J. H. RIDDELL.
Weird Stories. | Fairy Water.
Her Mother's Darling.
Prince of Wales's Garden Party.
The Uninhabited House.
The Mystery in Palace Gardens.
The Nun's Curse. | Idle Tales.
By F. W. ROBINSON.
Women are Strange.
The Hands of Justice.
By JAMES RUNCIMAN.
Skippers and Shellbacks.
Grace Balmaign's Sweetheart.
Schools and Scholars.
By W. CLARK RUSSELL.
Round the Galley Fire.
On the Fo'k'sle Head.
In the Middle Watch.
A Voyage to the Cape.
A Book for the Hammock.
The Mystery of the "Ocean Star."
The Romance of Jenny Harlowe.
An Ocean Tragedy.
My Shipmate Louise.
Alone on a Wide Wide Sea.
GEORGE AUGUSTUS SALA.
Gaslight and Daylight.
By JOHN SAUNDERS.
Guy Waterman. | Two Dreamers.
The Lion in the Path.
By KATHARINE SAUNDERS.
Joan Merryweather. | Heart Salvage.
The High Mills. | Sebastian.
Margaret and Elizabeth.
By GEORGE R. SIMS.
Rogues and Vagabonds.
The Ring o' Bells.
Mary Jane's Memoirs.
Mary Jane Married.
Tales of To-day. | Dramas of Life.
Tinkletop's Crime.
Zeph: A Circus Story.
By ARTHUR SKETCHLEY.
A Match in the Dark.
By HAWLEY SMART.
Without Love or Licence.
By T. W. SPEIGHT.
The Mysteries of Heron Dyke.
The Golden Hoop. | By Devious Ways.
Hoodwinked, &c. | Back to Life.
The Loudwater Tragedy.

Two-Shilling Novels—*continued.*
By R. A. STERNDALE.
The Afghan Knife.
By R. LOUIS STEVENSON.
New Arabian Nights. | Prince Otto.
BY BERTHA THOMAS.
Cressida. | Proud Maisie.
The Violin-player.
By WALTER THORNBURY.
Tales for the Marines.
Old Stories Re-told.
T. ADOLPHUS TROLLOPE.
Diamond Cut Diamond.
By F. ELEANOR TROLLOPE.
Like Ships upon the Sea.
Anne Furness. | Mabel's Progress.
By ANTHONY TROLLOPE.
Frau Frohmann. | Kept in the Dark.
Marion Fay. | John Caldigate.
The Way We Live Now.
The American Senator.
Mr. Scarborough's Family.
The Land-Leaguers.
The Golden Lion of Granpere.
By J. T. TROWBRIDGE.
Farnell's Folly.
By IVAN TURGENIEFF, &c.
Stories from Foreign Novelists.
By MARK TWAIN.
A Pleasure Trip on the Continent.
The Gilded Age.
Mark Twain's Sketches.
Tom Sawyer. | A Tramp Abroad.
The Stolen White Elephant.
Huckleberry Finn.
Life on the Mississippi.
The Prince and the Pauper.
A Yankee at the Court of King Arthur.
By C. C. FRASER-TYTLER.
Mistress Judith.
By SARAH TYTLER.
The Bride's Pass. | Noblesse Oblige.
Buried Diamonds. | Disappeared.
Saint Mungo's City. | Huguenot Family.
Lady Bell. | Blackhall Ghosts.
What She Came Through.
Beauty and the Beast.
Citoyenne Jaqueline.
By Mrs. F. H. WILLIAMSON.
A Child Widow.
By J. S. WINTER.
Cavalry Life. | Regimental Legends.
By H. F. WOOD.
The Passenger from Scotland Yard.
The Englishman of the Rue Cain.
By Lady WOOD.
Sabina.
CELIA PARKER WOOLLEY.
Rachel Armstrong; or, Love & Theology.
By EDMUND YATES.
The Forlorn Hope. | Land at Last.
Castaway.

OGDEN, SMALE AND CO. LIMITED, PRINTERS, GREAT SAFFRON HILL, E.C.

1247913R0

Printed in Great Britain by
Amazon.co.uk, Ltd.,
Marston Gate.